W9-DDD-202

VS COBOL II

A guide for programmers and managers

Second Edition

© 1990, Mike Murach & Associates, Inc.
All rights reserved.
Printed in the United States of America.
20 19 18 17 16 15 14 13 12 11 10 9 8 7 6 5 4

Library of Congress Cataloging-in-Publication Data

Prince, Anne.
    VS COBOL II : a guide for programmers and managers / Anne Prince.
    -- 2nd ed.
        p. cm.
    ISBN 0-911625-54-2 (alk. paper) : $25.00
    1. COBOL (Computer program language) 2. Virtual computer systems.
    I. Title.
QA76.73.C25P75   1989
005.2'22--dc20   89-13671
                                                                        CIP

VS COBOL II

A guide for programmers and managers

Second Edition

Anne Prince

Development team

Editor:	Sheila Lynch
Designer and Production Director:	Steve Ehlers
Production Assistant:	Cris Allen

Other products in our COBOL series

Structured ANS COBOL, Part 1 by Mike Murach and Paul Noll
Structured ANS COBOL, Part 2 by Mike Murach and Paul Noll

CICS for the COBOL Programmer, Part 1 by Doug Lowe
CICS for the COBOL Programmer, Part 2 by Doug Lowe

IMS for the COBOL Programmer, Part 1 by Steve Eckols
IMS for the COBOL Programmer, Part 2 by Steve Eckols

VSAM for the COBOL Programmer by Doug Lowe
VSAM: Access Method Services and Application Programming
    by Doug Lowe

Contents

Preface

If you're a COBOL programmer or a manager working in an MVS or VM environment, this book is for you. It will teach you everything you need to know about VS COBOL II, IBM's newest COBOL compiler...whether your shop has recently converted to VS COBOL II, is in the middle of converting, or is just considering conversion.

To be specific, this book will teach you how the features of VS COBOL II can make your programs run more efficiently. It will teach you how to code the new language elements of VS COBOL II, how to control the compilation and execution of your programs, and how to use the VS COBOL II debugger. And it will give you guidelines for converting to VS COBOL II.

In June of 1988, when this book was first published, only the first two releases of VS COBOL II were available; Release 3 wasn't available until December of 1988. Since Release 3 contains some important changes that I didn't cover in the first version of this book, this revised edition includes all the important Release 3 elements. However, because you may still be using Release 2, I have made it clear which elements are implemented by which releases. So you can use this book no matter what release you're using.

How to use this book

This book is designed to be as flexible as possible, so you can use it to suit your own needs. If you're a COBOL manager whose shop hasn't yet converted to VS COBOL II, it will help you evaluate the benefits of the new compiler so you can start to plan when and how to convert. If you're a manager or trainer whose shop is already using VS COBOL II, you can use this book as a training resource. And if you're a programmer, this book will teach you all the new elements and features of VS COBOL II as well as which OS/VS COBOL elements will no longer be available to you. Then, if you're working in a shop that has already installed VS COBOL II, you can start using the elements and features that will help you most. Otherwise, you can start writing programs that will be easy to convert later on.

No matter what your purpose is for reading this book, be sure not to skip chapter 1. It introduces you to VS COBOL II and all of its features; this is the background on which the rest of the book is based.

After chapter 1, though, the book is organized so you can read whatever chapters you're interested in, when you're interested in them. However, if you're going to read the entire book, I suggest you read it straight through. It's presented in a logical sequence from coding to compiling and testing to debugging to related subjects that only certain shops will be interested in (like CICS considerations and conversion suggestions).

Related books

This book does not teach you how to write COBOL programs. It teaches you how the elements of VS COBOL II can be applied to the programs you're already writing. So, if you're just beginning to learn COBOL or aren't familiar with its advanced features, you might be interested in our *Structured ANS COBOL* books. *Part 1* of this series is a course for novices. It teaches a beginner how to use a subset of COBOL for developing report preparation programs. *Part 2* is an advanced book that teaches an entry-level programmer how to use advanced COBOL elements to develop batch edit and update programs.

Perhaps the most important book we've ever done for COBOL programmers is called *How to Design and Develop COBOL Programs*. It shows experienced COBOL programmers how to design, code, and test programs that are easy to debug and maintain. And it shows them how to increase their productivity, often by 200 percent or more. As an accompanying reference, we offer *The COBOL Programmer's Handbook*, which summarizes the procedures and techniques presented in the text. It also presents seven model programs that you can use as guides for developing your own programs. Because this text and handbook present techniques and examples that will help you at any stage of your COBOL training, we recommend that you get them and use them throughout your training and career.

Beyond this, we offer books that teach COBOL programmers how to use CICS and IMS or DL/I on IBM mainframes. We have books on other subjects that the MVS COBOL programmer must know, like VSAM, TSO, assembler language, utilities, and JCL. We have books on VM/CMS command and concepts and on the CMS text editor, XEDIT. And we're publishing new books each year. So please check our current catalog for titles you may be interested in.

Conclusion

If your shop is considering converting to VS COBOL II, I hope this book will convince you of its advantages. And I hope it will give you some idea of how to approach the conversion. If you're in the process of converting to VS COBOL II or have already converted, I hope you'll find this book helpful in your training efforts.

I welcome *any* comments you may have about this book. If you feel that I should have covered any additional topics, if you discover any technical errors, or if you just have a question, please let me know. A postage-paid comment form is included at the back of this book. Thank you for your help.

Anne Prince
Fresno, California
October, 1989

Section

1

Introduction

This section presents an overview of VS COBOL II. If you're a manager who's in charge of converting to VS COBOL II...or who's trying to decide *whether* to convert...this section is critical. It presents all the features of VS COBOL II that you need to know about and shows you how they differ from OS/VS COBOL. While most of these features are expanded on later in the book, some of them aren't covered anywhere else. So to get a complete view of VS COBOL II, you must read this section.

If you're a programmer, it's not essential that you know everything presented in this section. In fact, you could probably get by without reading it at all, skipping directly to the chapters on language elements. But if you want the broad picture that will help you become as effective a programmer as possible under VS COBOL II, I urge you to read this section.

Chapter
one

What you should know about VS COBOL II

VS COBOL II is IBM's latest COBOL compiler for MVS and VM systems. At the time the first release was developed, the American National Standards Institute (ANSI) was working on a set of COBOL standards to update the 1974 ANS standards. Although the new standards hadn't yet been approved, there was agreement on a number of items. So IBM implemented the language elements that seemed certain to be included in the new standards in its first two releases of VS COBOL II.

Of course, when the new standards were finally approved in 1985, they also included a number of features that *weren't* a part of VS COBOL II. As a result, the first two releases of VS COBOL II don't even qualify as minimum-subset compilers under the 1985 standards (a minimum-subset compiler is one that satisfies the minimum requirements of the standards). But IBM has made available a new release of VS COBOL II that qualifies as a high-subset compiler under the 1985 standards.

In this chapter, I'll give you an overview of VS COBOL II by describing the features you'll find in *all* releases of the compiler. If you're a manager, this chapter will help you start to evaluate what impact VS COBOL II will have on your shop. If you're a programmer, this chapter will show you what new coding and debugging features are available with VS COBOL II to make your work easier.

To start, I'll present the features that are new in VS COBOL II; these features aren't available using OS/VS COBOL. Then, I'll tell you what features of OS/VS COBOL aren't supported by VS COBOL II. Although much of this material is expanded on later in this book, you shouldn't skip this chapter. Even if you're familiar with VS COBOL II, I think you'll discover some things in this chapter that you weren't aware of.

FEATURES OF VS COBOL II THAT AREN'T AVAILABLE WITH OS/VS COBOL

As you can see in figure 1-1, the new features provided by VS COBOL II fall into several categories. These include new language elements, performance improvements, compiler improvements, and improved debugging features. In this section, I'll introduce some of the specific features in each category. I won't say much about the language elements and debugging features, however, since the bulk of this book is devoted to presenting them in detail.

New language elements

There are two major improvements in the language elements offered by VS COBOL II. First, elements have been added that support structured programming techniques; second, CICS coding has been made easier. In addition to these improvements, there are also some other new language elements that you may find useful. I'll present those elements in chapter 3. For now, though, let me introduce you to structured programming and CICS coding.

Structured programming enhancements   The term *structured programming* refers to a collection of techniques that are designed to help improve both productivity and the quality of programs in your shop. These techniques include structured program design, structured module planning using pseudocode, structured coding, and top-down testing.

To support structured programming, VS COBOL II provides some new language elements that make structured coding easier. These elements include structured delimiters, the inline PERFORM statement, the PERFORM UNTIL WITH TEST AFTER statement, the EVALUATE statement, the SET TO TRUE statement, the CONTINUE statement, and the IF-THEN-ELSE statement. I'll present all of these elements in chapter 2.

Easier CICS coding   If you've ever written a program under CICS, you know how cumbersome it is to address data defined in the Linkage Section of a program. To do that, you have to use a special convention called Base Locator for Linkage to establish a system of pointers. VS COBOL II eliminates the need for this convention by using the ADDRESS special register. In chapter

```
New language elements
    Structured programming enhancements
    Easier CICS coding

Performance improvements
    31-bit addressing
    Reentrant programs
    Improved optimization
    Faster sorting

Compiler improvements
    Checking for out-of-range conditions
    Increased compiler limits

Improved debugging features
    VS COBOL II Debug
    Improved compiler listings
    Improved dump format

Other features
    Controls added for reserved words
    Controls added for compiler options
    More feedback from VSAM requests
    More flexibility for preloading COBOL programs under IMS/VS
    Extended Graphic Character Set
```

Figure 1-1   Features of VS COBOL II that aren't available under OS/VS COBOL

6, I'll present this register along with some other VS COBOL II features that make CICS programs easier to code.

Performance improvements

VS COBOL II provides several features that can improve the overall performance of your programs. These features include 31-bit addressing, reentrant programs, improved optimization, and faster sorting.

31-bit addressing   One of the biggest advantages of VS COBOL II over other compilers is that it allows programs to use the *31-bit addressing* of the MVS/XA operating system (*XA* stands for *extended architecture*). 31-bit addressing means that 31 bits are used to store an address instead of the 24 bits used by older operating systems. This, in turn, means that programs can access areas at larger addresses, programs can be loaded at larger addresses (so more programs can be running at a time), and the programs themselves can be larger.

In order for a VS COBOL II program to take full advantage of 31-bit addressing and to be executable above the 16-megabyte limit imposed by *24-bit addressing*, the program must use the *COBOL Library Management Facility* and must be reentrant. The COBOL Library Management Facility allows subroutines in the COBOL library to be shared by other programs that are executing at the same time. You invoke it by specifying the RESIDENT compiler option. And a reentrant program, as you'll see in a minute, is one that can satisfy multiple requests with a single copy of the program and can, therefore, be placed in a shared area of the system.

Reentrant programs   VS COBOL II allows you to specify that a program is *reentrant*. This means that only one copy of the program is needed to satisfy multiple requests for that program, saving both storage and processing time. To specify a program as reentrant, you code the RENT compiler option. I'll cover that option in chapter 4.

Improved optimization   The optimization features provided by VS COBOL II are much improved over those provided by OS/VS COBOL. To begin with, much of the optimization is automatic; under OS/VS COBOL, you have to specifically request that the optimization feature be used.

In addition, VS COBOL II provides some optional features not provided by OS/VS COBOL. When you request these features using the OPT compiler option, the compiler will: simplify, and in some cases, eliminate, branching; eliminate unnecessary linkage code; and handle redundant computations more efficiently.

VS COBOL II also provides optimization features related to system management. For example, frequently used subroutines that are compiled with the RESIDENT option can be loaded into storage once, as part of initialization, instead of being loaded each time they're needed. Another system management feature allows you better control over the space allocated for a particular application. By specifying the SPOUT run-time option, which is covered in chapter 4, you can determine how much space the application is using above and below 16 megabytes. Then you can use that information to adjust space management values related to the application.

Faster sorting   VS COBOL II supports the improved sorting capabilities provided by the IBM product *Data Facility Sort (DFSORT)*, Release 6 or later. In addition to doing the actual sorting, this facility provides for input and output processing. In contrast, OS/VS COBOL must perform the input/output processing for a sort itself. That makes the procedure much less efficient since the data has to be moved between OS/VS COBOL and the sort facility.

To request fast sorting under VS COBOL II, you use the FASTSRT compiler option. Be aware, though, that using this option puts some restrictions on how you code your COBOL programs. I'll cover those restrictions when I discuss the FASTSRT option in chapter 4.

Compiler improvements

VS COBOL II also provides two important compiler improvements over OS/VS COBOL: a check for out-of-range conditions for table references and increased compiler limits.

Checking for out-of-range conditions   Under OS/VS COBOL, index and subscript values aren't checked to see if they're beyond the boundaries of the tables they're associated with. So it's common for programs to abend due to a runaway subscript or index. For example, if you tried to access the 101st entry of a table containing only 100 entries, your program wouldn't inform you of the error, but would probably abend due to complications caused by the error.

Under VS COBOL II, however, a new compiler option called SSRANGE causes the compiler to check whether index and subscript values refer to entries beyond the end of a table. In addition, the compiler checks for out-of-range conditions for OCCURS DEPENDING ON values and reference modification values. (I'll present reference modification in chapter 3.) The check for out-of-range conditions is performed when the object code containing the index, subscript, OCCURS DEPENDING ON clause, or reference modifier is executed. If an error is detected, an error message is generated and the program continues.

Increased compiler limits   VS COBOL II removes many of the size restrictions of OS/VS COBOL. This is possible due to the additional space available with the extended architecture systems. Figure 1-2 presents a comparison between some of the limits imposed under OS/VS COBOL and those under VS COBOL II. As you can see, the limits have been relaxed significantly. Of course, you can take advantage of them only if you're working on an XA system.

Improved debugging features

VS COBOL II gives the programmer several tools that make debugging much easier. For one thing, it has its own debug facility, called *VS COBOL II Debug*,

Language element	OS/VS COBOL	VS COBOL II
Data Division	1M	No limit
File Section		
BLOCK CONTAINS integer	32K	1M*
RECORD CONTAINS integer	32K	1M*
Item length	32K	1M*
Working-storage Section	1M	128M
Level 77 data names	1 million	16 million
Level 01-49 data names	1 million	16 million
Elementary item size	32K	16M
Table size	32K	16M
Table element size	32K	8M
Linkage Section	1M	128M
Number of level 01-77		
data items	255	No limit

* Limit is 32K for QSAM files

Figure 1-2   Compiler limits for OS/VS COBOL and VS COBOL II

or *COBTEST*, that allows you to trace the execution of a program. In addition, it provides improved compiler listings and an improved dump format to aid in debugging.

VS COBOL II Debug   VS COBOL II Debug is similar to the OS/VS COBOL Interactive Debug product. However, its capabilities have been greatly expanded. The most significant difference is that in addition to line mode, VS COBOL II Debug can be used in batch and full-screen modes. I'll cover VS COBOL II Debug in detail in chapter 5.

Improved compiler listings   The compiler listings available with VS COBOL II have been improved over those provided with OS/VS COBOL. Not only is more information included on the listings, but the information is presented in a more readable format. I'll discuss the individual listings in detail in chapter 4.

Improved dump format   When a program terminates abnormally, it can be a nightmare trying to locate the problem using a storage dump. To assist you in these situations, VS COBOL II provides you with a formatted dump.

Although the formatted dump contains basically the same information as an unformatted dump, it's much more readable. You can request a formatted dump by specifying the FDUMP compiler option. I'll cover this option in detail in chapter 4.

Other features

VS COBOL II provides some other features you don't get with OS/VS COBOL. In particular, you should know about the controls that have been added for reserved words and compiler options, the additional feedback provided for VSAM requests, the additional flexibility provided for preloading COBOL programs under IMS/VS, and the Extended Graphic Character Set.

Controls added for reserved words   VS COBOL II allows an installation to tailor the reserved word list to its own specifications. Using this feature, you can restrict the use of reserved words, flag the use of reserved words, and create an alias for a reserved word. Although the benefit of specifying an alias is questionable, the other two features can be quite useful under certain circumstances. For example, if you're in charge of a shop that uses structured COBOL, you may want to restrict the use of GOTO statements. And, in any shop, you may want to flag words that you know will become obsolete in a future release of COBOL so that your programmers can avoid using them.

It's also possible for an installation to create and use more than one reserved word list. To specify which list you want to use for a particular program, you code the WORD compiler option. I'll have more to say about this option in chapter 4.

Controls added for compiler options   At most installations, it's important that you use certain compiler options for every program you compile. So in addition to specifying compiler defaults when a compiler is installed, VS COBOL II allows you to specify whether or not a default can be changed. Once you specify that an option cannot be changed, a conflicting option won't be accepted at compile time.

More feedback from VSAM requests   Under OS/VS COBOL, the only feedback you get from VSAM I/O requests is what's returned in the area specified in the FILE STATUS clause for the file. Many times, though, that information is too general for you to determine the cause of an error. Under VS COBOL II, two areas can be specified in the FILE STATUS clause. The first area contains the usual file status code. The second area contains more specific VSAM information. I'll show you how to use this information in chapter 3.

More flexibility for preloading COBOL programs under IMS/VS
Under IMS/VS, you can load a COBOL program into storage before it's requested for execution. That way the program doesn't have to be loaded each time it's requested. With OS/VS COBOL, however, programs that are preloaded need to be compiled with different options than programs that are not preloaded. Unfortunately, this leads to problems if you want to use a single program both ways. In contrast, VS COBOL II allows a program that's preloaded to be compiled with the same options as a program that's not preloaded. The only requirement for this is that you compile the program using the RENT and RESIDENT options.

Extended Graphic Character Set   Release 1.0 of VS COBOL II introduced a new character set, called the *Extended Graphic Character Set (EGCS)*. This character set allows a character to be represented by two consecutive bytes of data. These characters are used most frequently with applications that support large character sets, such as Kanji, a character set used in Japan.

With Release 2.0 of VS COBOL II, the Extended Graphic Character Set was improved. It now includes a subset called the *Double Byte Character Set (DBCS)*. This subset allows you to form certain double-byte character strings. Each character in the string can range in value from hex 41 to hex FE for both bytes. Because you would use this feature only for special applications, I won't cover it in detail in this book. If you need more information, see the IBM publication *VS COBOL II Application Programming: Language Reference.*

FEATURES OF OS/VS COBOL NOT SUPPORTED BY VS COBOL II

There are several features you should know about that are supported by OS/VS COBOL but not by VS COBOL II. First, some of the features of 1974 COBOL that are optional in the 1985 standards haven't been implemented in VS COBOL II. In addition, some other language elements (most of which were IBM extensions to the 1968 or 1974 standards) have been dropped, while others have been changed. Finally, ISAM files, BDAM files, and the Lister feature are no longer supported. These changes are summarized for you in figure 1-3.

```
1974 standard features
    Report Writer
    Communications support
    Advanced capabilities of the USE FOR DEBUGGING statement

Language elements (mostly IBM extensions to the 1968 and 1974 standards)

ISAM and BDAM files

The Lister feature
```

Figure 1-3   Features of OS/VS COBOL that aren't supported by VS COBOL II

1974 standard features

Unlike OS/VS COBOL, VS COBOL II does *not* support the use of Report Writer, communications with outside devices via messages (provided for by the CD entry and the ENABLE, DISABLE, RECEIVE, and SEND statements), or the advanced capabilities of the USE FOR DEBUGGING statement. The reason is that all these features are optional under the 1985 standards; in fact, the debugging feature is marked for deletion in the next set of standards. As a result, if you want to continue using Report Writer under VS COBOL II, you have to use a precompiler that's available from IBM. Similarly, communication support is available on most systems outside the COBOL compiler. And for advanced debugging functions, you can use the VS COBOL II debug tool, COBTEST, that I mentioned earlier in this chapter. It's a powerful debugger that I'll describe in detail in chapter 5.

Language elements

Many of the IBM extensions to the 1968 or 1974 standards that were a part of OS/VS COBOL have not been included in VS COBOL II. For example, the ON and TRANSFORM statements and the CURRENT-DATE and TIME-OF-DAY registers, which were originally extensions to the 1968 standards, have been dropped. And the EXAMINE, EXHIBIT, and NOTE statements, which were extensions to the 1974 standards, have been dropped. In addition, several elements that were treated as comments by OS/VS COBOL have been dropped entirely from VS COBOL II. And others, although they haven't been dropped, are now treated only as comments by VS COBOL II. In chapter 7, I'll show you specifically what statements will have to be changed when you convert to VS COBOL II.

Most of the language elements that were dropped have been replaced by other elements. For example, the TRANSFORM and EXAMINE statements have been replaced by the INSPECT statement, and the CURRENT-DATE and TIME-OF-DAY registers have been replaced by the DATE and TIME registers. If you're still using any of these extensions, you should switch to the newer elements right away, because sooner or later you'll be converting to VS COBOL II.

There are a few other language elements to which minor changes have been made. But, because they probably won't have any effect on your coding, I don't feel it's necessary to discuss each of them here. If you're interested, appendix A presents all of the new language elements of VS COBOL II. You can review it to find any additional changes I haven't discussed.

ISAM and BDAM files

ISAM and BDAM files are no longer supported under VS COBOL II. And all language elements related specifically to ISAM and BDAM have been dropped. These files have been replaced by VSAM key-sequenced and relative-record data sets (KSDS and RRDS). So, if your shop has not yet converted all its files to VSAM, you'll have to do so before you can convert the programs that access those files to VS COBOL II.

The Lister feature

Under OS/VS COBOL, the Lister feature was used to reformat source code for improved readability and to create formatted cross-references. Because of the improved compiler listings available with VS COBOL II, however, the Lister feature is no longer necessary. As a result, it isn't supported by VS COBOL II.

DISCUSSION

If you're a COBOL programmer, you've probably heard a lot about the new language elements of VS COBOL II. But chances are you didn't know about many of the other improvements I've introduced in this chapter. These features can not only make programming easier for you, but they can make your programs more efficient too.

If you're a manager, you should now have a good idea of how VS COBOL II will affect your shop. In fact, after reading this chapter, you may have already decided to convert to VS COBOL II. But whether you've made that decision or not, you should continue reading to find out how the new language elements and program development features will affect your programmers.

The next two sections of this book explain the new language elements and program development features in more detail. Then, the last section presents some related topics you might be interested in knowing about. In particular, chapter 7 will give managers some recommendations on when to convert to VS COBOL II and how to plan the conversion.

Terminology

structured programming	DFSORT
31-bit addressing	VS COBOL II Debug
XA	COBTEST
extended architecture	Extended Graphic Character Set
24-bit addressing	EGCS
COBOL Library Management Facility	Double Byte Character Set
reentrant program	DBCS
Data Facility Sort	

Objectives

1. Describe the basic features of VS COBOL II as it relates to OS/VS COBOL, including new language elements, performance improvements, compiler improvements, and debugging improvements.

2. Identify the features of OS/VS COBOL you're currently using, if any, that aren't supported by VS COBOL II.

2

VS COBOL II
language elements

In section 1, you were introduced to all the features of VS COBOL II you should know about. Now, in sections 2 and 3, I'll cover in greater depth the features that will affect the way you code and develop your programs. So if you're a programmer, you'll want to concentrate on these sections.

In this section, I'll expand on the language elements that were introduced in section 1. Chapter 2 will present the language elements for structured programming. And chapter 3 will present some additional elements you may find useful. Then, in section 3, you'll learn about some of the program development features of VS COBOL II.

Chapter
two

VS COBOL II elements for structured programming

The purpose of many of the new elements of VS COBOL II is to make it easier for you to design and code structured programs. The basic theory behind structured programming is that any program can be made up of only a few, well-defined structures. Each structure may consist of a number of statements, but it can have only one entry point and one exit point. As a result, you do away with the uncontrolled branching that makes programs difficult to design, code, test, and (especially) maintain.

To implement the theory, a collection of techniques has been developed, including structured program design, structured module planning, structured coding, and top-down testing. You probably use at least some of these techniques in some form in your shop right now. But if you'd like to know more about them, I recommend our book *How to Design and Develop COBOL Programs*. It teaches you everything you need to know to create structured COBOL programs efficiently and effectively.

In this chapter, you'll learn the most important of the new structured programming elements implemented in VS COBOL II. I'll show you how they work and give you recommendations for their use. As you'll see, these new elements won't have a dramatic effect on the way you design and code your programs, but they'll be useful at times.

Structured delimiters

Figure 2-1 shows the verbs that have *structured delimiters* under VS COBOL II. Simply stated, the purpose of a structured delimiter is to show where a statement ends. So, in the first example in figure 2-1, the READ statement ends with the END-READ delimiter; however, the IF condition is still in effect for the MOVE statement that follows.

In technical terms, structured delimiters are known as *explicit scope terminators*. They are an addition to the only *implicit scope terminator*, the period. Because I think the term "structured delimiter" is more meaningful in terms of how these elements are used, I'll use that term throughout this book.

In general, structured delimiters are useful only when one conditional statement is used within another one. This is illustrated by the examples in figure 2-1. If a statement isn't used within another statement, it doesn't need a structured delimiter because the period at the end of the statement is the delimiter. As a result, structured delimiters should have only a minor effect on your coding and little or no effect on the way you design programs. (The only exception to this is the END-PERFORM statement used with an inline PERFORM, which I'll say more about in a minute.)

Of all the structured delimiters, you'll probably use the END-IF delimiter the most. Because structured programming makes extensive use of *nested IF statements* (IF statements coded within IF statements), the END-IF delimiter can help you improve the readability of your modules, as illustrated in figure 2-2. In the top example, the programmer had to code the IF NOT EMPLOYEE-EOF condition twice because the only way she could end the second IF statement was with a period. In the bottom example, the programmer ends the second IF statement with an END-IF, making the code for the module easier to read.

You should notice in figure 2-2 that the structured delimiter in the second example is aligned with the IF statement it ends. This makes it obvious which IF statement it's associated with. Whenever you use structured delimiters, you should align them this way.

With the exception of END-IF, I don't think you'll use delimiters much. If you isolate I/O statements in their own modules (we recommend this in our structured programming techniques), you won't ever need the delimiters for the I/O verbs. And you should have only an occasional need for delimiters on the computational verbs and the other miscellaneous verbs. As a general rule, then, you should use structured delimiters only when they improve readability ...and this should be infrequently.

Input/output verbs

```
READ                    REWRITE                 RETURN
WRITE                   DELETE                  START
```

Example

```
IF CONDITION-A
    READ TRANREC
        INVALID KEY
            MOVE 'Y' TO INVALID-KEY-SW
    END-READ
    MOVE TR-RECORD-KEY TO OLD-RECORD-KEY.
```

Computational verbs

```
ADD                     MULTIPLY                COMPUTE
SUBTRACT                DIVIDE
```

Example

```
IF CONDITION-A
    ADD B TO C
        ON SIZE ERROR
            MOVE ZERO TO C
    END-ADD
    ADD C TO D.
```

Miscellaneous verbs

```
IF                      EVALUATE                STRING
PERFORM                 SEARCH                  UNSTRING
CALL
```

Example

```
IF CONDITION-A
    IF CONDITION-B
        PERFORM 100-PROCESS-CONDITION-B
    ELSE
        PERFORM 200-PROCESS-OTHER-CONDITION
    END-IF
    PERFORM 300-PROCESS-CONDITION-A.
```

Figure 2-1   Verb list for structured delimiters

Coding without END-IF

```
 100-PRODUCE-EMPLOYEE-LINE.
*
     PERFORM 110-READ-EMPLOYEE-RECORD.
     IF NOT EMPLOYEE-EOF
         IF SR-ACTIVE-EMPLOYEE
             PERFORM 120-PRINT-ACTIVE-LINE
         ELSE
             PERFORM 150-PRINT-INACTIVE-LINE.
     IF NOT EMPLOYEE-EOF
         PERFORM 160-ACCUMULATE-GRAND-TOTAL.
*
```

Coding with END-IF

```
 100-PRODUCE-EMPLOYEE-LINE.
*
     PERFORM 110-READ-EMPLOYEE-RECORD.
     IF NOT EMPLOYEE-EOF
         IF SR-ACTIVE-EMPLOYEE
             PERFORM 120-PRINT-ACTIVE-LINE
         ELSE
             PERFORM 150-PRINT-INACTIVE-LINE
         END-IF
         PERFORM 160-ACCUMULATE-GRAND-TOTAL.
*
```

Figure 2-2   How END-IF can improve the readability of a module

The inline PERFORM

The *inline PERFORM* is a structure that many structured programming advo-
cates have wanted for years. When you use an inline PERFORM, you code the
performed function right after the PERFORM statement rather than placing it
in a separate paragraph, as you would using a traditional PERFORM statement.
Then, you end the function with the END-PERFORM delimiter. (The END-
PERFORM delimiter is required with an inline PERFORM.) This is illustrated
by the example in figure 2-3.

As you can see in part 1 of the figure, without the inline PERFORM,
module 000 must call module 200 with a PERFORM VARYING statement.
But in part 2, module 000 simply calls module 200 to load the price table. Then,
module 200 uses an inline PERFORM VARYING statement to load the table.
For functions like this, I believe the coding with the inline PERFORM is
preferable to the coding without it.

Coding without an inline PERFORM

```
 000-PREPARE-PRICE-LISTING.
*
     .
     .
     PERFORM 200-LOAD-PRICE-TABLE
         VARYING PRICE-TABLE-INDEX FROM 1 BY 1
         UNTIL PTABLE-EOF.
     .
     .
*
 200-LOAD-PRICE-TABLE.
*
     PERFORM 210-READ-PRICE-TABLE-RECORD.
     IF NOT PTABLE-EOF
         MOVE PT-ITEM-NUMBER
             TO ITEM-NUMBER (PRICE-TABLE-INDEX)
         MOVE PT-ITEM-PRICE
             TO ITEM-PRICE (PRICE-TABLE-INDEX)
     ELSE
         SET PRICE-TABLE-INDEX DOWN BY 1
         SET PT-ENTRY-COUNT TO PRICE-TABLE-INDEX.
*
 210-READ-PRICE-TABLE-RECORD.
*
     READ PTABLE RECORD INTO PRICE-TABLE-RECORD
         AT END
             MOVE 'Y' TO PTABLE-EOF-SW.
*
```

Figure 2-3   How an inline PERFORM can improve the code of a load-table module (part 1 of 2)

The problem with the inline PERFORM is that it makes it relatively easy for you to code more than one function in a single COBOL paragraph. And that can lead to complex paragraphs that are difficult to read, test, and maintain...just the opposite of what you're trying to achieve using structured programming. As a result, I don't think you should use inline PERFORMs much. As I see it, you should use them only when the use of traditional PERFORMs would force you to divide a function in a way that you wouldn't otherwise divide it. Then, the use of an inline PERFORM can help you consolidate the code in a single module so you improve both the structure and coding of your program.

There's one more thing you should keep in mind when considering whether to use an inline PERFORM. If you're using it to improve the efficiency of your program by eliminating unnecessary branching, you should realize that

Coding with an inline PERFORM

```
 000-PREPARE-PRICE-LISTING.
*
      .
      .
     PERFORM 200-LOAD-PRICE-TABLE.
      .
      .
*
 200-LOAD-PRICE-TABLE.
*
     PERFORM
         VARYING PRICE-TABLE-INDEX FROM 1 BY 1
         UNTIL PTABLE-EOF
             PERFORM 210-READ-PRICE-TABLE-RECORD
             IF NOT PTABLE-EOF
                 MOVE PT-ITEM-NUMBER
                     TO ITEM-NUMBER (PRICE-TABLE-INDEX)
                 MOVE PT-ITEM-PRICE
                     TO ITEM-PRICE (PRICE-TABLE-INDEX)
             ELSE
                 SET PRICE-TABLE-INDEX DOWN BY 1
                 SET PT-ENTRY-COUNT TO PRICE-TABLE-INDEX
     END-PERFORM.
*
 210-READ-PRICE-TABLE-RECORD.
*
     READ PTABLE RECORD INTO PRICE-TABLE-RECORD
         AT END
             MOVE 'Y' TO PTABLE-EOF-SW.
*
```

Figure 2-3   How an inline PERFORM can improve the code of a load-table module (part 2 of 2)

the VS COBOL II compiler can improve your program's efficiency automatically. That was one of the improved optimization features I mentioned in chapter 1. So, if you're concerned with efficiency, just use the OPT compiler option; don't use inline PERFORMs.

The PERFORM UNTIL statement WITH TEST AFTER

In a PERFORM UNTIL statement, the condition is tested *before* the performed module is called. Then, if the condition is true, the module isn't called. Although this is acceptable most of the time, there are times when it would be

Coding with test before

```
 100-GENERATE-DEPT-STATISTICS.
*
         .
         .
     PERFORM 130-SEARCH-DEPT-TABLE
         VARYING DT-INDEX FROM 1 BY 1
         UNTIL DT-ENTRY-FOUND
            OR DT-INDEX > DT-TABLE LIMIT.
     SET DT-INDEX DOWN BY 1.
         .
         .
*
 130-SEARCH-DEPT-TABLE.
*
     IF DEPT-LOOKUP = DT-ENTRY (DT-INDEX)
         MOVE 'Y' TO DT-ENTRY-FOUND-SW.
```

Coding with test after

```
*
 100-GENERATE-DEPT-STATISTICS.
*
         .
         .
     PERFORM 130-SEARCH-DEPT-TABLE
         WITH TEST AFTER
         VARYING DT-INDEX FROM 1 BY 1
         UNTIL DT-ENTRY-FOUND
            OR DT-INDEX = DT-TABLE LIMIT.
         .
         .
*
 130-SEARCH-DEPT-TABLE.
*
     IF DEPT-LOOKUP = DT-ENTRY (DT-INDEX)
         MOVE 'Y' TO DT-ENTRY-FOUND-SW.
*
```

Figure 2-4   How WITH TEST AFTER can improve the code of a search function

nice to have the statement test the condition *after* the module is called. And that's what the WITH TEST AFTER language of VS COBOL II provides for.

Figure 2-4 illustrates how this statement can be useful. Without this clause, the search module derives an index that is one larger than the index of the desired table entry. As a result, the search module has to set the index down by 1 before passing control back to its calling module. But when the WITH

TEST AFTER clause is used, the index has the desired value when the table entry is found.

The flowcharts in figure 2-5 show the operation of PERFORM statements with tests before and after. When you use a before test, the index named in the VARYING clause is increased after the called module or inline statements are executed. In contrast, when you use an after test, the index is *not* increased if the condition is true after the called module or the inline statements are executed. This explains why you have to reduce the index in the example in figure 2-4 by one when the before test is used, but not when the after test is used.

If you use the PERFORM statement WITH TEST AFTER, you'll need to be careful how you code any limiting values. For example, suppose you're loading a table with a maximum of 100 entries. With the standard PERFORM statement, your code would look something like this:

```
PERFORM 130-SEARCH-DEPT-TABLE
    VARYING DT-INDEX FROM 1 BY 1
    UNTIL DT-ENTRY-FOUND
        OR DT-INDEX > 100
    .
    .
```

Using the PERFORM WITH TEST AFTER, however, your code would look something like this:

```
PERFORM 130-SEARCH-DEPT-TABLE
    WITH TEST AFTER
    VARYING DT-INDEX FROM 1 BY 1
    UNTIL DT-ENTRY-FOUND
        OR DT-INDEX = 100
    .
    .
```

In other words, because the test is done after the execution of the performed statements, you want to stop when the index is equal to the limit, not when it's one greater than the limit. If you coded it with the greater-than test, the program would attempt to load an entry beyond the end of the table.

Something else you should be aware of if you use WITH TEST AFTER is that the performed statements are always executed at least once. That's because the stated condition isn't tested until after the first execution. In most cases, that's probably what you'll want anyway. But in some cases, you may have to test the condition before the performed statements are executed.

Because the WITH TEST AFTER clause has limited application, you probably won't use it much. In fact, you can do anything with the traditional

PERFORM VARYING with test before

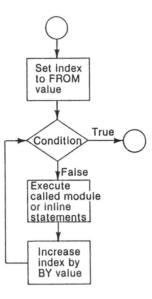

PERFORM VARYING with test after

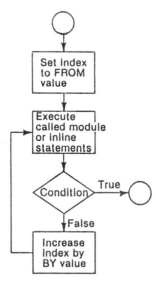

Figure 2-5   Flowcharts for the logic of PERFORM VARYING statements with before and after tests

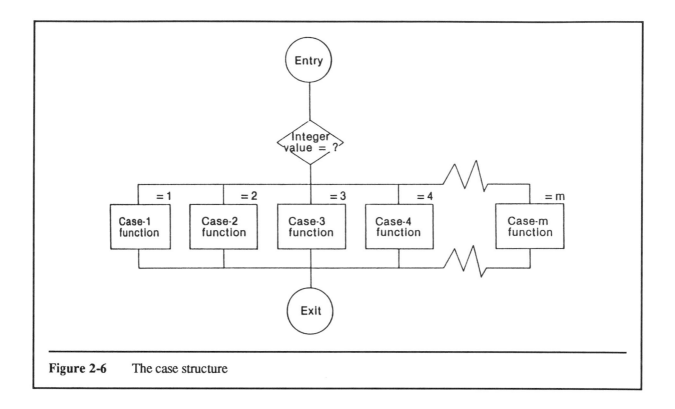

Figure 2-6   The case structure

before test that you can do WITH TEST AFTER. Nevertheless, you should use this clause whenever it improves the clarity of your code.

The EVALUATE statement

One of the purposes of the EVALUATE statement is to implement the *case structure* of structured programming, illustrated in figure 2-6. As you can see, one function is performed for each case depending on the value of the integer field that is tested at the start of the structure. If the integer field contains a one, the function for case 1 will be performed; if the integer field contains a two, the function for case 2 will be performed; and so on.

In the past, it was common to code the case structure using the GOTO/DEPENDING statement or a linear nest of IF statements (which I'll say more about in a minute). With VS COBOL II, you can also implement the case structure with an EVALUATE statement. In addition to the case structure, though, the EVALUATE statement can be used to code complex logical structures, including the structures for most decision tables. As you can see by its format, given in figure 2-7, this statement is quite complicated.

```
         ┌ identifier-1 ┐        ┌ identifier-2 ┐
         │ literal-1    │        │ literal-2    │
EVALUATE │ expression-1 │ [ALSO  │ expression-2 ⌋ ...
         │ TRUE         │        │ TRUE         │
         └ FALSE        ┘        └ FALSE        ┘

  ┌ ┌ WHEN
  │ │
  │ │   ┌ ANY                                                                    ┐
  │ │   │ condition-1                                                            │
  │ │   │ TRUE                                                                   │
  │ │   │ FALSE                                                                  │
  │ │   │        ┌ identifier-3           ┐ ┌ ┌ THROUGH ┐ ┌ identifier-4           ┐ ┐ │
  │ │   │ [NOT]  │ literal-3              │ │ │ THRU    │ │ literal-4              │ │ │
  │ │   └        └ arithmetic-expression-1┘ └ └         ┘ └ arithmetic-expression-2┘ ┘ ┘
  │   [ALSO
  │      ┌ ANY                                                                   ┐
  │      │ condition-2                                                           │
  │      │ TRUE                                                                  │
  │      │ FALSE                                                                 │  ]...}...
  │      │        ┌ identifier-5           ┐ ┌ ┌ THROUGH ┐ ┌ identifier-6           ┐ ┐│
  │      │ [NOT]  │ literal-5              │ │ │ THRU    │ │ literal-6              │ ││
  │      └        └ arithmetic-expression-3┘ └ └         ┘ └ arithmetic-expression-4┘ ┘┘
        imperative-statement-1 ...

  [WHEN OTHER imperative-statement-2]

  [END-EVALUATE]
```

Figure 2-7   The format of the EVALUATE statement

Rather than explain the operation of the EVALUATE statement in detail, I'm just going to present a couple of examples of it in use. As you'll see, it isn't too difficult to use if you keep its application simple.

Figure 2-8 shows how the EVALUATE statement can be used to implement a simple case structure. Notice that by using the word OTHER, you can perform a function if the field has a value other than those specified. Also, by using the word THRU (or THROUGH), you can code conditions that are more difficult to code in a *linear nest*.

In case you're not familiar with the linear nest, it's simply a string of nested IF statements coded without indentation. It's typically used to check a single field for a succession of independent values. If you compare the EVALUATE statement in figure 2-8 with the linear nest above it, I think you'll agree that the EVALUATE statement is easier to read and understand.

The case structure as implemented by nested IF statements in linear form

```
IF ITR-TRAN-CODE = 1
    PERFORM 240-EDIT-CODE-1-FIELDS
ELSE IF ITR-TRAN-CODE = 2
    PERFORM 250-EDIT-CODE-2-FIELDS
ELSE IF ITR-TRAN-CODE = 3
    PERFORM 260-EDIT-CODE-3-FIELDS
ELSE IF ITR-TRAN-CODE = 4
    PERFORM 270-EDIT-CODE-4-FIELDS
ELSE IF ITR-TRAN-CODE = 5
    PERFORM 280-EDIT-CODE-5-FIELDS
ELSE IF ITR-TRAN-CODE NOT < 6 AND NOT > 10
    PERFORM 290-EDIT-COMMON-FIELDS
ELSE MOVE MARK TO ITL-TYPE-CODE-ERROR
    MOVE 'N' TO VALID-TRAN-SW
    ADD 1 TO INVALID-TRAN-CODE-COUNT.
```

The case structure as implemented by an EVALUATE statement

```
EVALUATE ITR-TRAN-CODE
    WHEN 1          PERFORM 240-EDIT-CODE-1-FIELDS
    WHEN 2          PERFORM 250-EDIT-CODE-2-FIELDS
    WHEN 3          PERFORM 260-EDIT-CODE-3-FIELDS
    WHEN 4          PERFORM 270-EDIT-CODE-4-FIELDS
    WHEN 5          PERFORM 280-EDIT-CODE-5-FIELDS
    WHEN 6 THRU 10  PERFORM 290-EDIT-COMMON-FIELDS
    WHEN OTHER      MOVE MARK TO ITL-TYPE-CODE-ERROR
                    MOVE 'N' TO VALID-TRAN-SW
                    ADD 1 TO INVALID-TRAN-CODE-COUNT.
```

Figure 2-8   A simple case structure as implemented by nested IF statements and by an EVALUATE statement

Incidentally, I didn't include an example of the case structure implemented with GOTO/DEPENDING because we don't recommend its use. As I see it, either of the coding alternatives in figure 2-8 is preferable to the use of GOTO/DEPENDING.

Figure 2-9 shows an EVALUATE statement that handles a more complex set of conditions. Here, each action depends on the values in three fields. For instance, module 310 is performed when EXPERIENCE-CATEGORY has a value of 1, COLLEGE-DEGREE-CATEGORY has a value of B, and SALARY-REQUIREMENT-CATEGORY has a value of 1. If the word ANY is used, it means that any value in that field is acceptable. For instance, module 350 is performed when EXPERIENCE-CATEGORY has a value of 2, COLLEGE-DEGREE-CATEGORY has a value of P, and SALARY-

```
   WORKING-STORAGE SECTION.
 *
 01  APPLICANT-CATEGORY-FIELDS.
 *
     05   EXPERIENCE-CATEGORY          PIC X.
          88   NO-EXPERIENCE                        VALUE '1'.
          88   UNDER-5-YEARS                        VALUE '2'.
          88   5-AND-OVER-YEARS                     VALUE '3'.
     05   COLLEGE-DEGREE-CATEGORY      PIC X.
          88   NO-DEGREE                            VALUE 'N'.
          88   BACHELORS-DEGREE                     VALUE 'B'.
          88   MASTERS-DEGREE                       VALUE 'M'.
          88   DOCTORAL-DEGREE                      VALUE 'P'.
     05   SALARY-REQUIREMENT-CATEGORY  PIC X.
          88   UNDER-20-THOUSAND                    VALUE '1'.
          88   FROM-20-TO-35-THOUSAND               VALUE '2'.
          88   OVER-35-THOUSAND                     VALUE '3'.
 *
     .
     .
     .
 *
 PROCEDURE DIVISION.
 *
     .
     .
     .
 *
 300-EVALUATE-APPLICANT-DATA.
 *
     EVALUATE EXPERIENCE-CATEGORY
         ALSO COLLEGE-DEGREE-CATEGORY
         ALSO SALARY-REQUIREMENT-CATEGORY
     WHEN '1'      ALSO 'B'       ALSO '1'       PERFORM 310-ACTION-1
     WHEN '1'      ALSO 'M'       ALSO '2'       PERFORM 320-ACTION-2
     WHEN '1'      ALSO 'P'       ALSO '3'       PERFORM 330-ACTION-3
     WHEN '2'      ALSO NOT 'P'   ALSO NOT '3'   PERFORM 340-ACTION-4
     WHEN '2'      ALSO 'P'       ALSO ANY       PERFORM 350-ACTION-5
     WHEN '3'      ALSO NOT 'P'   ALSO ANY       PERFORM 360-ACTION-6
     WHEN '3'      ALSO 'P'       ALSO ANY       PERFORM 370-ACTION-7
     WHEN OTHER                                  PERFORM 380-DEFAULT.
 *
```

Figure 2-9   An EVALUATE statement that operates on three fields so it can direct the processing of a decision table

REQUIREMENT-CATEGORY has any value. With code like this, you can use the EVALUATE statement to specify the logic for most decision tables.

Figure 2-10 shows another way the EVALUATE statement could have been coded to process the decision table in figure 2-9. Here, the EVALUATE

```
300-EVALUATE-APPLICANT-DATA.
*
    EVALUATE TRUE ALSO TRUE
                  ALSO TRUE
    WHEN NO-EXPERIENCE ALSO BACHELORS-DEGREE
                      ALSO UNDER-20-THOUSAND
        PERFORM 310-ACTION-1
    WHEN NO-EXPERIENCE ALSO MASTERS-DEGREE
                      ALSO FROM-20-TO-35-THOUSAND
        PERFORM 320-ACTION-2
    WHEN NO-EXPERIENCE ALSO DOCTORAL-DEGREE
                      ALSO OVER-35-THOUSAND
        PERFORM 330-ACTION-3
    WHEN UNDER-5-YEARS ALSO NOT DOCTORAL-DEGREE
                       ALSO NOT OVER-35-THOUSAND
        PERFORM 340-ACTION-4
    WHEN UNDER-5-YEARS ALSO DOCTORAL-DEGREE
                       ALSO ANY
        PERFORM 350-ACTION-5
    WHEN 5-AND-OVER-YEARS ALSO NOT DOCTORAL-DEGREE
                          ALSO ANY
        PERFORM 360-ACTION-6
    WHEN 5-AND-OVER-YEARS ALSO DOCTORAL-DEGREE
                          ALSO ANY
        PERFORM 370-ACTION-7
    WHEN OTHER
        PERFORM 380-DEFAULT.
*
```

Figure 2-10   A variation of the EVALUATE statement to process the decision table defined in figure 2-9

statement tests for three TRUE conditions, one from each applicant category, and the WHEN clauses state the conditions to be met for each case. I think this coding is much clearer than the coding in figure 2-9 because you use the condition names instead of the condition codes. As a result, you don't need to have the table in front of you to know what conditions are being tested.

You can tell from these examples that the EVALUATE statement can help improve the readability of some programming functions. However, it's limited in application, so you probably won't use it much. Also, keep in mind that you don't ever *have* to use the EVALUATE statement, because you can get the same results with a sequence of IF statements or nested IF statements.

One danger in using the EVALUATE statement is that you can create code that is extremely difficult to read. In fact, I haven't begun to show you all the different ways that this statement can be coded. My general recommendation, then, is to use this statement when it improves the clarity of your code, but don't hesitate to replace an EVALUATE statement with IF statements should the EVALUATE statement become confusing.

The SET TO TRUE statement

The SET TO TRUE statement is designed to be used with condition names. By using this statement, you can set a condition to true without knowing the value required by the condition. This is illustrated in figure 2-11. As you can see, using the SET TO TRUE statement is equivalent to moving the value of a condition to a field.

If you code your switches and flags so the values assigned to the conditions are directly related to the condition names, your coding will be quite readable. As a result, the SET TO TRUE statement won't do much to improve the clarity of your code. If, however, the values aren't directly related to the condition names, the SET TO TRUE statement can make it easier for you to write the code in your Procedure Divisions.

In figure 2-11, for example, numeric values are arbitrarily assigned to condition names. In a case like this, it's easier to remember a condition name than the value assigned to it. So it's also easier to code and read the program if you use SET TO TRUE statements for turning conditions on.

The CONTINUE statement

The CONTINUE statement is a no-operation statement. It can be used to satisfy the syntax of another statement while showing that no operation should be performed. For instance, figure 2-12 illustrates the use of the CONTINUE statement within an EVALUATE statement. You might code a statement like this to provide for all transaction codes from 1 through 6 even though some of them aren't used at the time you code your program. Later on, you can replace the CONTINUE statements with the code your program requires. In this example, no operation is performed for transaction codes 3 and 5.

You might also want to use the CONTINUE statement in a nest of IF statements to show when no operation is to be performed. This is illustrated in figure 2-13. Notice that I could have used an END-IF statement in place of the CONTINUE statement in this example. Under OS/VS COBOL, however, it wouldn't have been possible to code this structure in a single sentence.

Field description with condition names

```
 DATA DIVISION.
*
       .
       .
    05   COMMISSION-STATUS        PIC X.
         88   TRAINEE             VALUE '1'.
         88   ASSISTANT           VALUE '2'.
         88   ASSOCIATE           VALUE '3'.
         88   MANAGER             VALUE '4'.
*
       .
       .
```

Turning a condition on with a MOVE statement

```
 PROCEDURE DIVISION.
*
       .
       .
    MOVE '3' TO COMMISSION-STATUS.
       .
       .
*
```

Turning a condition on with a SET TO TRUE statement

```
 PROCEDURE DIVISION.
*
       .
       .
    SET ASSOCIATE TO TRUE.
       .
       .
*
```

Figure 2-11   The SET TO TRUE statement

I think the CONTINUE statement is useful when it's used as in these two examples. In many such cases, it can help you improve the readability of a set of statements. But remember that you can usually code what you want in a readable style without using the CONTINUE statement.

```
EVALUATE ITR-TRAN-CODE
    WHEN 1     PERFORM 240-EDIT-CODE-1-FIELDS
    WHEN 2     PERFORM 250-EDIT-CODE-2-FIELDS
    WHEN 3     CONTINUE
    WHEN 4     PERFORM 260-EDIT-CODE-4-FIELDS
    WHEN 5     CONTINUE
    WHEN 6     PERFORM 270-EDIT-CODE-6-FIELDS
    WHEN OTHER MOVE MARK TO ITL-TYPE-CODE-ERROR
               MOVE 'N' TO VALID-TRAN-SW
               ADD 1 TO INVALID-TRAN-CODE-COUNT.
```

Figure 2-12   The CONTINUE statement used within an EVALUATE statement

```
  300-PROCESS-MAINTENANCE-TRAN.
*
      PERFORM 310-READ-INVENTORY-TRAN.
      IF NOT MNTTRAN-EOF
          PERFORM 320-READ-INVENTORY-MASTER
          IF RECORD-FOUND
              IF MT-CHANGE
                  PERFORM 330-CHANGE-INVENTORY-MASTER
              ELSE
                  IF MT-DELETION
                      PERFORM 350-DELETE-INVENTORY-MASTER
                  ELSE
                      CONTINUE
          ELSE
              IF MT-ADDITION
                  PERFORM 360-ADD-INVENTORY-MASTER.
*
```

Figure 2-13   The CONTINUE statement used in a set of nested IF statements

The IF-THEN-ELSE statement

Under VS COBOL II, the IF-ELSE statement can optionally be implemented
with the IF-THEN-ELSE statement. The addition of THEN relates the statement directly to one of the basic structures of structured programming, the
IF-THEN-ELSE structure, and provides for consistency with other program-

ming languages. From a practical point of view, it can also make your code more readable in some cases in which you use the END-IF delimiter.

For example, figure 2-14 shows the code that was originally presented in figure 2-2 to illustrate the END-IF statement. It also shows the same code using the IF-THEN-ELSE statement. I think the IF-THEN-ELSE statement makes the code more readable because it sets off the code that's subordinate to the IF and makes the pairing of the IF and END-IF more apparent. When used in this manner, I think it's useful. Otherwise, it's just a matter of preference.

Discussion

In this chapter, I've tried to present all the important new code of VS COBOL II that's related to structured programming. In most cases, these elements don't provide new functions; they just provide new ways to do old functions. Because of that, you may not need to use these elements very often. However, in some cases these elements can make your coding task easier and make the resulting code more readable. When they serve this purpose, I think they're useful.

Terminology

structured delimiter   inline PERFORM
explicit scope terminator   case structure
implicit scope terminator   linear nest
nested IF statements

Objective

Use the language elements presented in this chapter in your COBOL programs.

Coding with IF-ELSE structure

```
 100-PRODUCE-EMPLOYEE-LINE.
*
     PERFORM 110-READ-EMPLOYEE-RECORD.
     IF NOT EMPLOYEE-EOF
         IF SR-ACTIVE-EMPLOYEE
             PERFORM 120-PRINT-ACTIVE-LINE
         ELSE
             PERFORM 150-PRINT-INACTIVE-LINE
         END-IF
         PERFORM 160-ACCUMULATE-GRAND-TOTAL.
*
```

Coding with IF-THEN-ELSE structure

```
 100-PRODUCE-EMPLOYEE-LINE.
*
     PERFORM 110-READ-EMPLOYEE-RECORD.
     IF NOT EMPLOYEE-EOF
         IF SR-ACTIVE-EMPLOYEE
             THEN
                 PERFORM 120-PRINT-ACTIVE-LINE
             ELSE
                 PERFORM 150-PRINT-INACTIVE-LINE
         END-IF
         PERFORM 160-ACCUMULATE-GRAND-TOTAL.
*
```

Figure 2-14   How the IF-THEN-ELSE structure can make your code more readable

Chapter
three

Other VS COBOL II elements

In addition to the structured programming elements presented in the last chapter, there are some other new VS COBOL II elements you should know about. Some of these elements were implemented by the first two releases of VS COBOL II. I'll present those elements in the first topic of this chapter. Then, in topic 2, I'll cover those elements that weren't implemented until the third release of VS COBOL II.

As you read this chapter, you should be aware that there are some additional elements included in VS COBOL II that I will not cover here. To find out what these are, I suggest you refer to appendix A of this book. It's a complete reference summary of all the VS COBOL II language elements.

Topic 1   Elements implemented by Releases 1 and 2 of VS COBOL II

This topic presents the COBOL elements implemented by Releases 1 and 2 of VS COBOL II. Except as noted otherwise, all the elements presented in this topic are implemented by both releases and continue to be implemented under Release 3. Several are elements you'll probably use from time to time, while others are elements you probably won't use, but may want to know about.

VS COBOL II elements you will probably use

The FILE STATUS clause for VSAM feedback information   As I mentioned in chapter 1, VS COBOL II provides you with a way to get additional feedback from VSAM I/O requests. To do this, you code a second operand on the FILE STATUS clause for the file like this:

```
FILE STATUS IS file-status-code VSAM-code
```

where VSAM-code is defined in working storage as a six-byte group item. The format of this item is presented in figure 3-1.

As you can see in the figure, the first two bytes of this item are used for a VSAM return code, the second two bytes are used for a VSAM function code, and the last two bytes are used for a VSAM feedback code. When an error occurs on an I/O request for the file, the appropriate VSAM codes are placed in these areas. You can then use these codes to determine the actual cause of the error.

The VSAM return code provides information similar to the information provided by the file status code. Figure 3-2 presents the possible VSAM return codes and their meanings. As you can see, a return code of 0 indicates that the request was successfully completed, a return code of 4 indicates that the request was unsuccessful because an I/O request was already pending for the same file, a return code of 8 indicates a logical error, and a return code of 12 indicates a physical error. Although the same basic information is available from the file status code, the VSAM return code is important because it determines the possible values of the function code and feedback code.

If the VSAM return code indicates that a logical or physical error occurred, the VSAM function code indicates the function that was being attempted. Figure 3-3 presents these function codes and their meanings. If you're familiar with VSAM, these codes should be self-explanatory.

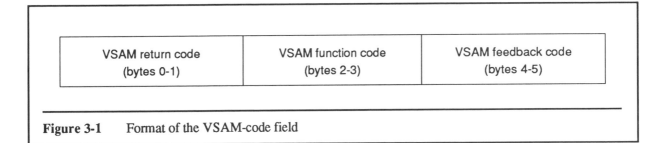

VSAM return code (bytes 0-1)	VSAM function code (bytes 2-3)	VSAM feedback code (bytes 4-5)

Figure 3-1   Format of the VSAM-code field

Code	Explanation
0	The request has been successfully completed.
4	A request is already active for the file specified.
8	A logical error has occurred; check the feedback code for specific information.
12	A physical error has occurred; check the feedback code for specific information.

Figure 3-2   VSAM return codes for I/O requests

The VSAM feedback code gives more specific information about the I/O request. For example, if a logical error is detected, a feedback code of 96 means that you attempted to change the key of reference while updating a record. And a feedback code of 68 means that the type of processing you attempted wasn't specified in the OPEN statement for the file. Because so many different error codes are possible, I won't try to list them all here. If you need to find out what they are, refer to the *OS/VS VSAM Programmer's Guide.*

The LENGTH special register   The LENGTH special register makes it possible to refer to the length of data items in your programs. A separate register exists implicitly for each data item referred to by the LENGTH OF phrase and is defined as PIC 9(9) with computational usage. You can use a LENGTH OF phrase anywhere a numeric data item with the same picture can be used. For example, you can use it in a MOVE statement like this:

```
MOVE LENGTH OF LAST-NAME TO NAME-LENGTH
```

Code	Explanation	Upgrade set status
0	An attempt was made to access a base cluster.	Correct
1	An attempt was made to access a base cluster.	May be incorrect
2	An attempt was made to access an alternate index of a base cluster.	Correct
3	An attempt was made to access an alternate index of a base cluster.	May be incorrect
4	An attempt was made to update the upgrade set for a base cluster.	Correct
5	An attempt was made to update the upgrade set for a base cluster.	May be incorrect

Figure 3-3   VSAM function codes for I/O requests

or in an ADD statement like this:

```
ADD LENGTH OF FIRST-NAME TO NAME-LENGTH
```

Although you can use the LENGTH special register in a variety of statements, you probably won't need it very often. If you do use it, it will probably be in one of two situations: on a CALL statement to pass a length to a subprogram or with a CICS command to specify the length of a record. I'll discuss the use of the LENGTH special register with the CALL statement now, and its use in CICS programs in chapter 6.

The BY CONTENT phrase of the CALL statement   Figure 3-4 presents the format of the CALL statement under VS COBOL II. As you can see, the statement now includes the END-CALL delimiter, as I mentioned in chapter 2. But the most significant change is that you can now code either BY REFERENCE or BY CONTENT in the USING phrase (BY REFERENCE is the default).

The BY REFERENCE phrase with a data name works just as the USING phrase does in OS/VS COBOL: the address of the data item is passed to the subprogram, and the subprogram uses that address to access the data item when

```
CALL    {Literal-1    }
        {identifier-1 }

                 {[BY REFERENCE]   {identifier-2          }
        [USING   {                 {[ADDRESS OF] record-name}  ...  }
                 {                 {Literal-2             }          }  ...]
                 {BY CONTENT       {LENGTH OF identifier-3}  ...     }

        [ON OVERFLOW imperative-statement]

[END-CALL]
```

Figure 3-4   The format of the CALL statement

needed. The ADDRESS OF option is new. It's not something you'll use very often, but when you do, you'll use it in conjunction with several other VS COBOL II elements. As a result, I'm going to explain it later in this chapter.

For now, I want to concentrate on the BY CONTENT phrase. It allows you to pass a value directly to a subprogram instead of moving the value to a field in the calling program and then passing that field. If you specify a literal here, its value is passed to the subprogram. If you code the LENGTH OF option, the calling program uses the LENGTH special register to pass the length of the data item specified to the subprogram.

I think you'll find that both options of the BY CONTENT phrase will come in handy from time to time. For example, if you have a subprogram that performs one of several functions based on a code that's passed to it, you can pass that code directly as a literal. Or if you want to code a subprogram that processes data items of variable length, you can use the LENGTH OF option to pass the length of the data item to the subprogram.

The INITIALIZE statement   The INITIALIZE statement assigns values to a field that is either an elementary item or a group item. Its format is illustrated in figure 3-5. In its simplest form, it is coded as in this example:

```
INITIALIZE INVENTORY-DATA
```

Then, if INVENTORY-DATA is a group item, all numeric and numeric-edited fields within it are set to zeros, and all alphabetic, alphanumeric, and alphanumeric-edited fields are set to spaces. Similarly, if INVENTORY-DATA is an elementary item, it is set to spaces or zeros depending on how it's defined.

```
INITIALIZE   identifier-1 [identifier-2]...

                      (ALPHABETIC          )
                      |ALPHANUMERIC        |              (identifier-3)
        [REPLACING    |NUMERIC             | DATA BY      |            |  ]
                      |ALPHANUMERIC-EDITED |              (literal-1   )
                      (NUMERIC-EDITED      )

                      (ALPHABETIC          )
                      |ALPHANUMERIC        |              (identifier-4)
                      |NUMERIC             | DATA BY      |            |  ]
                      |ALPHANUMERIC-EDITED |              (literal-2   )
                      (NUMERIC-EDITED      )
```

Figure 3-5   The format of the INITIALIZE statement

If you don't want the fields to be initialized to spaces or zeros, you can code one or more REPLACING phrases. These phrases imply a series of moves with identifier-1 as the receiving field and identifier-3, identifier-4, etc., or literal-1 , literal-2, etc., as the sending fields. In this case, you can initialize specific types of fields with whatever data you want. Any field types you don't specify are ignored.

For instance, this statement initializes only the alphanumeric fields and the alphanumeric-edited fields within a group item:

```
INITIALIZE INVENTORY-FIELDS
      REPLACING ALPHANUMERIC DATA BY SPACE
                ALPHANUMERIC-EDITED DATA BY SPACE
```

When this statement is executed, it will ignore alphabetic fields, numeric fields, and numeric-edited fields. And again, whether or not the REPLACING phrase is specified, index data items, elementary filler data items, and fields that are redefined within the area named INVENTORY-FIELDS are ignored.

If you use INITIALIZE REPLACING to initialize an elementary item, you must be sure the item is the same type as that indicated in the REPLACING phrase. For example, if you want to initialize a field defined as PIC S9(5) with +99999, you have to specify NUMERIC in the REPLACING phrase. Otherwise, the INITIALIZE statement won't work as you intended.

In our COBOL programming texts, we recommend that you initialize fields in working storage with VALUE clauses whenever possible. As a result, you shouldn't have much need for the INITIALIZE statement. In some programs, though, this statement makes it easy for you to define a table area or some other large area. It's also useful when you have to re-initialize the fields within a program.

Because the INITIALIZE statement makes it so easy for you to initialize fields within records, you should use it with some caution. If you use it carelessly, it can cause serious inefficiencies within a program. For instance, you can initialize a 50,000-byte table with a single INITIALIZE statement, whether it needs to be initialized or not.

One of our readers commented that in general, the INITIALIZE statement on his company's system was extremely inefficient. He said that it took as much as eight times longer to initialize a table using INITIALIZE than it did using MOVE. So again, I urge you to use the INITIALIZE statement with caution.

VS COBOL II elements that you probably won't use

Nested COPY statements   VS COBOL II allows you to nest COPY statements. In other words, source code that's copied into a program using a COPY statement can itself contain a COPY statement. There are only two limitations: the COPY statements cannot contain the REPLACING phrase and a specific COPY member can be referred to only once in a nested COPY.

Even with the limitations that have been placed on nested copying, I don't recommend its use. It's too easy to lose track of what's being copied and where it's coming from. In particular, I don't recommend nested copying with more than two levels of nesting. And frankly, I can't think of an application that would benefit from using nested COPY statements.

Complex OCCURS DEPENDING ON clauses   VS COBOL II allows for an OCCURS DEPENDING ON clause to be coded subordinate to another OCCURS DEPENDING ON clause. In addition, a data item containing an OCCURS DEPENDING ON clause that is part of a group item can be followed by additional data items that are not subordinate to it but are part of the group item. The record description in figure 3-6 illustrates these options.

In the figure, you can see that the record description contains two OCCURS DEPENDING ON clauses. The group item associated with the first one defines invoice segments for a customer; the number of invoice segments depends on CR-INVOICE-COUNT. The group item associated with the second one defines product segments for each invoice; the number of product segments for each invoice segment depends on CR-PRODUCT-COUNT. Following the product segment is the data item CR-PRODUCT-TOTAL. CR-PRODUCT-TOTAL is part of the invoice segment, but not a part of the product segment. Because of this, the location of CR-PRODUCT-TOTAL in storage is variable; it depends on the number of occurrences of the product segment.

```
    01   CUSTOMER-RECORD.
    *
         05   CR-ROOT-SEGMENT.
              10   CR-CUSTOMER-NO          PIC X(6).
              10   CR-INVOICE-COUNT        PIC S99.
              10   CR-PRODUCT-COUNT        PIC S99.
         05   CR-INVOICE-SEGMENT           OCCURS 1 TO 20 TIMES
                                           DEPENDING ON CR-INVOICE-COUNT.
              10   CR-INVOICE-DATE         PIC X(6).
              10   CR-INVOICE-NUMBER       PIC X(5).
              10   CR-PRODUCT-SEGMENT      OCCURS 1 TO 10 TIMES
                                           DEPENDING ON CR-PRODUCT-COUNT.
                   15   CR-PRODUCT-CODE    PIC X(4).
                   15   CR-UNIT-PRICE      PIC S9(3)V99.
                   15   CR-QUANTITY        PIC S9(3).
              10   CR-PRODUCT-TOTAL        PIC S9(5)V99.
    *
```

Figure 3-6   Complex use of OCCURS DEPENDING ON

Actually, you wouldn't want to use nested OCCURS DEPENDING ON clauses for the example in figure 3-6. This is because the data item referenced by a DEPENDING ON clause can't be variably located—that is, it can't be subordinate to a DEPENDING ON clause. So CR-PRODUCT-COUNT has to be defined before the first OCCURS DEPENDING ON clause. And that means each invoice segment will have the same number of product segments, which probably isn't what you want.

If all this seems confusing, it is. That's why we recommend you don't use complex OCCURS DEPENDING ON clauses unless the application is well suited for it. In fact, we recommend you avoid using any OCCURS DEPENDING ON clauses. That's because variable-length data items require special processing that leads to inefficient object code.

Incidentally, the complex usage of the OCCURS DEPENDING ON clause isn't supported by the first release of VS COBOL II. It was only added with the second release. So if you're still using Release 1 of VS COBOL II, you won't have the capabilities I just described.

The SORT-CONTROL special register   When you code a sort operation in a COBOL program, you can specify certain parameters to make the sort more efficient. To do this under OS/VS COBOL, you use the SORT-FILE-SIZE, SORT-CORE-SIZE, and SORT-MODE-SIZE special registers. The SORT-FILE-SIZE register specifies the number of records being sorted. The SORT-CORE-SIZE register specifies the amount of main storage to be used. And the SORT-MODE-SIZE register specifies the most frequently occurring record length of the records being sorted in a variable-length file. You can also use the special register SORT-MESSAGE to specify the name of the message file for a sort or merge operation (the default is SYSOUT). These registers are passed to the sort program, DFSORT, when it is executed.

These special sort registers aren't supported under the first release of VS COBOL II. Instead, you specify these values by coding control statements that are placed in a separate file and referenced by the JCL that executes DFSORT. The default name for this control file is IGZSRTCD. If you want to place the control statements in a file other than IGZSRTCD, you specify the name of the file in the SORT-CONTROL special register. DFSORT will then look for control statements in the file you specify.

The second release of VS COBOL II supports both methods for specifying sort parameters. You should realize, though, that any values you code in control statements in the SORT-CONTROL file override any values you code in your program using sort special registers. For more information on coding sort control statements, refer to *DFSORT Application Programming: Guide*.

New elements for handling storage addresses: Pointer data items, the ADDRESS special register, and the CALL and SET statements   VS COBOL II gives you several new language elements that let you handle storage addresses directly in your COBOL programs. First, you can use a new USAGE clause, USAGE IS POINTER, to define a field as a pointer data item. Pointer data items are used to hold addresses and are defined implicitly as four-byte, nonnumeric data items (you don't code PICTURE clauses for them). If you want to initialize a pointer data item to a value of nonnumeric zero, you use a new VALUE clause, VALUE IS NULL. You can use pointer data items only in relational conditions, in the USING phrases of CALL BY REFERENCE statements, and in SET statements.

One specific pointer data item you should know about is the ADDRESS special register. Like other special registers, it isn't defined explicitly in a program. Instead, a separate ADDRESS register exists implicitly for each 01- or 77-level field in the Linkage Section to hold the address of that field.

When you code ADDRESS OF in the USING BY REFERENCE phrase of the CALL statement (see figure 3-4), the calling program uses the ADDRESS register to pass the address of the record name you specify to the subprogram. However, the subprogram can't automatically access the data at that address (as it can if you pass an address using the data-name option of the BY REFERENCE phrase). Instead, you have to establish addressability to the subprogram using the SET statement.

When you use the SET statement to handle storage addresses, it has the format shown in figure 3-7. As you can see, you can code the name of a pointer data item in this statement or you can code ADDRESS OF plus a data name

```
SET  {pointer-data-item-1        } [{pointer-data-item-2        }] ...
     {ADDRESS OF identifier-1     }  {ADDRESS OF identifier-2     }

     TO {identifier-3             }
        {NULL                     }
        {ADDRESS OF identifier-4  }
```

Figure 3-7   The format of the SET statement for manipulating pointer data items

when you want to use the value in an ADDRESS register. Most often, you'll code either the SET or TO field using ADDRESS OF.

To illustrate how all these address-related elements work together, suppose you pass the address of a record area to a subprogram with this statement:

```
CALL SUBPROG USING BY REFERENCE ADDRESS OF RECORD-AREA
```

when the subprogram Procedure Division header is this:

```
PROCEDURE DIVISION USING RECORD-ADDRESS
```

Then, you can establish addressability to the record area from within the subprogram using this statement:

```
SET ADDRESS OF RECORD-AREA TO RECORD-ADDRESS
```

Here, both RECORD-ADDRESS and RECORD-AREA have to be defined in the Linkage Section of the subprogram, with RECORD-AREA at the 01 or 77 level. In addition, RECORD-ADDRESS has to be defined as a pointer data item.

Note in the format in figure 3-7 that you can also use the SET statement to initialize pointer data items. For example, if you want to initialize the ADDRESS register of a record called INVENTORY-RECORD that's defined in the Linkage Section of a program, you can code a SET statement like this:

```
SET ADDRESS OF INVENTORY-RECORD TO NULL
```

Or, if you want to initialize a pointer data item called RECORD-ADDRESS that's defined in the Working-Storage Section of a program, you can code this SET statement:

```
SET RECORD-ADDRESS TO NULL
```

In either case, the field is set to a value of nonnumeric zero.

Frankly, you won't want to manipulate storage addresses in most of the COBOL programs you write. In fact, unless you're working in CICS, you probably won't use pointer data items, the ADDRESS register, or the new format of the SET statement at all. The ADDRESS register is especially useful in CICS programs, though. So I'll talk about it more in chapter 6 when I discuss the VS COBOL II considerations for CICS.

The Extended Graphic Character Set   In chapter 1, I introduced you to the Extended Graphic Character Set, which allows you to define double-byte data items and literals. You define these data items using a new USAGE clause, USAGE IS DISPLAY-1. The PICTURE clause associated with an unedited double-byte data item can contain only the letter "G," which represents a single character of two bytes. For an edited double-byte data item, the PICTURE clause can also contain the letter "B," which represents a two-byte blank. Unless you're using Kanji data or scientific notations that require two bytes for a character, you'll probably never use the Extended Graphic Character Set.

Discussion

If you're using Release 1 or 2 of VS COBOL II, the elements presented in this topic along with those presented in chapter 1 should be all you need to know to start coding with VS COBOL II. On the other hand, if you're using Release 3 of VS COBOL II, or if you plan on converting to it in the near future, read the next topic before you begin coding. It presents additional elements available with Release 3 that you should know about.

Terminology

VSAM return code
VSAM function code
VSAM feedback code
pointer data item

Objective

Apply the language elements presented in this chapter to your COBOL programs whenever appropriate.

Topic 2   Elements implemented by Release 3 of VS COBOL II

I mentioned in chapter 1 that the first two releases of VS COBOL II don't qualify as standard compilers under the 1985 standards. That's because they don't contain some of the elements required by the standards, even at the lowest level. Release 3, however, does include the elements that are necessary to conform to these standards. In the first part of this topic, then, I'll introduce you to the 1985 standards and present those elements as implemented by Release 3 of VS COBOL II. Then, I'll present two additional elements of Release 3 you should know about.

If you're already using Release 3, you'll want to be sure to read this topic so that you can take advantage of its new elements. But even if you're not using Release 3 yet, you should read this topic. Because of the enhancements that were included in this release, it's likely that you'll be converting to it before long. And if you still haven't converted to VS COBOL II, it's likely that Release 3 will be the release you'll convert to when you do convert.

ELEMENTS OF THE 1985 STANDARDS IMPLEMENTED BY RELEASE 3

The 1985 standards are a long overdue revision of the 1974 ANS COBOL standards. They are the industry standards on which Release 3 of VS COBOL II is based. Therefore, it's important that you know a little bit about them. So before I present the new elements implemented by Release 3, I'll introduce the different modules that make up the standards.

An introduction to the 1985 standards

Figure 3-8 presents the *functional processing modules* of the 1985 COBOL standards. As you can see, all the modules with the exception of Report Writer consist of two levels; the Report Writer module has only one level. The second level of a module always contains more COBOL elements than the first level. For example, the simple DIVIDE statement is part of level 1 of the nucleus module, while the DIVIDE statement with the REMAINDER clause is part of level 2.

Compilers are classified according to how fully they implement each module in the standards. If you look at figure 3-8, you can see that for a compiler to qualify as a minimum subset of the 1985 standards, it must contain

Module name	1985 standards	Minimum subset	Intermediate subset	High subset
Nucleus	2 levels	Level 1	Level 1	Level 2
Sequential I/O	2 levels	Level 1	Level 1	Level 2
Relative I/O	2 levels	None	Level 1	Level 2
Indexed I/O	2 levels	None	Level 1	Level 2
Inter-program communication	2 levels	Level 1	Level 1	Level 2
Sort/merge	2 levels	None	Level 1	Level 2
Source text manipulation	2 levels	None	Level 1	Level 2
Report Writer	1 level	None	None	None
Communication	2 levels	None	None	None
Debug	2 levels	None	None	None
Segmentation	2 levels	None	None	None

Figure 3-8   The modules of the 1985 standards required for minimum, intermediate, and high subset compilers

the first level of the nucleus, sequential I/O, and inter-program communication modules. For a compiler to qualify as an intermediate subset, it must contain the first level of the relative I/O, indexed I/O, sort/merge, and source text manipulation modules in addition to the modules required for a minimum subset. And a high-subset compiler must contain both the first and second level of each of these modules.

If you're familiar with the 1974 standards, there are three things you should notice about the modules that make up the 1985 standards. First, there's no table handling module. In the new standards, table handling has been included as part of the nucleus module. Second, there's a new module, *source text manipulation*. Actually, this isn't a new module; it's an expanded version of the library module of the 1974 standards. It consists of the COPY statement and the REPLACE statement. I'll cover the REPLACE statement later in this topic. Third, the last four modules, Report Writer, communication, debug, and segmentation, are optional; they aren't required even for a high subset compiler.

Figure 3-9 presents the specific elements of the 1985 standards that have been implemented by Release 3 of VS COBOL II. As you can see, the majority of these elements are part of the nucleus module. However, there are also some changes to the sequential, relative, and indexed I/O modules, the inter-program communication module, the sort/merge module, and the source text manipulation module.

The nucleus module

Many of the changes in the standards that are implemented by VS COBOL II Release 3 are part of the nucleus module. Although most of these changes won't have a dramatic effect on the way you code your programs, some of them can make your programs easier to read and understand. So use these features in the new programs you write whenever possible.

The SET ON/OFF statement   The SET ON/OFF statement makes it possible to set external switches associated with specific hardware and software devices. To set an external switch on, you code a statement in this format:

```
SET mnemonic-name TO ON
```

And to set a switch off, you code a statement in this format:

```
SET mnemonic-name TO OFF
```

In either case, you must define mnemonic-name and its on and off conditions in the SPECIAL-NAMES paragraph. Since most systems no longer use external switches, you'll probably never use this statement.

New ADD statement format   Under the first two releases of VS COBOL II, the word TO is illegal when the GIVING clause is used in an ADD statement. Under Release 3, however, you can use the word TO with the GIVING clause, although it's optional. For example, you can code the following statement:

```
ADD SUBTOTAL-1 TO SUBTOTAL-2 GIVING GRAND-TOTAL
```

NOT clauses   Many COBOL statements provide clauses for specific conditions like the AT END condition in a sequential READ statement or the

Element	Explanation
Nucleus level 1	
SET ON/OFF statement	New statement. Allows setting of external switches.
ADD statement	New format. The keyword TO is allowed with the GIVING format.
NOT clauses	New element. Provides for checking of specific conditions that do *not* occur.
Relative subscripts	New element. Provides for relative subscripts to be used for referring to table entries.
GREATER THAN OR EQUAL TO (>=) LESS THAN OR EQUAL TO (<=)	New relational operators.
Class tests	New class tests added. ALPHABETIC-UPPER and ALPHABETIC-LOWER provide testing for uppercase and lowercase letters in alphanumeric fields. You can also create your own class names in the SPECIAL-NAMES paragraph.
Omission of FILLER	New element. Coding of FILLER is not required.
Nonnumeric literals	Enhanced element. Provides for a minimum length of 160 characters for nonnumeric literals.
BINARY PACKED-DECIMAL	New usages. Provide for binary and packed-decimal fields.
Nucleus level 2	
ACCEPT DAY-OF-WEEK statement	New form of ACCEPT statement. Provides for access to the system day of the week.
Reference modification	New element. Provides for accessing a selected portion of a record or field.
De-editing numeric items	New feature of the MOVE statement. Provides for de-editing numeric fields by moving them from a numeric-edited field to a numeric field.
Table handling	Enhanced element. Provides for tables of up to seven levels.

Figure 3-9   Elements of the 1985 standards implemented by Release 3 of VS COBOL II (part 1 of 2)

Element	Explanation
INSPECT statement	Enhanced element. Provides for the replacement of multiple values using the CONVERTING phrase.
VALUE clause	Enhanced element. VALUE can now be specified for data items containing or subordinate to an OCCURS clause.
Sequential, relative, indexed I/O level 2	
VARYING IN SIZE phrase	New element. Provides for specifying the lengths of records in a variable-length file.
Inter-program communication level 2	
CALL BY CONTENT	Enhanced element. Provides for passing the content of a data item.
Nested source programs	New element. Provides for nesting of one source program within another.
Global names	New element. Provides for data names and file names that can be referenced by any program in a nest.
External names	New element. Provides for data names and file names that are associated with an entire run unit.
Common program	New element. Provides for programs that can be invoked by any program in which it's directly or indirectly contained.
Initial program	New element. Provides for the initialization of called programs.
Sort/merge level 1	
DUPLICATES phrase	New element. Determines the order in which records containing duplicate sort keys are sorted.
GIVING phrase	Enhanced element. Provides for multiple files to be specified in the GIVING phrase.
Source text manipulation level 2	
REPLACE statement	New element. Provides for replacing text in your program at the time it's compiled.

Figure 3-9   Elements of the 1985 standards implemented by Release 3 of VS COBOL II (part 2 of 2)

Clause	Statements
NOT ON SIZE ERROR	ADD SUBTRACT MULTIPLY DIVIDE COMPUTE
NOT AT END	READ RETURN
NOT INVALID KEY	READ START WRITE DELETE REWRITE
NOT ON OVERFLOW	STRING UNSTRING
NOT ON EXCEPTION	CALL

Figure 3-10   NOT clauses and the statements to which they apply

ON SIZE ERROR condition in an arithmetic statement. Under the 1985 standards, these statements also provide a clause that is executed when the condition doesn't occur. For instance, you can code a NOT AT END clause in a sequential READ statement and a NOT ON SIZE ERROR clause in an arithmetic statement. The NOT clauses that are implemented by Release 3 of VS COBOL II are summarized in figure 3-10.

In general, the NOT AT END and NOT INVALID KEY clauses are useful when you code I/O statements. For instance, figure 3-11 illustrates the use of these clauses in sequential and random READ statements. Without these clauses, the coding for the same functions is a bit less clear, so I recommend the use of these clauses as shown.

Similarly, you will probably find that the other NOT clauses are useful in some situations. Often, you can use the condition clause to set a switch one way and the NOT clause to set the switch the other way. For instance, you can use the ON SIZE ERROR clause to turn an error switch on, while you use the NOT ON SIZE ERROR clause to turn the error switch off.

A sequential read module using NOT AT END

```
310-READ-INVENTORY-RECORD.
*
    READ INVMAST RECORD INTO INVENTORY-MASTER-RECORD
        AT END
            SET INVMAST-EOF TO TRUE
        NOT AT END
            ADD 1 TO RECORD-COUNT.
```

A random read module using NOT INVALID KEY

```
310-READ-INVENTORY-RECORD.
*
    MOVE TR-PART-NO TO IM-PART-NO.
    READ INVMAST RECORD INTO INVENTORY-MASTER-RECORD
        INVALID KEY
            MOVE 'N' TO RECORD-FOUND-SW
        NOT INVALID KEY
            MOVE 'Y' TO RECORD-FOUND-SW.
```

Figure 3-11   Using NOT clauses in sequential and random read modules

---

Relative subscripts   Under Release 3 of VS COBOL II, you can use *relative subscripting* to refer to table entries. This is analogous to relative indexing when indexes are used. For example, you can reference a table entry like this:

```
ITEM-PRICE(ITEM-SUB + 1)
```

where ITEM-SUB is defined as a subscript.

New relational operators   Four new relational operators have been added in Release 3 of VS COBOL II. They are GREATER THAN OR EQUAL TO, >=, LESS THAN OR EQUAL TO, and <=. Although GREATER THAN OR EQUAL TO is equivalent to NOT LESS THAN, it can improve readability in some cases. Similarly, LESS THAN OR EQUAL TO is equivalent to NOT GREATER THAN, but it can improve readability in some cases.

Expanded class tests   Under any release of VS COBOL II, you can code a class test to determine whether an alphanumeric field is numeric or alphabetic. Under Release 3, you can also use the class test to find out whether a field contains lowercase (ALPHABETIC-LOWER) or uppercase (ALPHA-

BETIC-UPPER) letters. Then, ALPHABETIC refers to a field that contains lowercase letters, uppercase letters, or both. These new class tests correspond with the addition of lowercase letters to the COBOL character set.

With Release 3, you can also use a class test to find out whether a field consists of only the characters you define for a class name in the SPECIAL-NAMES paragraph of the Environment Division. Although you may find occasional use for these special class tests, you certainly won't use them much. In fact, I recommend you avoid using class names since they can reduce the readability of your Procedure Divisions by putting some of the program logic in the Environment Division. That's why I won't take the time to show you how to code class names in the Environment Division. If class names are used in your shop, you can quickly learn how to use them on your own.

Omission of FILLER   As you know, you can use FILLER in place of a data name for a field you aren't going to refer to in a program. Under Release 3 of VS COBOL II, though, you don't have to code the word FILLER if you are describing a record or field that you aren't going to refer to. However, we recommend that you always code FILLER so there won't be any confusion about your intent. If you omit the FILLERs, it's hard to tell when you mistakenly omit a data name.

Length of nonnumeric literals   Under the first two releases of VS COBOL II, a nonnumeric literal can have a maximum length of 120 characters. Under Release 3, 160 characters are provided for nonnumeric literals. This is the minimum length required by the 1985 standards.

New usages   Because only one computational usage (COMPUTA-TIONAL, or COMP) was provided by the 1974 standards, the first two releases of VS COBOL II had to use extensions to provide for the different types of usages available on an IBM mainframe. For example, COMP-3 is used to define a packed-decimal data item and COMP is used to define a binary data item. Now, Release 3 provides for both types of storage with two new usages: BINARY and PACKED-DECIMAL. So, you'll probably see COMP and COMP-3 being replaced by BINARY and PACKED-DECIMAL. This will make it much more obvious what type of data representation is being used.

The ACCEPT DAY-OF-WEEK statement   Under Release 3 of VS COBOL II, you can use the ACCEPT statement not only to access the system date and time, but the day of the week as well. To do that you use this format of the ACCEPT statement:

```
ACCEPT data-name FROM DAY-OF-WEEK
```

In this case, you must define data-name as a one-digit elementary item. After the statement has been executed, a value of 1 in the receiving field represents Monday; a value of 2, Tuesday; and so on.

Reference modification   Under the first two releases of VS COBOL II, you can refer only to the entire record or field that is represented by a record name or a field name. Under Release 3, though, you can use *reference modification* to refer to a portion of a record or field. For instance, this code

```
IM-ITEM-NO (3:2)
```

refers to two characters in the field named IM-ITEM-NO, starting with the third character from the left. Similarly,

```
IM-ITEM-NO (2)
```

refers to all the characters in the field starting with the second character from the left.

When you use reference modification, the first integer in the parentheses after a data name indicates the starting position within the field. As a result, the range of this value must be from one through the number of characters within the field. Then, the second integer represents the number of characters to be operated on. You must code this value to refer only to characters within the field. You can omit this second integer to refer to all the remaining characters in the field. If you use indexing or subscripting with a data name, you code the reference modification parentheses following the indexing or subscripting parentheses.

Reference modification is useful because it gives you more control over the characters within a field. As a result, it can help you improve the coding of some character manipulation routines.

De-editing numeric items   When you move a numeric field to a numeric-edited field, it gets edited. Under Release 3 of VS COBOL II, the MOVE statement provides for the opposite condition too—it de-edits a numeric-edited item when you move the item to a numeric field. You might never have to use this facility of 1985 COBOL, but perhaps you'll run into an application someday that requires it.

Seven-level tables   Under the first two releases of VS COBOL II, you can define a table with a maximum of three levels. And for most applications, three levels is sufficient. However, under Release 3 of VS COBOL II, you can now code tables with up to seven levels.

New INSPECT statement format   Under the first two releases of VS COBOL II, if you wanted to replace multiple characters with other characters using the INSPECT statement, you had to code multiple REPLACING phrases. Under Release 3, however, you can do the same thing using a single CONVERTING phrase. For example, instead of coding

```
INSPECT FIELD-1
    REPLACING ALL 'X' BY 'Y' AFTER INITIAL 'R'
                   'B' BY 'Z' AFTER INITIAL 'R'
                   'C' BY 'Q' AFTER INITIAL 'R'
```

you can code

```
INSPECT FIELD-1
    CONVERTING 'XBC' TO 'YZQ' AFTER INITIAL 'R'
```

Both statements accomplish the same thing, but the second one is much simpler to code.

New use for VALUE clause   Under Release 3 of VS COBOL II, you can code a VALUE clause on a data description entry that contains or is subordinate to an OCCURS clause. For example, you might code something like this:

```
01  PRICE-TABLE.
*
    05  PRICE-GROUP         OCCURS 16 TIMES
                            INDEXED BY PRICE-TABLE-INDEX.
        10  ITEM-NUMBER     PIC X(3)    VALUE SPACE.
        10  ITEM-PRICE      PIC S99V99  VALUE ZERO.
```

In this case, all 16 occurrences of ITEM-NUMBER are initialized to space, and all 16 occurrences of ITEM-PRICE are initialized to zero.

As you can see in the example above, this use of the VALUE clause makes it easy to initialize a table of values. By using VALUE clauses for a table description, you eliminate the need to initialize the table in the Procedure Division. So I recommend that you use this clause whenever you use a table that needs to be initialized at the beginning of a program.

The sequential, relative, and indexed I/O modules

Under Release 3 of VS COBOL II, you can use the VARYING IN SIZE phrase for a sequential, relative, or indexed file to specify the record size of a variable-length record. Under the first two releases of VS COBOL II, you use the RECORDS CONTAINS clause to do that. For example, the clause

```
RECORD CONTAINS 26 TO 368 CHARACTERS
```

can be written as

```
RECORD IS VARYING IN SIZE
    FROM 26 TO 368 CHARACTERS
    DEPENDING ON data-name
```

in Release 3. The difference in these two phrases is in how they're implemented.

When you use the RECORD CONTAINS clause, you must define each possible record length in the record description entry. You can accomplish this using multiple record descriptions, one for each possible record length, or using an OCCURS DEPENDING ON clause in the record description. When you use the RECORD IS VARYING IN SIZE clause, this isn't necessary. Instead, you specify the record size in the DEPENDING ON phrase. In the example above, the record can contain any number of characters between and including 26 and 368.

There probably aren't many instances in which you'll need to use the RECORD IS VARYING IN SIZE clause. Most files that have variable-length records either have multiple record descriptions or have records that contain a variable number of segments. When that's the case, I think RECORD CONTAINS and OCCURS DEPENDING ON are easier to use than RECORD IS VARYING IN SIZE. However, I see no problem with your using RECORD IS VARYING IN SIZE if you prefer it. In any case, you should be familiar with RECORD IS VARYING IN SIZE so you can use it if you ever have an application for which RECORD CONTAINS and OCCURS DEPENDING ON aren't appropriate.

The inter-program communication module

The inter-program communication module of the 1985 standards has been greatly expanded from the 1974 standards. In addition to providing for transferring control between programs and passing data back and forth, the new standards also provide for the nesting of source programs, the use of global and external names, and common and initial programs.

In general, most of these features are useful only if you implement the modules of your programs as subprograms. Since most shops don't develop programs that way, I'll describe these features briefly just to familiarize you with the concepts. If you want to know more about these features, consult the VS COBOL II manuals.

New CALL BY CONTENT format   In topic 1, I introduced the CALL BY CONTENT statement. As you'll recall, this statement allows you to pass a literal value or the length of a data item directly to a subprogram. Under Release 3, you can also pass the value of a data item using CALL BY CONTENT. For example, if you coded the statement

```
CALL UPDATE USING BY CONTENT UPDATE-FLAG
```

the value of UPDATE-FLAG would be passed to the subprogram.

The difference between passing a data item BY CONTENT and BY REFERENCE (the default) is that BY CONTENT passes the value of the data item and BY REFERENCE passes the address of the data item. So when you pass a data item BY REFERENCE, the calling program and the subprogram both refer to the same area of storage when they refer to the data item. But when you use BY CONTENT, the subprogram stores the passed value in a separate location. That way, if the value is changed during the execution of the subprogram, it doesn't affect the original value of the data item.

There probably aren't too many situations in which you'll need to use this format of the CALL BY CONTENT statement. In many cases, you'll want the subprogram to change the original value of the data item. But if you want to save the original value, this CALL statement format can be useful.

Nested source programs   Release 3 of VS COBOL II provides for the capability of *nesting a source program* within another source program. In other words, an entire COBOL program, consisting of an Identification Division, Environment Division, Data Division, and Procedure Division, can be contained within another program and can be invoked by the containing program.

Figure 3-12 presents the structure of a nested program. There are three things you should notice here. First, the nested program must be coded following the last statement of the program in which it's nested. Second, both the contained program and the containing program must be followed by an END PROGRAM header. On this header, you specify the name of the program you're ending as it's coded on the PROGRAM-ID paragraph. Third, you can

```
     IDENTIFICATION DIVISION.
     *
      PROGRAM-ID.      program-name-1.
     *
       .
       .
      ENVIRONMENT DIVISION.
     *
       .
       .
      DATA DIVISION.
     *
       .
       .
      PROCEDURE DIVISION.
     *
       .
       .
          CALL program-name-2.
       .
       .
      IDENTIFICATION DIVISION.
     *
      PROGRAM-ID.      program-name-2.
     *
       .
       .
      ENVIRONMENT DIVISION.
     *
       .
       .
      DATA DIVISION.
     *
       .
       .
      PROCEDURE DIVISION.
     *
       .
       .
          END PROGRAM program-name-2.
          END PROGRAM program-name-1.
```

Containing
program

Contained
program

Figure 3-12   The structure for nesting programs

invoke a contained program with a CALL statement, just as if it was a
subprogram. The program name you specify on the CALL statement must be
the same as the name coded on the PROGRAM-ID paragraph of the program
you're calling.

As I said at the beginning of this section, you'll probably use this feature only if your shop requires you to implement the modules of your programs as subprograms. Then, coding each module as a nested program is a viable alternative to coding each as a separately compiled program. But if you use subprograms only to perform general purpose functions, as in most shops, continue coding them as separately compiled modules. That way, they can be called from any program. In contrast, a nested program can be called only from the program in which it's nested.

Global names   A *global name* is a data name or file name that can be referred to by the program in which it's defined or by any program contained in the program in which it's defined. In other words, if you define a name as global, it is accessible from any contained program. This eliminates the need to pass data between programs as you do when you use subprograms.

To identify a data name or file name as global, you code the GLOBAL clause on the data description entry. The GLOBAL clause must be specified at the 01 level. If there are any data names subordinate to the global name, they are also global. For example, in the data description entry

```
01  CURRENT-DATE          GLOBAL.
*
    05  CURRENT-MONTH   PIC 99.
    05  CURRENT-DAY     PIC 99.
    05  CURRENT-YEAR    PIC 99.
```

all four data names are defined as global and can be referred to by any program that's contained in the program that defines them. Note that you do not have to redefine the data names in a contained program for that program to access the data item.

External names   Every file or data item is associated with an area of storage. That storage can be defined as either internal or external to a program. If the storage is internal, it's referred to by an *internal name*, which is associated only with the program that defines it. If the storage is external, it's referred to by an *external name*, which is associated not with any particular program, but with the run unit. Then, it can be accessed by any program in the run unit that describes it.

To define a data item or file as external, you code the EXTERNAL clause on its definition like this:

```
01  CURRENT-DATE    PIC 9(6)   EXTERNAL.
```

This clause can be coded for a data description entry only at the 01 level. If you define any data items subordinate to an external item, those items are also external. Unlike global data items, you must define an external data item in every program in which it's used.

Common programs   A *common program* is a program contained within another program that can be invoked from the containing program or from any other program contained directly or indirectly in the containing program. For example, suppose the program INV3500 contains the programs INV3510 and INV3520. And suppose that INV3510 contains the program INV3511. If you define INV3520 as a common program, you can invoke it not only from INV3500, but from INV3510 and INV3511 as well.

     To define a program as common, you code the COMMON clause on the PROGRAM-ID paragraph like this:

```
PROGRAM-ID.    AR2311 IS COMMON.
```

Note that you can code the COMMON clause only on a program that is contained within another program.

Initial programs   An *initial program* is one that is in its initial state, just as it was the first time it was executed in a run unit. So each time you execute an initial program, all the data in its Working-Storage Section is initialized as well as any data in the Working-Storage Sections of any programs contained within it. In addition, all files defined as internal are closed.

     To define a program as initial, you code the INITIAL clause on the PROGRAM-ID paragraph like this:

```
PROGRAM-ID.    AR2311 IS INITIAL.
```

The sort/merge module

Two enhancements have been made to the sort/merge feature in Release 3 of VS COBOL II. The first enhancement is the addition of the DUPLICATES phrase. The presence or absence of this phrase determines the order in which records are sorted when they have identical keys. If you specify the phrase, duplicates are left in the same order as they occur in the input file. If you omit it, the sequence is undefined. Unless it's important that records with duplicate keys be kept in the same order as in the input file, you shouldn't code the DUPLICATES phrase since it makes the sort process less efficient.

The format of the DUPLICATES phrase is:

```
WITH DUPLICATES IN ORDER
```

You code it after the ON ASCENDING/DESCENDING KEY phrase and before the INPUT PROCEDURE, USING, OUTPUT PROCEDURE, or GIVING phrases, if they're present. For example, the statement

```
SORT SORTFILE
    ON ASCENDING KEY SR-LAST-ORDER-DATE
    WITH DUPLICATES
    USING INVMAST
    OUTPUT PROCEDURE IS 1000-PRINT-ORDER-REPORT
```

causes any records in INVMAST with the same last order date to remain in the same order in which they're read.

The sort/merge feature also allows you to specify multiple files in the GIVING phrase. For example, the statement

```
SORT SORTFILE
    ON ASCENDING KEY SR-CURRENT-MONTHLY-SALES
    INPUT PROCEDURE IS 1000-GET-CURRENT-PRODUCTS
    GIVING INVMST1 INVMST2
```

creates two output files, each containing the same records.

The source text manipulation module

As you learned earlier in this chapter, the library module under the 1974 standards has been replaced by the source text manipulation module under the 1985 standards. Both modules contain the COPY statement. However, the 1985 source text manipulation module also contains the REPLACE statement, which is implemented by VS COBOL II Release 3.

The REPLACE statement is used at compile time to replace text in your program with the text you specify. This is similar to specifying the REPLACING clause on a COPY statement except that you can use a REPLACE statement to replace text anywhere in your program; it's not limited to text copied in using the COPY statement.

When you use the REPLACE statement, you specify two things: the text you want to replace and the text that is to replace it. For example, to replace the text S9(5) by X(5), you code

```
REPLACE ==S9(5)== BY ==X(5)==
```

The double equal signs and the word BY are required.

You can also limit the scope of a REPLACE statement using the REPLACE OFF format. To do that, you code the REPLACE statement before the first occurrence of the text you want to replace. Then, you code the REPLACE OFF statement after the last occurrence of the text you want to replace. As a result, only the text between the two statements is replaced.

As I see it, there aren't too many applications for the REPLACE statement. With the global replace feature that most editors have today, it's usually just as easy to change the source code directly as it is to code a REPLACE statement. So, I don't recommend its use.

OTHER ELEMENTS IMPLEMENTED BY RELEASE 3

In addition to the language elements that were implemented by Release 3 of VS COBOL II based on the 1985 standards, there are two other non-standard changes you'll want to know about. I'll present those elements here.

Hexadecimal notation

One of the new features of VS COBOL II Release 3 is the support of hexadecimal notation. You can now code a hexadecimal value as a nonnumeric literal. To do that, you enclose the value in quotes (or apostrophes if the APOST option is in effect) and precede it with the character X. For example, this is a valid hexadecimal literal:

```
X"40404040"
```

A hexadecimal literal can contain up to 320 hexadecimal digits, which is equivalent to 160 EBCDIC characters.

Optional division headers

Under Release 3 of VS COBOL II, only the IDENTIFICATION DIVISION header is required. All the others, ENVIRONMENT DIVISION, DATA DIVISION, and PROCEDURE DIVISION, are optional. This was done mainly to simplify the coding of contained programs, which may not contain code in one or more of these divisions.

DISCUSSION

As you have seen in this topic, the features that are implemented by Release 3 of VS COBOL II are significant. Although you will use some of them only for special purposes, you'll use others quite frequently, especially those that are part of the nucleus module.

One thing I didn't present in this chapter is the way some of the elements are executed under Release 3 in contrast to how they're executed under Release 2. For example, because lowercase letters were non-COBOL characters under Releases 1 and 2, they were not treated the same as uppercase letters. Under Release 3, however, lowercase letters are part of the COBOL character set and are treated the same as uppercase letters. So if you ever recompile a Release 1 or 2 program that contains lowercase letters with a Release 3 compiler, it may not execute the same.

If you won't ever need to recompile a Release 2 program under Release 3, you don't have to worry about these differences. But if you're using Release 2 now and plan to convert to Release 3, it's likely that at some time you'll need to modify one of your Release 2 programs and recompile it with the Release 3 compiler. In that case, you should be aware of the differences in the way some of the elements are executed. In the next chapter, I'll present these differences along with two compiler options that have been added to Release 3 to help identify them.

Terminology

functional processing module
source text manipulation module
relative subscripting
reference modification
nested source programs
global name
internal name
external name
common program
initial program

Objective

Apply the Release 3 language elements presented in this topic to your COBOL programs whenever appropriate.

Section

3

VS COBOL II
program development features

If you've read section 2, you should have a pretty good idea of how to code your VS COBOL II programs. But there are some additional things you should know about VS COBOL II before you begin testing and debugging your programs. So, this section will present the most important program development features of VS COBOL II. Chapter 4 presents compiler and run-time considerations. And chapter 5 presents the VS COBOL II debugger, COBTEST. After you've finished these chapters, you'll know everything you need to use VS COBOL II to develop COBOL programs.

Chapter
four

Compiler and run-time considerations

In this chapter, I'll present the new features of VS COBOL II that affect the compilation and execution of your programs. These features fall into five categories: procedures for compiling, link-editing, and executing your programs; compiler options; compiler-directing statements; compiler listings; and run-time options.

PROCEDURES FOR COMPILING, LINK-EDITING, AND EXECUTING YOUR PROGRAMS

In general, the procedures for compiling, link-editing, and executing VS COBOL II programs are the same as those for OS/VS COBOL programs. However, there are some differences you should be aware of. To illustrate those differences, I'll present the general procedures for compiling, link-editing, and executing VS COBOL II programs in three different environments: MVS, TSO, and CMS. If you're working in another environment, be sure to check the procedures for your particular system.

Using MVS JCL and cataloged procedures

When you develop programs under MVS, you'll probably use the cataloged procedures provided with the system to compile, link-edit, and execute your

Procedures			Step names	
Compile-only	COB2UC		Compile	COB2
Compile-and-link	COB2UCL		Link	LKED
Compile-link-and-go	COB2UCLG		Go	GO
Compile-and-go	COB2UCG			

Figure 4-1   Cataloged procedures for batch program development in VS COBOL II

programs. Figure 4-1 shows the procedures for VS COBOL II along with the step names used by the procedures. As you can see, the procedure names are very similar to those for OS/VS COBOL. And, in fact, the procedures themselves are very similar. However, there are some differences, which I'll discuss as I present each of the procedures. Except for the compile step, the procedure step names are the same for VS COBOL II as for OS/VS COBOL. (If you don't have much experience with MVS job control language, I recommend you get a copy of our book, *MVS JCL*. It explains in detail the types of statements you'll find in the cataloged procedures that follow.)

The compile-only procedure   Sometimes, you'll want to invoke the VS COBOL II compiler by itself, without link-editing or executing the application program. One reason for doing that is to let the compiler point out any syntax errors so you can correct them before you submit a compile-link-and-go or compile-and-go job to compile and execute the program. Another reason is to compile a subprogram you want stored in an object library. To do either, you use the COB2UC procedure, presented in figure 4-2.

Note in this figure that the name of the VS COBOL II compiler is IGYCRCTL. If you ever need to execute the compiler without using a cataloged procedure, IGYCRCTL is the program you'll run.

The main difference between the COB2UC procedure and the equivalent procedure under OS/VS COBOL is the default output. The default for COB2UC is to create an object module, while the default for the OS/VS COBOL procedure is to create punch output. Under VS COBOL II, the object module is created by specifying OBJECT as a run-time parameter and by defining a SYSLIN data set. (The OBJECT option of VS COBOL II is equivalent to the LOAD option of OS/VS COBOL.)

You should also notice that the procedure includes a STEPLIB statement. This statement defines a library that contains modules required by the VS COBOL II compiler. In figure 4-2, this library is named SYS1.COB2COMP. The name may be different in your shop.

The COB2UC procedure

```
XXCOB2UC PROC
***     PROC FOR COBOL II - COMPILE ONLY
XXCOB2    EXEC  PGM=IGYCRCTL,PARM='OBJECT,MAP',
XX              REGION=1024K
XXSTEPLIB  DD   DSNAME=SYS1.COB2COMP,DISP=SHR
XXSYSPRINT DD   SYSOUT=*
XXSYSLIN   DD   DSNAME=&&LOADSET,UNIT=SYSDA,
XX              DISP=(MOD,PASS),SPACE=(TRK,(3,3))
XXSYSUT1   DD   UNIT=SYSDA,SPACE=(CYL,(1,1))
XXSYSUT2   DD   UNIT=SYSDA,SPACE=(CYL,(1,1))
XXSYSUT3   DD   UNIT=SYSDA,SPACE=(CYL,(1,1))
XXSYSUT4   DD   UNIT=SYSDA,SPACE=(CYL,(1,1))
XXSYSUT5   DD   UNIT=SYSDA,SPACE=(CYL,(1,1))
XXSYSUT6   DD   UNIT=SYSDA,SPACE=(CYL,(1,1))
XXSYSUT7   DD   UNIT=SYSDA,SPACE=(CYL,(1,1))
```

Invoking JCL

```
//DLOWE2A   JOB   USER=DLOWE2,PASSWORD=XXXXXXXX
//          EXEC COB2UC,PARM.COB2='APOST,OBJECT'
//COB2.SYSLIN DD DSNAME=MMA2.INVENTRY.OBJLIB(INV3520),DISP=SHR
//COB2.SYSIN  DD DSNAME=MMA2.INVENTRY.COBOL(INV3520),DISP=SHR
//COB2.SYSLIB DD DSNAME=MMA2.COPYLIB.COBOL2,DISP=SHR
```

Figure 4-2   The COB2UC procedure

For any compilation under VS COBOL II, six work data sets are required: SYSUT1, SYSUT2, SYSUT3, SYSUT4, SYSUT6, and SYSUT7. If you use COPY statements in your program, an additional data set, SYSUT5, is required. As you can see, SYSUT5 is included in the cataloged procedure.

Finally, you should notice the space allocations for the compile step and the work data sets. For the compile step, the size of the region has been increased from 128K under OS/VS COBOL to 1024K. (The minimum size for a region under VS COBOL II is 512K.) And for the work data sets, space is now allocated in cylinders rather than in blocks.

The bottom part of figure 4-2 shows typical JCL used to invoke the COB2UC procedure. Here, SYSIN names a member of a partitioned data set as the source program. SYSLIB identifies a COPY library named MMA2.COPYLIB.COBOL2. And SYSLIN overrides the temporary data set specified in the procedure, storing the object module as INV3520 in the library named MMA2.INVENTRY.OBJLIB.

The compile-and-link procedure   To compile and link a program, you use the COB2UCL procedure, shown in figure 4-3. Except for the differences I mentioned when discussing the COB2UC procedure, the COB2UCL procedure is almost identical to the equivalent OS/VS COBOL procedure. Both procedures compile a program and then link-edit the resulting object module to create a load module. The only thing you should notice is that there is no SEP operand coded on the UNIT parameter of the DD statement for SYSUT1 as there is in the OS/VS COBOL procedure. This operand was coded for efficiency purposes and specified that a different channel be used when accessing the SYSUT1 data set than was used for the SYSLIN and SYSLMOD data sets. SEP is no longer a valid operand under MVS/XA.

The bottom part of figure 4-3 presents typical JCL for invoking the COB2UCL procedure. Because you'll usually want to store the load module created by the link-edit step in a permanent load library, you'll want to override the SYSLMOD DD statement to indicate the member and library. In figure 4-3, I stored the load module as INV3520 in MMA2.INVENTRY.LOADLIB.

The LKED.SYSLIB DD statement identifies any object libraries used to resolve subprogram references. As you can see, the procedure supplies one subprogram library: SYS1.COB2LIB. This library contains essential COBOL subroutines, so it must be available when the object module is link-edited. If you want to specify additional subprogram libraries, you need to concatenate them with this library. In figure 4-3, I concatenated the library MMA2.INVENTRY.OBJLIB.

The compile-link-and-go procedure   To compile, link-edit, and execute a VS COBOL II program you use the COB2UCLG procedure, shown in figure 4-4. The compile and link-edit steps are the same as in the COB2UCL procedure. Then, in the execute step, there are four data sets specified that aren't included in the equivalent OS/VS COBOL procedure: STEPLIB, SYSABOUT, SYSDBOUT, and SYSUDUMP. STEPLIB defines a library that contains modules necessary to execute a VS COBOL II program. SYSABOUT is required if a SNAP dump is requested. (A SNAP dump contains information that's essential if you're debugging a program using a system dump. This information includes the base locators for different areas of the program, which you can use to locate data items in the system dump. If you use a formatted dump, however, you won't need the SNAP dump because the value of each data item is printed right along with its name and description.) SYSDBOUT is required if a formatted dump is requested or if the batch debugger is being used. And SYSUDUMP is required if the DUMP compiler option is specified, unless SYSABEND or SYSMDUMP are defined. (You'll learn more about compiler options and output later in this chapter.)

The COB2UCL procedure

```
XXCOB2UCL PROC
***     PROC FOR COBOL II - COMPILE AND LINK
XXCOB2    EXEC  PGM=IGYCRCTL,PARM='OBJECT,MAP',REGION=1024K
XXSTEPLIB DD    DSNAME=SYS1.COB2COMP,DISP=SHR
XXSYSPRINT DD   SYSOUT=*
XXSYSLIN  DD    DSNAME=&&LOADSET,UNIT=SYSDA,DISP=(MOD,PASS),
XX              SPACE=(TRK,(3,3))
XXSYSUT1  DD    UNIT=SYSDA,SPACE=(CYL,(1,1))
XXSYSUT2  DD    UNIT=SYSDA,SPACE=(CYL,(1,1))
XXSYSUT3  DD    UNIT=SYSDA,SPACE=(CYL,(1,1))
XXSYSUT4  DD    UNIT=SYSDA,SPACE=(CYL,(1,1))
XXSYSUT5  DD    UNIT=SYSDA,SPACE=(CYL,(1,1))
XXSYSUT6  DD    UNIT=SYSDA,SPACE=(CYL,(1,1))
XXSYSUT7  DD    UNIT=SYSDA,SPACE=(CYL,(1,1))
XXLKED    EXEC  PGM=IEWL,PARM='LIST,XREF,LET,MAP',COND=(5,LT,COB2),
XX              REGION=96K
XXSYSLIN  DD    DSNAME=&&LOADSET,DISP=(OLD,DELETE)
XX        DD    DDNAME=SYSIN
XXSYSLMOD DD    DSNAME=&&GOSET(GO),DISP=(,PASS),UNIT=SYSDA,
XX              SPACE=(CYL,(1,1,1))
XXSYSLIB  DD    DSNAME=SYS1.COB2LIB,DISP=SHR
XXSYSUT1  DD    UNIT=SYSDA,SPACE=(CYL,(1,1))
XXSYSPRINT DD   SYSOUT=*
```

Invoking JCL

```
//DLOWE2A   JOB  USER=DLOWE2,PASSWORD=XXXXXXXX
//          EXEC COB2UCL,PARM.COB2='APOST,OBJECT',REGION.LKED=
//COB2.SYSIN   DD DSNAME=MMA2.INVENTRY.COBOL(INV3520),DISP=SHR
//COB2.SYSLIB  DD DSNAME=MMA2.COPYLIB.COBOL2,DISP=SHR
//LKED.SYSLMOD DD DSNAME=MMA2.INVENTRY.LOADLIB(INV3520),DISP=SHR
//LKED.SYSLIB  DD
//            DD DSNAME=MMA2.INVENTRY.OBJLIB,DISP=SHR
```

Figure 4-3   The COB2UCL procedure

In the invoking JCL shown in the bottom part of figure 4-4, you can see that I supplied three DD statements for the GO step. The first, SYSOUT, defines the output data set used to print messages produced by COBOL DISPLAY statements. The others, INVMAST and INVLIST, allocate files processed by the program.

The compile-and-go procedure   For most program development purposes, you won't use the compile-link-and-go procedure. Instead, you'll use the simpler compile-and-go procedure. The difference between the two is

The COB2UCLG procedure

```
XXCOB2UCLG PROC
***     PROC FOR COBOL II - COMPILE, LINK, AND GO
XXCOB2     EXEC   PGM=IGYCRCTL,PARM='OBJECT,MAP',REGION=1024K
XXSTEPLIB  DD     DSNAME=SYS1.COB2COMP,DISP=SHR
XXSYSPRINT DD     SYSOUT=*
XXSYSLIN   DD     DSNAME=&&LOADSET,UNIT=SYSDA,DISP=(MOD,PASS),
XX                SPACE=(TRK,(3,3))
XXSYSUT1   DD     UNIT=SYSDA,SPACE=(CYL,(1,1))
XXSYSUT2   DD     UNIT=SYSDA,SPACE=(CYL,(1,1))
XXSYSUT3   DD     UNIT=SYSDA,SPACE=(CYL,(1,1))
XXSYSUT4   DD     UNIT=SYSDA,SPACE=(CYL,(1,1))
XXSYSUT5   DD     UNIT=SYSDA,SPACE=(CYL,(1,1))
XXSYSUT6   DD     UNIT=SYSDA,SPACE=(CYL,(1,1))
XXSYSUT7   DD     UNIT=SYSDA,SPACE=(CYL,(1,1))
XXLKED     EXEC   PGM=IEWL,PARM='LIST,XREF,LET,MAP',COND=(5,LT,COB2),
XX                REGION=96K
XXSYSLIN   DD     DSNAME=&&LOADSET,DISP=(OLD,DELETE)
XX         DD     DDNAME=SYSIN
XXSYSLMOD  DD     DSNAME=&&GOSET(GO),DISP=(,PASS),UNIT=SYSDA,
XX                SPACE=(CYL,(1,1,1))
XXSYSLIB   DD     DSNAME=SYS1.COB2LIB,DISP=SHR
XXSYSUT1   DD     UNIT=SYSDA,SPACE=(CYL,(1,1))
XXSYSPRINT DD     SYSOUT=*
XXGO       EXEC   PGM=*.LKED.SYSLMOD,COND=(5,LT,LKED)
XXSTEPLIB  DD     DSNAME=SYS1.COB2LIB,DISP=SHR
XXSYSABOUT DD     SYSOUT=A
XXSYSDBOUT DD     SYSOUT=A
XXSYSUDUMP DD     SYSOUT=A
```

Invoking JCL

```
//DLOWE2A  JOB   USER=DLOWE2,PASSWORD=XXXXXXXX
//         EXEC COB2UCLG,PARM.COB2='APOST,OBJECT',REGION.LKED=
//COB2.SYSIN    DD DSNAME=MMA2.INVENTRY.COBOL(INV3520),DISP=SHR
//COB2.SYSLIB   DD DSNAME=MMA2.COPYLIB.COBOL2,DISP=SHR
//LKED.SYSLMOD  DD DSNAME=MMA2.INVENTRY.LOADLIB(INV3520),DISP=SHR
//LKED.SYSLIB   DD
//             DD DSNAME=MMA2.INVENTRY.OBJLIB,DISP=SHR
//GO.SYSOUT     DD SYSOUT=A
//GO.INVMAST    DD DSNAME=MMA2.INVMAST.DATA,DISP=SHR
//GO.INVLIST    DD SYSOUT=A
```

Figure 4-4   The COB2UCLG procedure

The COB2UCG procedure

```
XXCOB2UCG PROC
***     PROC FOR COBOL II - COMPILE AND GO
XXCOB2    EXEC  PGM=IGYCRCTL,PARM='OBJECT,MAP',REGION=1024K
XXSTEPLIB  DD   DSNAME=SYS1.COB2COMP,DISP=SHR
XXSYSPRINT DD   SYSOUT=*
XXSYSLIN   DD   DSNAME=&&LOADSET,UNIT=SYSDA,DISP=(MOD,PASS),
XX              SPACE=(TRK,(3,3))
XXSYSUT1   DD   UNIT=SYSDA,SPACE=(CYL,(1,1))
XXSYSUT2   DD   UNIT=SYSDA,SPACE=(CYL,(1,1))
XXSYSUT3   DD   UNIT=SYSDA,SPACE=(CYL,(1,1))
XXSYSUT4   DD   UNIT=SYSDA,SPACE=(CYL,(1,1))
XXSYSUT5   DD   UNIT=SYSDA,SPACE=(CYL,(1,1))
XXSYSUT6   DD   UNIT=SYSDA,SPACE=(CYL,(1,1))
XXSYSUT7   DD   UNIT=SYSDA,SPACE=(CYL,(1,1))
XXGO      EXEC PGM=LOADER,PARM='MAP,LET',COND=(5,LT,COB2)
XXSYSLIB   DD   DSNAME=SYS1.COB2LIB,DISP=SHR
XXSYSLIN   DD   DSNAME=*.COB2.SYSLIN,DISP=(OLD,DELETE)
XXSYSLOUT  DD   SYSOUT=A
XXSYSABOUT DD   SYSOUT=A
XXSYSDBOUT DD   SYSOUT=A
XXSYSUDUMP DD   SYSOUT=A
```

Invoking JCL

```
//DLOWE2A  JOB  USER=DLOWE2,PASSWORD=XXXXXXXX
//         EXEC COB2UCG,PARM.COB2='APOST,OBJECT'
//COB2.SYSIN  DD DSNAME=MMA2.INVENTRY.COBOL(INV3520),DISP=SHR
//COB2.SYSLIB DD DSNAME=MMA2.COPYLIB.COBOL2,DISP=SHR
//GO.SYSLIB   DD
//           DD DSNAME=MMA2.INVENTRY.OBJLIB,DISP=SHR
//GO.SYSOUT   DD SYSOUT=A
//GO.INVMAST  DD DSNAME=MMA2.INVMAST.DATA,DISP=SHR
//GO.INVLIST  DD SYSOUT=A
```

Figure 4-5   The COB2UCG procedure

that the compile-link-and-go procedure creates a permanent load module while the compile-and-go procedure does not.

The compile-and-go procedure, COB2UCG, is shown in figure 4-5. As you can see, the compile step in the COB2UCG procedure is the same as it is in the COB2UCLG procedure. And the execute step combines the functions of the link-edit and execute steps in COB2UCLG. The only differences from the equivalent OS/VS COBOL procedure are that a REGION parameter isn't coded in the execute step and the SYSABOUT, SYSDBOUT, and SYSUDUMP data sets are coded as in the COB2UCLG procedure. Because the REGION parameter isn't specified, the step is limited to the default size of 256K unless overridden by the JCL that invokes the procedure.

The bottom part of figure 4-5 shows typical JCL to invoke the COB2UCG procedure. As you can see, the data sets required by the procedure are identical to those required for the COB2UCLG procedure. The only difference is that the step name for the SYSLMOD and SYSLIB data sets is GO instead of LKED.

Using TSO commands and command procedures

To compile an OS/VS COBOL program under TSO, you use the COBOL command. This command invokes the *COBOL prompter*, which prepares certain required data sets and invokes the standard COBOL compiler for foreground processing. However, an equivalent command isn't provided under VS COBOL II. So you have to know how to allocate the required data sets and invoke the COBOL compiler on your own. That's what I'll show you first in this section. Then, I'll show you how to link-edit and execute a program once it's compiled. Finally, I'll show you how you can use command procedures for compiling, link-editing, and executing your programs.

TSO commands for compiling a program   Before you can execute the VS COBOL II compiler under TSO, you need to allocate the required data sets. To do that, you use the TSO ALLOCATE command. The data sets that can be allocated are presented in figure 4-6. As you can see, most of the data sets are the same as the ones you use when you compile a program under MVS. The only one you wouldn't use under MVS is SYSTERM. It provides for diagnostic and progress messages to be written to your TSO terminal.

The top portion of figure 4-7 shows sample ALLOCATE commands for data sets used by the compiler. The first seven commands allocate the seven work data sets: SYSUT1, SYSUT2, SYSUT3, SYSUT4, SYSUT5, SYSUT6, and SYSUT7. The next two ALLOCATE commands allocate SYSPRINT and SYSTERM, which route any output from the compiler to a print file and your terminal. Following these commands is the ALLOCATE command for the object module to be created by the compiler (SYSLIN). Usually, you'll want to give this data set the same name as the source file except for the type qualifier, which should be OBJ. In figure 4-7, I specified the name TEST.OBJ for the object file. The last ALLOCATE command is for the input data set (SYSIN), which contains your source program (in this case, INV3520).

After you've allocated all of the required data sets, you use the CALL command to invoke the compiler. It's the last command in the top portion of figure 4-7. On the CALL command, you specify the name of the program to

ddname	Explanation
SYSIN	Data set that contains the source program used as input to the compiler.
SYSPRINT	Data set to which output listings and messages from the compiler are written.
SYSTERM	Used to display diagnostics and progress messages issued by the compiler at the terminal.
SYSPUNCH	Data set to which punched output is written.
SYSLIN	Object module created by the compiler that's used as input to the linkage editor.
SYSUT1	Work data set required by the compiler.
SYSUT2	Work data set required by the compiler.
SYSUT3	Work data set required by the compiler.
SYSUT4	Work data set required by the compiler.
SYSUT5	Work data set required by the compiler if COPY statements are present in the source program.
SYSUT6	Work data set required by the compiler.
SYSUT7	Work data set required by the compiler.
SYSLIB	Library containing members to be copied into the source program during compilation.
SYSUDUMP SYSABEND	Data set to which dump output is written. Either SYSUDUMP or SYSABEND is required if the DUMP compiler option is specified.

Figure 4-6   Data sets used for compilation under TSO

be executed (IGYCRCTL), the name of the library in which the program resides (SYS1.COB2COMP), and any compiler options you want in effect. Note in figure 4-7 that I had to specify the compiler option OBJECT to create an object module.

TSO commands for link-editing and executing a program   Once you've compiled your program, you need to link-edit it using the TSO LINK command. Before you do that, however, you need to allocate the library

Sample TSO commands to compile a program

```
ALLOCATE DDNAME(SYSUT1) CYLINDERS SPACE(1,1)
ALLOCATE DDNAME(SYSUT2) CYLINDERS SPACE(1,1)
ALLOCATE DDNAME(SYSUT3) CYLINDERS SPACE(1,1)
ALLOCATE DDNAME(SYSUT4) CYLINDERS SPACE(1,1)
ALLOCATE DDNAME(SYSUT5) CYLINDERS SPACE(1,1)
ALLOCATE DDNAME(SYSUT6) CYLINDERS SPACE(1,1)
ALLOCATE DDNAME(SYSUT7) CYLINDERS SPACE(1,1)
ALLOCATE DDNAME(SYSPRINT) DSNAME(*)
ALLOCATE DDNAME(SYSTERM) DSNAME(*)
ALLOCATE DDNAME(SYSLIN) DSNAME(TEST.OBJ) TRACKS SPACE(3,3)
ALLOCATE DDNAME(SYSIN) DSNAME(TEST.COBOL2(INV3520))
CALL 'SYS1.COB2COMP(IGYCRCTL)' 'OBJECT,TERMINAL,APOST'
```

Sample TSO commands to link-edit a program

```
ALLOCATE DDNAME(SYSLIB) DSNAME('SYS1.COB2LIB') SHR
LINK TEST
```

Sample TSO commands to execute a program

```
ALLOCATE DDNAME(INVMAST) DSNAME(INVMAST.DATA)
ALLOCATE DDNAME(INVLIST) DSNAME(*)
CALL TEST
```

Figure 4-7   Sample TSO commands for compiling, link-editing, and executing a program

SYS1.COB2LIB to SYSLIB. This library contains modules required by VS COBOL II to link your program. The command for allocating this library is illustrated in the middle portion of figure 4-7.

After you've allocated the SYSLIB data set, you issue a LINK command. On the LINK command, you specify the names of the modules you want to link. In figure 4-7, I specified only one module, TEST, which is the module that was created by the compiler. Note that you don't have to specify the type qualifier if it's OBJ; OBJ is the default.

If your program calls any subprograms, you need to specify the library they're in using the LIB option of the LINK command. For example, if the program in figure 4-7 called a subprogram stored in the data set SUBPROG.OBJ, you would code this LINK command:

```
LINK TEST LIB(SUBPROG.OBJ)
```

Then, the SUBPROG.OBJ library would be searched for any called programs.

You can also specify the name of the load module to be created by the linkage editor on the LINK command. For example, when I completed the testing of INV3520, I could store it as a member in a partitioned data set with this command:

```
LINK TEST LOAD(INVENTRY(INV3520))
```

If you omit the LOAD option, the linkage editor creates the load module as a member in a library whose name is the same as the input data set's, but whose type qualifier is LOAD. For example, in figure 4-7, the load module is stored in the library named TEST.LOAD. The default member name is TEMPNAME.

To execute a program that's been link-edited, you need to allocate any data sets used by the program and then invoke the program using the CALL command. On the CALL command, you specify the name of the program along with any parameters you want to pass to it. The bottom portion of figure 4-7 shows the commands required to execute INV3520. Here, the first two commands allocate the data sets required by the program: INVMAST and INVLIST. Then, the CALL command executes INV3520. Notice that the program is identified simply by specifying the library in which it's stored: TEST. Since I didn't specify a type qualifier, LOAD is assumed. And since I didn't specify a member name, TEMPNAME is assumed.

After you finish compiling, linking, and executing a program, you'll usually want to release the space you've allocated for the required data sets. To do that, you use the FREE command. For example, to release the space allocated to the compiler data sets in figure 4-7, I could issue these commands:

```
FREE DDNAME(SYSUT1,SYSUT2,SYSUT3,SYSUT4,SYSUT5,SYSUT6,SYSUT7)
FREE DDNAME(SYSPRINT,SYSTERM,SYSIN,SYSLIN)
```

In addition, you'll probably want to delete the object module that's created by the compiler. If you allocate this file without specifying a disposition, as in figure 4-7, it's automatically cataloged. So, you can delete it with this command:

```
DELETE DDNAME(SYSLIN)
```

Probably the only time you won't delete an object module is when it's for a subprogram. Then, you'll want to save it so you can link it with other programs.

Another way to link-edit and execute a program is using the LOADGO command. The LOADGO command combines the functions of the LINK and

CALL commands. For example, to link-edit and execute the program in figure 4-7, I could have entered the command

```
LOADGO TEST
```

The main difference between the LOADGO command and the LINK and CALL commands is that the LOADGO command doesn't create a load module.

In some cases, the LOADGO command may save you some time because you don't have to link-edit and execute your program separately. In general, though, I recommend you use the LINK and CALL commands rather than the LOADGO command for two reasons. First, it's more efficient to create a load module with the LINK command if you're going to execute your program more than once between compilations. And second, your program has to be processed by the LINK command if you want to debug it using VS COBOL II Debug. (I'll show you how to use the debugger in chapter 5.)

Command procedures for compiling, link-editing, and executing your programs   If you use the techniques I've just presented for compiling, link-editing, and executing your programs, you'll probably find yourself entering the same series of commands repeatedly. To avoid having to do this, you can store the commands in a *command procedure*, or *CLIST*. Then, you can invoke the CLIST to cause its commands to be executed. Although I won't go into the details of how to code a CLIST in this book, I would like to show you an example of a CLIST for compiling, link-editing, and executing a VS COBOL II program. If you want to learn more about CLISTs, I recommend our book *MVS TSO*.

Figure 4-8 presents a CLIST that will compile, link-edit, and execute a COBOL program. As you can see, it's almost identical to the commands presented in figure 4-7. Actually, you could create a CLIST by coding the commands exactly as they appear in figure 4-7. However, if you did that, you'd be able to compile only the program that's specified in the SYSIN data set. In contrast, the CLIST in figure 4-8 allows you to code the program name as a variable. It does that by defining the variable MEMBER on the PROC statement and then using it in the form &MEMBER in the DSNAME operand of the ALLOCATE command for the SYSIN data set. Then, when you invoke the CLIST, you specify the name of the member you want to compile.

To illustrate, suppose the CLIST shown in figure 4-8 is stored as a member named COB2CLG in the library COBOL2.CLIST. To execute the CLIST to compile the program INV3520, you would issue this command:

```
EXEC COBOL2.CLIST(COB2CLG) INV3520
```

```
PROC 1 MEMBER
ALLOCATE DDNAME(SYSUT1) CYLINDERS SPACE(1,1)
ALLOCATE DDNAME(SYSUT2) CYLINDERS SPACE(1,1)
ALLOCATE DDNAME(SYSUT3) CYLINDERS SPACE(1,1)
ALLOCATE DDNAME(SYSUT4) CYLINDERS SPACE(1,1)
ALLOCATE DDNAME(SYSUT5) CYLINDERS SPACE(1,1)
ALLOCATE DDNAME(SYSUT6) CYLINDERS SPACE(1,1)
ALLOCATE DDNAME(SYSUT7) CYLINDERS SPACE(1,1)
ALLOCATE DDNAME(SYSPRINT) DSNAME(*)
ALLOCATE DDNAME(SYSTERM) DSNAME(*)
ALLOCATE DDNAME(SYSLIN) DSNAME(TEST.OBJ) TRACKS SPACE(3,3)
ALLOCATE DDNAME(SYSIN) DSNAME(TEST.COBOL2(&MEMBER))
CALL 'SYS1.COB2COMP(IGYCRCTL)' 'OBJECT,TERMINAL,APOST'
ALLOCATE DDNAME(SYSLIB) DSNAME('SYS1.COB2LIB') SHR
LINK TEST
CALL TEST
```

Figure 4-8   A CLIST that will compile, link-edit, and execute a VS COBOL II program

Then, anywhere the variable &MEMBER occurred in the CLIST, it would be replaced by INV3520. So the procedure would compile the program INV3520 in the library TEST.COBOL2. Since the variable isn't used anywhere else in the CLIST, the remaining commands would execute just as if you had entered them at your terminal.

The only other difference between the CLIST in figure 4-8 and the commands in figure 4-7 is that the ALLOCATE commands for the data sets used by the program you're executing (in this case, INVMAST and INVLIST) aren't included in the CLIST. That's because the required data sets will be different for each program you execute. So if you use a CLIST like the one in figure 4-8 to compile, link-edit, and execute your programs, you'll need to allocate the appropriate data sets *before* you execute the CLIST.

The CLIST presented in figure 4-8 should be all you need for compiling, link-editing, and executing most of your programs. However, you'll probably want other CLISTs that compile, compile and link, and compile and execute a program. Using the CLIST in figure 4-8 as a guide, you should have no problem creating these other CLISTs.

In addition, you may want to make your CLISTs more versatile. For example, if you have more than one production library, you might want to code the entire data set specification for SYSIN as a variable. Then, you would specify the data set and member name on the EXEC statement that invokes the CLIST. Or, you might want to code the load module name as a variable. In any case, I think you can see how useful CLISTs can be for program development.

Using CMS commands

The procedure for compiling, link-editing, and executing VS COBOL II programs under CMS is almost identical to the procedure for OS/VS COBOL. The biggest difference is that instead of using the COBOL command to compile a program, you use the COBOL2 command. You still use the LOAD and START commands to load and execute your programs and the LOAD and GENMOD commands to create program modules. However, there are a few minor differences you should be aware of. So I'll present those differences now, as I show you the general procedures for compiling, link-editing, and executing VS COBOL II programs and creating program modules.

CMS commands for compiling VS COBOL II programs   As I've already mentioned, you use the COBOL2 command to compile your VS COBOL II programs under CMS. The top part of figure 4-9 shows a sample COBOL2 command. On it, you specify the name of the CMS file you want to compile along with any compiler options you want in effect. For example, in figure 4-9, the source file named INV3520 is compiled using the options OBJECT and APOST. Notice that you enter only the file name; the file type COBOL is assumed.

   If you specify compiler options on the COBOL2 command, there are a couple of things you should be aware of. First, the length of each option is limited to eight characters. If the option is longer than that, it has to be abbreviated. (To find out what the abbreviations are, refer to *VS COBOL II Application Programming: Supplement for CMS Users.*) Second, if you code an option that uses parentheses, you should replace the parentheses with blanks. That's because a right parenthesis indicates the end of the command. For example, if you coded this command:

```
COBOL2 INV3520 (OBJECT FLAG(E,E) APOST
```

the APOST option would be ignored. Instead, you should code the command like this:

```
COBOL2 INV3520 (OBJECT FLAG E,E  APOST
```

   You should also realize that the DATA and FASTSRT options have no effect under CMS. However, if the program you're compiling will be executed under MVS, you can still specify these options. Also, the OSDECK option isn't supported by VS COBOL II. It was used under OS/VS COBOL to create an object deck that was formatted properly for use under MVS. But now, since

Sample CMS commands to compile a program

```
GLOBAL MACLIB INVCOPY
COBOL2 INV3520 (OBJECT APOST
```

Sample CMS commands to load and execute a program

```
GLOBAL TXTLIB VSC2LTXT
GLOBAL TXTLIB COB2SUBS
FILEDEF INVMAST DISK INVMAST DATA A
FILEDEF INVLIST PRINTER
LOAD INV3520
START
```

Sample CMS commands to create and execute a program module

```
GLOBAL TXTLIB COB2SUBS
LOAD INV3520 DATEDIT
GENMOD INV3520
FILEDEF INVMAST DISK INVMAST DATA A
FILEDEF INVLIST PRINTER
INV3520
```

Figure 4-9   Sample CMS commands for compiling a program, loading and executing a program, and creating and executing a program module

the object decks created by the VS COBOL II compiler under CMS are identical to the ones created under MVS, this option is no longer necessary.

If you use COPY statements in your programs, you'll need to identify the libraries that contain the COPY members before you invoke the compiler. These members must be stored in macro libraries, which have the file type MACLIB. To identify these libraries, you use the GLOBAL command. For example, in the top part of figure 4-9, I coded the command

```
GLOBAL MACLIB INVCOPY
```

Then, every time the compiler processes a COPY statement, the INVCOPY library is searched for the appropriate member.

When you compile a program under CMS, the object code that's generated is stored in a CMS TEXT file. That file is given the same name as the source file. For example, if the source file is named INV3520, the object code is stored in a file named INV3520 TEXT.

CMS commands for loading and executing VS COBOL II programs
Before you can load and execute a VS COBOL II program under CMS, you
need to have access to the VS COBOL II library. This library may be stored
in a CMS TXTLIB, a CMS LOADLIB, or both. Be sure to check with a
systems programmer for the names of the appropriate libraries.

To access the VS COBOL II library, you need to issue GLOBAL
commands for the CMS libraries in which it resides. In the middle part of figure
4-9, I coded the command

```
GLOBAL TXTLIB VSC2LTXT
```

since the VS COBOL II library is stored in VSC2LTXT TXTLIB on my
system. Because the VS COBOL II library must be available every time you
execute a VS COBOL II program, you'll probably want your logon procedure
to include the appropriate command to access the library.

Of course, you also need to define the files required by the program before
you can execute it. To do that, you use the CMS FILEDEF command. In the
middle part of figure 4-9, I coded two FILEDEF commands to define the two
CMS files used by the program: INVMAST and INVLIST.

After a program is compiled, you can load it into storage and execute it
using the CMS LOAD and START commands. On the LOAD command, you
simply specify the name of the file containing the object code you want to load;
the file type TEXT is assumed. Then, you issue the START command with no
operands. For example, in the middle part of figure 4-9 I coded the commands

```
LOAD INV3520
START
```

Note that because the loader is being invoked and not the linkage editor, no
permanent load module is created.

If the program you're loading contains any subprogram calls, the loader
will look for CMS TEXT files with the appropriate file names. However, if the
subprograms are stored in TXTLIBs, you'll need to identify those libraries
before you load the program. To do that, you use the GLOBAL command. For
example, in the middle part of figure 4-9 I issued the command:

```
GLOBAL TXTLIB COB2SUBS
```

Then, when the program is loaded, if the subprogram isn't found in a TEXT
file, the loader will search the COB2SUBS library.

CMS commands for creating program modules   After you've thoroughly tested and debugged a program, you'll want to create a *program*

module. A program module is the CMS equivalent of a load module; it's ready to be loaded and executed. Program modules have the file type MODULE.

To create a program module, you must first load all of the TEXT files or TXTLIB members the module will consist of into storage using the LOAD command. Of course, if you use TXTLIB members, you'll need to specify the appropriate text library by coding a GLOBAL command. To illustrate the loading procedure, consider the example in the bottom part of figure 4-9. Here, the TEXT file named INV3520 and the TXTLIB member named DATEDIT are both loaded into storage. Because DATEDIT is stored as a TXTLIB member, I had to code the GLOBAL command to identify the text library.

After you've loaded the TEXT files and TXTLIB members, you use the GENMOD command to combine them into a program module. In the bottom part of figure 4-9, I coded this command:

```
GENMOD INV3520
```

So the files that were previously loaded into storage (INV3520 and DATEDIT) are combined into a program module named INV3520.

Once you've created a program module, you can execute it by simply entering the module name. For example, in the bottom part of figure 4-9, I coded this command to execute the program module named INV3520:

```
INV3520
```

COMPILER OPTIONS

Compiler options give the programmer some control over how a program is compiled. Now, with the compiler options provided by VS COBOL II, a programmer has more control than ever before. As you can see in figure 4-10, these options fall into six categories: controlling object code generation; controlling object code execution; controlling maps, listings, and diagnostics; controlling the compiler's use of virtual storage; selecting a reserved word list; and providing a formatted dump. Unless noted otherwise, these options are available with all three releases of VS COBOL II.

In addition to the compiler options I'll present in this section, you should realize that the names of some of the old compiler options under OS/VS COBOL have been changed. Although their functions are the same, you need to familiarize yourself with the new names. A complete list of the VS COBOL II compiler options is given in appendix B of this book.

Before I present the VS COBOL II compiler options, I need to point out that the defaults indicated in figure 4-10 and mentioned throughout this section

Function	Option	Description
Control object code generation	NAME NONAME	Release 3 only. Determines whether linkage editor NAME control cards are generated during compilation. The default is NONAME.
	CMPR2 NOCMPR2	Release 3 only. Determines whether compilation results are compatible with Release 2. The default is NOCMPR2.
Control object code execution	DATA(24) DATA(31)	Determines if storage obtained for data areas during program execution is located below 16M (DATA(24)) or anywhere in storage (DATA(31)). The default is DATA(31).
	FASTSRT NOFASTSRT	Indicates if DFSORT is to perform the processing of input and output files. The default is NOFASTSRT.
	PFDSGN NOPFDSGN	Releases 1 and 2 only. Indicates if signed fields will use the preferred sign format. The default is NOPFDSGN.
	NUMPROC(PFD) NUMPROC(NOPFD) NUMPROC(MIG)	Release 3 only. Determines if and how signed decimals are to be converted to the preferred format. The default is NUMPROC(NOPFD).
	RENT NORENT	Determines if your program is reentrant. The default is NORENT.
	SRANGE NOSSRANGE	Determines if out-of-range conditions are checked during program execution. The default is NOSSRANGE.
	TRUNC(STD) TRUNC(OPT) TRUNC(BIN)	Release 3 only. Determines how results stored in a binary receiving field are truncated. The default is TRUNC(STD).

Figure 4-10   New compiler options available with VS COBOL II (part 1 of 2)

Function	Option	Description
Control maps, listings, and diagnostics	FLAG(x[,y])	Determines what messages are printed in the diagnostics listing (x) and what messages are imbedded in the source listing (y). See figure 4-12 for the values that are valid for x and y. The default is FLAG(I).
	FLAGSTD(x[yy][,z]) NOFLAGSTD	Release 3 only. Identifies the language elements in a program that do not conform to the specified subset of the 1985 standards. The x identifies the subset, yy identifies optional modules, and z indicates if obsolete elements are flagged. The default is NOFLAGSTD.
	FLAGSAA NOFLAGSAA	Release 3 only. Identifies the language elements in a program that do not conform to SAA requirements. The default is NOFLAGSAA.
	LANGUAGE(ENGLISH) LANGUAGE(UENGLISH) LANGUAGE(JAPANESE)	Release 3 only. Determines the language in which compiler output is printed. The default is LANGUAGE(ENGLISH).
	FLAGMIG NOFLAGMIG	Release 3 only. Identifies the language elements of Release 2 that may execute differently under Release 3. The default is NOFLAGMIG.
Control the compiler's use of virtual storage	SIZE(nnnnn) SIZE(nnnK) SIZE(MAX)	Indicates the amount of storage needed for compilation. The *nnnnn* is number of bytes, *nnn*K is increments of 1K, and MAX is limited only by the space available in your user region. The default is SIZE(MAX).
Select a reserved word list	WORD(xxxx) [*]NOWORD	Determines if a reserved word list other than the system default is used. The default is *NOWORD.
Provide a formatted dump	FDUMP NOFDUMP	Determines if a formatted dump is created when an abnormal termination occurs. The default is NOFDUMP.

Figure 4-10   New compiler options available with VS COBOL II (part 2 of 2)

are IBM defaults. Since individual installations can change these defaults, you should check to see what they are in your shop.

Controlling object code generation

There are two options available only with Release 3 of VS COBOL II that affect the way the compiler generates object code. These options are NAME and CMPR2.

The NAME option   You can use the NAME option under Release 3 of VS COBOL II to generate linkage editor NAME control cards during compilation. The NAME control card determines whether a program is link-edited by itself into a load module or link-edited with other programs previously compiled in the same batch compilation. This is particularly useful if you are compiling multiple programs with a single invocation of the compiler. If you don't want to create load modules, specify NONAME or let it default.

The CMPR2 option   The CMPR2 option was added to Release 3 of VS COBOL II to aid in the migration from Release 2 to Release 3. As I mentioned in the last chapter, there are certain language elements that don't execute the same way under Release 3 as they do under Release 2. But if you specify the CMPR2 option when you compile a Release 2 program under Release 3, the results of the compilation are compatible with the results under Release 2. So your programs execute identically without any changes. Figure 4-11 lists the elements that are affected by the CMPR2 option and briefly describes the differences in the way they execute.

The drawback to specifying CMPR2 is that if you do, you can't use any Release 3 elements in your program. In other words, you can't generate code that's compatible with Release 2 and use Release 3 elements at the same time. So if you're converting a Release 2 program to Release 3 and the program doesn't contain any of the elements in figure 4-11, be sure to specify NOCMPR2 or let it default. That way, you can use whatever Release 3 elements you want. However, if the program contains any of the elements in figure 4-11, you'll have to make the changes necessary for it to execute the same under Release 3 as it did under Release 2 before you can add Release 3 elements. To help determine what changes are required, you can use the FLAGMIG compiler option.

Element	With CMPR2 option	With NOCMPR2 option
ALPHABET clause	ALPHABET is not recognized as a keyword.	ALPHABET is a valid keyword in the SPECIAL-NAMES paragraph.
ALPHABETIC class	This class doesn't include lowercase letters.	This class includes lowercase letters.
CALL statement	The ON OVERFLOW condition detects only an out-of-space error.	The ON OVERFLOW condition occurs whenever the called subprogram can't be made available.
Comparisons	The numeric value of a numeric item with the PICTURE symbol P is used when the item is compared to a nonnumeric item.	The character value of a numeric item with the PICTURE symbol P is used when the item is compared to a nonnumeric item.
COPY statement	Non-COBOL characters are allowed in COPY text. Lowercase letters are not treated the same as uppercase letters.	Non-COBOL characters are not allowed in COPY text. Lowercase letters are treated the same as uppercase letters.
EXIT PROGRAM statement	The last-used state for PERFORM ranges is retained following the execution of the EXIT PROGRAM statement. EXIT PROGRAM, STOP RUN, or GOBACK must be coded to terminate a program.	The end of all PERFORM ranges is assumed following the execution of the EXIT PROGRAM statement. EXIT PROGRAM is implicit at the end of a called program.
File status codes	Release 2 file status codes are returned. (See appendix D for a complete list of file status codes.)	Release 3 file status codes are returned. (See appendix D for a complete list of file status codes.)
GOBACK statement	The last-used state for PERFORM ranges is retained following the execution of the GOBACK statement.	The end of all PERFORM ranges is assumed following execution of the GOBACK statement.

Figure 4-11   Language elements that execute differently depending on the setting of the CMPR2/NOCMPR2 compiler option (part 1 of 4)

Element	With CMPR2 option	With NOCMPR2 option
PERFORM VARYING statement	When multiple VARYING identifiers are specified, a true condition for any but the first test condition causes the VARYING identifier associated with that condition to be set to its FROM value before the previous VARYING identifier is incremented with its BY value.	When multiple VARYING identifiers are specified, a true condition for any but the first test condition causes the VARYING identifier associated with the previous condition to be incremented with its BY value before the current VARYING identifier is set to its FROM value.
PICTURE clause	A PICTURE string that contains only the symbols A and B is classified as ALPHABETIC.	A PICTURE string that contains only the symbols A and B is classified as ALPHANUMERIC-EDITED.
Program collating sequence	The program collating sequence is applied to comparisons that are performed implicitly during the execution of an INSPECT, STRING, or UNSTRING statement.	The program collating sequence is applied only to comparisons specified explicitly in relation conditions and condition-name conditions and to SORT and MERGE operations.
READ statement	The record used for a READ INTO statement may not be the same as under NOCMPR2 if the file being read contains multiple records that are not all alphanumeric.	The record used for a READ INTO statement may not be the same as under CMPR2 if the file being read contains multiple records that are not all alphanumeric.
RECORD CONTAINS clause	The format of a record is determined by its 01- level record definition. The 01-level record definition must match the RECORD CONTAINS clause.	A RECORD CONTAINS clause that contains a single integer always indicates fixed-length records. The 01-level record definition doesn't have to match the RECORD CONTAINS clause exactly.

Figure 4-11   Language elements that execute differently depending on the setting of the CMPR2/NOCMPR2 compiler option (part 2 of 4)

Element	With CMPR2 option	With NOCMPR2 option
RETURN statement	The record used for a RETURN INTO statement may not be the same as under NOCMPR2 if the file being returned contains multiple records that are not all alphanumeric.	The record used for a RETURN INTO statement may not be the same as under CMPR2 if the file being returned contains multiple records that are not all alphanumeric.
Reserved words	Release 3 reserved words aren't recognized.	Release 3 reserved words are recognized. The new reserved words are: ALPHABET, ALPHABETIC-LOWER, ALPHABETIC-UPPER, BINARY, CLASS, COMMON, CONVERTING, DAY-OF-WEEK, DBCS, END-RECEIVE, EXTERNAL, GLOBAL, ORDER, PACKED-DECIMAL, PADDING, PURGE, REPLACE, and STANDARD-2.
SET statement	The SET condition-name TO TRUE statement is performed according to the rules of the MOVE statement.	The SET condition-name TO TRUE statement is performed according to the rules of the VALUE clause.
SIZE ERROR phrase	The SIZE ERROR condition is activated when a size error occurs on intermediate results of a MULTIPLY or DIVIDE statement.	The SIZE ERROR condition is not activated when a size error occurs on intermediate results of a MULTIPLY or DIVIDE statement.
UNSTRING statement	Subscripts, length, and location information are evaluated during the execution of an UNSTRING statement and may depend on the results stored in the receiving data items.	Subscripts, reference modification, length, and location information are evaluated before the execution of an UNSTRING statement.
UPSI Switches	You can reference UPSI switches directly in the Procedure Division.	You can reference UPSI switches only by their mnemonic-name or condition-name.

Figure 4-11 Language elements that execute differently depending on the setting of the CMPR2/NOCMPR2 compiler option (part 3 of 4)

Element	With CMPR2 option	With NOCMPR2 option
Variable-length group moves	The move uses the actual length of the sending field for the receiving field. You must set an OCCURS DEPENDING ON data item before you use it.	If the group contains its own OCCURS DEPENDING ON object, the move uses the maximum length for the receiving field. You don't always have to set the OCCURS DEPENDING ON data item before you use it.

Figure 4-11   Language elements that execute differently depending on the setting of the CMPR2/NOCMPR2 compiler option (part 4 of 4)

Controlling object code execution

Seven of the compiler options provided by VS COBOL II affect the way the object code for a program is executed. They are the DATA, FASTSRT, PFDSGN, NUMPROC, RENT, SSRANGE, and TRUNC options.

The DATA option   The DATA option is used to specify whether or not storage obtained for data areas during program execution is restricted to the area below 16 megabytes. You can specify DATA(24) for 24-bit processing (below 16 MB) or DATA(31) for 31-bit processing. Since the default is DATA(31), the only time you should need to specify this option is when your program passes data to another program that uses 24-bit processing.

The FASTSRT option   In chapter 1, I mentioned that the IBM product Data Facility Sort (DFSORT), Release 6 or later, provides for input and output processing in addition to actually sorting the file's records. That makes the sort operation more efficient because data doesn't have to be moved between the COBOL program and DFSORT. To use this feature of DFSORT, your program must be compiled with the FASTSRT option.

For a sort in your COBOL program to qualify for the FASTSRT option, it must meet two basic requirements. First, it must use either a USING phrase, a GIVING phrase, or both. That means your sort cannot contain both an input and output procedure, but may contain one or the other. Second, the sort can specify only one input file on the USING phrase and only one output file on the GIVING phrase. If these or any of the other requirements for input and output files aren't met, the sort will be performed as if the FASTSRT option had not been coded, and an informational message will be issued. On the other hand, if FASTSRT is not specified and the requirements for using the FASTSRT option are met, an informational message is issued to indicate that the option should be used.

The PFDSGN option   The PFDSGN option is available with Releases 1 and 2 of VS COBOL II. It affects the way signed fields defined with USAGE DISPLAY (external decimal) and USAGE COMP-3 (internal decimal) are handled in your programs. If you specify PFDSGN, the compiler assumes all such fields are defined with "preferred signs." The preferred signs are hex C for signed positive fields or zero, hex D for signed negative fields, and hex F for unsigned or alphanumeric fields.

Using PFDSGN can make your programs more efficient because the data doesn't have to be converted to the preferred sign format before it's processed. However, if you use it, fields should contain preferred signs or they may not be processed properly. Data initialized with a VALUE clause and data generated by arithmetic statements always contain preferred signs. However, redefining a field or initializing it with a group MOVE may alter the sign. So if you specify PFDSGN, you should avoid using REDEFINES. And you should use the INITIALIZE statement to initialize fields rather than using a group MOVE.

Unless processing efficiency is extremely important, I recommend you code the NOPFDSGN option or let it default. Then, data is always converted to the preferred sign format before it's processed.

The NUMPROC option   Under Release 3 of VS COBOL II, the PFDSGN option has been replaced by the NUMPROC option. The NUMPROC(PFD) option is equivalent to the PFDSGN option, and the NUMPROC(NOPFD) option is equivalent to NOPFDSGN. The default is NUMPROC(NOPFD). In addition, a third option, NUMPROC(MIG), is available. This option was added to aid in converting from OS/VS COBOL to VS COBOL II. It places certain restrictions on the conversion of signed decimals to the preferred format. These restrictions make the resulting code compatible with code generated by the OS/VS COBOL compiler.

The RENT option   As I mentioned in chapter 1, the RENT option is used to make your programs reentrant. That means that one copy of a program can be used to satisfy multiple requests. So, if several users will be requesting a program at the same time, it should be compiled with the RENT option.

Also, if a program is to be executed above 16 megabytes, it must be reentrant. And all CICS/OS/VS programs must be reentrant, as well as programs preloaded with IMS/VS. If you code RENT, the RESIDENT option is automatically put into effect. (The RESIDENT option requests the use of the COBOL Library Management Facility, which causes COBOL subroutines to be accessed dynamically instead of being link-edited with the program you're executing.)

The SSRANGE option   I also mentioned in chapter 1 that you can check for out-of-range conditions during program execution. You request this feature by coding the SSRANGE option. Then, if a subscript, index, or OCCURS DEPENDING ON clause refers to an entry beyond the end of a table, an error message is displayed and the program continues. In addition, under Release 3 of VS COBOL II, the SSRANGE option checks characters referred to by reference modification to be sure they are within the range of the referenced data item.

Although the SSRANGE option requires additional processing time, I recommend you code it during the testing of any program that uses subscripts, indexes, the OCCURS DEPENDING ON clause, or reference modification. Once a program is tested, you can remove the SSRANGE option or code the NOSSRANGE run-time option. I'll present the NOSSRANGE run-time option later in this chapter.

The TRUNC option   Although the TRUNC option was available under the first two releases of VS COBOL II, its format has been changed and its operation enhanced under Release 3. Under Releases 1 and 2, you specified the TRUNC option (or let it default) if you wanted the final intermediate result of an arithmetic expression or the sending field in a move statement to be truncated to the number of digits in the receiving field. This option applies only to receiving fields you defined as binary. If you specified NOTRUNC, the compiler assumed that the result conformed to its definition.

Under VS COBOL II Release 3, the TRUNC option is replaced by the TRUNC(STD) option, and the NOTRUNC option is replaced by TRUNC(OPT); the default is TRUNC(STD). In addition, a third option, TRUNC(BIN), is available. This option places additional restrictions on the way binary fields are handled. In particular, binary receiving fields are truncated only at halfword, fullword, or doubleword boundaries, and binary sending fields are always treated as halfwords, fullwords, or doublewords.

Controlling maps, listings, and diagnostics

There are five compiler options that affect the output that's generated by the compiler. The first one, FLAG, is available under all three releases of VS

Message code	Return code	Message type	Description
I	0	Informational	Indicates a condition that doesn't affect the execution of your program.
W	4	Warning	Indicates a condition that could potentially cause an error to occur during program execution.
E	8	Error	Indicates a definite error. Although the compiler attempts to correct these errors, your program may not execute properly.
S	12	Severe	Indicates a severe error. Although the compiler attempts to correct these errors, your program probably won't execute properly.
U	16	Unrecoverable	Indicates an error from which the compiler cannot recover.

Figure 4-12   Diagnostic codes and their meanings

COBOL II. The other four, FLAGSTD, FLAGSAA, LANGUAGE, and FLAGMIG, are available only under Release 3.

The FLAG option   The FLAG option has been improved under VS COBOL II. In addition to specifying the severity level at which you want to print diagnostic messages, you can also specify the severity level at which you want syntax error messages to be imbedded in the source listing. You do that by coding a second operand on the FLAG option.

The codes that are valid for both operands of the FLAG option are presented in figure 4-12. (These codes have been changed from those used for OS/VS COBOL, so be sure you use the right ones.) For example, if you code the option

```
FLAG(W,S)
```

a message will be printed in the diagnostics listing for statements causing a return code of 4 (warning) or greater, and a message will be imbedded in the source listing for statements causing a return code of 12 (severe) or greater.

The only restriction when coding the FLAG option is that the severity level coded for the second operand cannot be lower than the severity level coded for the first operand.

Figure 4-13 shows how messages imbedded in the source listing appear under Release 2 of VS COBOL II. In this case, the option FLAG(W,E) was specified. As you can see, the line number to which the error message is related is printed, followed by the message code and the message itself. There are some minor differences in the imbedded error messages under Release 3, but nothing that needs to be mentioned here.

If you request that messages be imbedded in the source listing, you should realize that the message may not always directly follow the statement to which it refers. That's because an error in one statement is not always detected until additional statements are processed. Each message that is imbedded in the source listing is identified in the diagnostic listing by an asterisk (*). You'll see an example of that later in this chapter.

The FLAGSTD option   Because Release 3 of VS COBOL II is based on the 1985 standards, the FLAGSTD option was added to identify language elements present in a program that do not conform to those standards. This can be helpful if you're converting programs from OS/VS COBOL to Release 3 of VS COBOL II or from Release 1 or 2 of VS COBOL II to Release 3. If you code this option, the NOCMPR2 compiler option must also be in effect.

There are three parameters you can code on the FLAGSTD option. The first parameter specifies the subset of the standards you want to check your program against. (You'll recall from the description of the standards in the last chapter that there are three levels or subsets of compilers: minimum, intermediate, and high.) The second parameter specifies which optional modules you want to check your program against. And the third parameter specifies whether you want to flag obsolete language elements.

For the first parameter, you must code M, I, or H. If you code FLAGSTD(M), any elements that are not in the minimum subset are flagged; if you code FLAGSTD(I), any elements that are not in the intermediate subset are flagged; and if you code FLAGSTD(H), any elements that are not in the high subset are flagged. During compilation, if an element is found that doesn't conform to the specified subset of the standards, an informational message is printed in the source program listing that identifies the language element. If you want to suspend the printing of these informational messages, code NOFLAGSTD or let it default.

The second parameter is optional and is coded immediately following the first parameter, without any intervening blanks. For this parameter you can code D, N, S, DN, or DS. If you specify D, elements from the optional debug module are not flagged as not conforming. If you specify N, elements from

```
000202          PROCEDURE DIVISION.
000203     *
000204          000-PREPARE-INVESTMENT-LISTING.
000205     *
000206          OPEN INPUT INVMAST
000207              OUTPUT INVLIST.
000208          PERFORM 100-FORMAT-REPORT-HEADING.
000209          PERFORM 300-PREPARE-INVESTMENT-LINE
000210              UNTIL INVMAST-EOF.

==000210==>  IGYPS2121-S    < INVMAST-EOF >  WAS NOT DEFINED AS A DATA-NAME.  THE STATEMENT WAS DISCARDED.

==000210==>  IGYPS2096-S   AN INCOMPLETE SINGLE CONDITION WAS FOUND IN A CONDITIONAL EXPRESSION.
                           THE OPERAND(S) WAS DISCARDED.

000211          PERFORM 500-PRINT-TOTAL-LINES.
000212          CLOSE INVMAST
000213              INVLIST.
000214          DISPLAY 'INV3520 I  1  NORMAL EOJ'.
000215          STOP RUN.
```

Figure 4-13   Diagnostic messages imbedded in a source listing

level 1 of the segmentation module are not flagged. And if you specify S, elements from level 2 of the segmentation module are not flagged. You can also code DN or DS to specify combinations of these two modules.

If you want to flag obsolete language elements, you can code O as the third parameter on the FLAGSTD option. If you code this option, it must be separated from the preceding options by a comma.

The FLAGSAA option   If you're writing programs that are to be ported across IBM systems and you're using Release 3 of VS COBOL II, you might want to code the FLAGSAA option to flag language elements that are not part of the COBOL interface for IBM's *Systems Application Architecture (SAA)*. SAA is a set of products and conventions that IBM is developing to provide consistency between the different IBM environments. If you code FLAGSAA, elements that do not conform to the SAA requirements are flagged with a warning level message. To use FLAGSAA, the CMPR2 option must be in effect. In addition, you can't code the FLAGSAA option with the FLAGSTD option. If you do, the FLAGSAA option is ignored.

The LANGUAGE option   The LANGUAGE option is available only under Release 3 of VS COBOL II. It allows you to specify that the compiler output be printed in a specific language. The default, LANGUAGE(ENGLISH), prints compiler output in mixed case English. The LANGUAGE(UENGLISH) option prints output in uppercase English. And the LANGUAGE(JAPANESE) option prints output in Japanese. If you use the LANGUAGE(JAPANESE) option, you must have the Japanese National Language Feature installed.

The FLAGMIG option   You can use the FLAGMIG option in conjunction with the CMPR2 option under Release 3 of VS COBOL II to flag those language elements in a Release 2 program that execute differently under Release 3. When one of these elements is identified, a warning level message is printed in the compiler listing that indicates the potential problem. You can then use this information to update your programs accordingly before recompiling without the CMPR2 option. There is also a conversion aid available from IBM that will automatically convert many of these language elements.

Controlling the compiler's use of virtual storage: The SIZE option

The SIZE option is used to request the amount of storage needed for compilation. You can specify the amount of storage in bytes (nnnnn) or in increments of 1K (nnnK), or you can specify that all the space in your user region be made available (MAX). If you specify MAX or let it default, the compiler will acquire as much storage as it needs. Except under unusual circumstances, then, you shouldn't need to code the SIZE option.

Selecting a reserved word list: The WORD option

In chapter 1, I mentioned that an installation can not only tailor the reserved word list to its own specifications, but can also create and use multiple reserved word lists. To request that a reserved word list other than the system default be used, you code the WORD option. The format of the WORD option is WORD(xxxx), where xxxx represents the characters that follow the prefix IGYC in the name of the reserved word list. (IGYC must be the first four characters of the name.) So if you created a reserved word list named IGYCRW1, you would request that list by coding WORD(RW1).

If you don't code the WORD option, the default *NOWORD is in effect. NOWORD means that the system default is used. The preceding asterisk means that the option cannot be overridden.

Providing a formatted dump: The FDUMP option

The FDUMP option requests that a formatted dump be created whenever a program terminates abnormally. As I mentioned in chapter 1, a formatted dump contains basically the same program information as an unformatted dump, but it's in a more readable form. Figure 4-14 presents a portion of a sample formatted dump.

The first thing you should notice is that the line number and the verb number of the statement being executed when the abend occurred is given near the beginning of the formatted dump. That makes it easy to locate the error. In contrast, if you use a standard dump, the address of the statement has to be calculated in hex using the load address given in the output from the linkage editor or loader and the offset given in the dump.

The most significant difference, however, is the format of the Data Division dump. If you look at the Data Division dump in figure 4-14, you'll see that each data item in the Data Division is printed on a separate line. The entry for each data item contains the line number on which it's defined, its *normalized level number* (numbered sequentially from 01 so that if you used 01 and 05 levels in your program, they'd become 01 and 02 levels in the dump), its name, and its picture or an indication that it's a group item (AN-GR for alphanumeric group). And, for each elementary data item, the content of the

```
                    ---VS COBOL II FORMATTED DUMP AT ABEND ---

                          PROGRAM      INV3520

       COMPLETION CODE = S0CB      PSW AT ABEND = 078D20000000E61A

       LINE NUMBER/VERB NUMBER BEING EXECUTED:   000273/1

                        GP REGISTERS AT ENTRY TO ABEND

       REGS  0-3      00000000   00009E70   0000E4DA   00012DC8

       REGS  4-7      00012C68   5000E520   0000E064   00012F19

       REGS  8-11     00009E70   0000E0A8   00012FA0   0000E2E0

       REGS  12-15    0000E090   00012A10   50014A70   12B6F1EC


                        DATA DIVISION DUMP OF INV3520



       00018 FD INV3520 INVMAST                        FD
       FILE SPECIFIED AS:
          ORGANIZATION=SEQUENTIAL   ACCESS MODE=SEQUENTIAL
          RECFM=FIXED
       CURRENT STATUS OF FILE IS:
          OPEN STATUS=INPUT
          QSAM STATUS CODE=00

       00022 01 INV3520.INVENTORY-MASTER-RECORD        AN-GR

       00024 02 INV3520.IM-DESCRIPTIVE-DATA            AN-GR

       00025 03 INV3520.IM-ITEM-NO                     9(5)
             DISP     ===>00001

       00026 03 INV3520.IM-ITEM-DESC                   X(20)
             DISP     ===>GENERATOR

       00027 03 INV3520.IM-UNIT-COST                   999V99
             DISP     ===>112.00

       00028 03 INV3520.IM-UNIT-PRICE                  999V99
             DISP     ===>174.50
                  .
                  .
                  .
             --- END OF VS COBOL II FORMATTED DUMP AT ABEND ---
```

Figure 4-14   A sample formatted dump

item at the time of the abend is given. In addition, the Data Division dump lists the characteristics and status of each file that's defined in the program.

If you compare this to a standard dump, I think you'll agree that it's much easier to locate program information in the formatted dump. However, the formatted dump contains only program information; it doesn't include a system storage dump. In most cases, that should be sufficient. But if the problem is caused by something outside of your program, you may need a system dump to determine the cause.

If you request a formatted dump, you should know that the output isn't written to the SYSUDUMP, SYSMDUMP, or SYSABEND data set like a standard dump. Instead, it's written to the SYSDBOUT data set. So be sure you allocate this data set if you want a formatted dump.

COMPILER-DIRECTING STATEMENTS

A compiler-directing statement causes the compiler to take a specified action during compilation. Three new compiler-directing statements are provided by VS COBOL II: *CBL, *CONTROL, and TITLE.

The *CBL and *CONTROL statements

The *CBL and *CONTROL statements are used interchangeably to control the output created by the compiler. They are used in conjunction with the SOURCE, MAP, and LIST compiler options. The SOURCE option causes a source listing to be generated; the MAP option causes a listing of all data items defined in the program to be generated; and the LIST option causes an assembler-language expansion of your source code to be generated. If any of these compiler options is in effect, you can use the *CBL or *CONTROL statement to select the portions of the program the listings should be generated for.

For example, if you want to print an assembler-language expansion for a particular statement in your program but not for the rest of the program, you have to do four things. First, you specify the LIST compiler option. Second, you turn the LIST option off at the beginning of your program by coding

```
*CBL NOLIST
```

or

```
*CONTROL NOLIST
```

Third, you code

```
*CBL LIST
```

or

```
*CONTROL LIST
```

immediately preceding the statement for which you want an assembler-language expansion printed. Fourth, you code *CBL or *CONTROL following the statement to turn the LIST option off again.

When you use the *CBL or *CONTROL statement, you code it starting in column 7 followed by a space or a comma and one or more options. There cannot be any other statements on the line and the statement cannot be continued. The *CBL and *CONTROL statements cannot be used to override options that have been fixed by your installation.

The TITLE statement

The TITLE statement is used to change the heading on page 2 through the end of a source listing. To use this option, you code the TITLE statement with a literal of up to 65 characters. For example, if you code

```
TITLE 'PROCEDURE DIVISION'
```

immediately preceding the Procedure Division header, "PROCEDURE DIVISION" appears at the top of each succeeding page along with the program name, the date and time of compilation, and the page number. The TITLE statement also forces a new page immediately. You'll see an example of the TITLE statement later in this chapter.

The TITLE statement is coded in any column starting in column 8. It cannot be continued on additional lines. Multiple TITLE statements can be used in a single program.

COMPILER LISTINGS

The compiler listings provided by VS COBOL II have been improved over the listings provided by OS/VS COBOL. In general, they're now formatted so they're easier to read. And some of the listings present information that wasn't provided before.

Because Release 3 listings have been further improved from the Release 2 listings, I'll present examples of both in this section when there is a significant difference. Figures 4-15 through 4-22 present some sample compiler output including the source statement listing, cross-reference listing, imbedded cross reference, Data Division listing, nested program listing, and diagnostic message listing.

The source statement listing

A *source statement listing*, as its name implies, is a listing of your source program. You request a source listing by specifying the SOURCE compiler option or letting it default. Figure 4-15 is a sample source statement listing from Release 2 of VS COBOL II; figure 4-16 is a listing from Release 3.

In both examples, I used the TITLE statement to print the heading "INVENTORY LISTING PROGRAM." I used the *CBL statement to suppress the printing of all of the source listing except for the Procedure Division. (Notice that the compiler-directing statements don't appear in the source listing.) And, I used the FLAG compiler option to imbed error messages (E-level and higher) in the source listing.

There are two additional features you should notice in the Release 3 listing in figure 4-16. First, a scale line is included at the top of the page. This scale line indicates the different areas of the source listing. Second, two columns have been added to the listing. The first one, labeled PL in the scale line, identifies the nesting level of the program. Since there are no programs nested in the program in figure 4-16, this column is blank. The second column, labeled SL in the scale line, indicates the statement nesting level. As you can see in figure 4-16, the statement nesting level corresponds to the indentation I used in the program.

The cross-reference listing

A *cross-reference listing* is a sorted listing of the data names and procedure names used in your program. You request a cross-reference listing by specifying the XREF compiler option. This option is equivalent to the SXREF option of OS/VS COBOL. (You no longer have the option of printing an unsorted cross-reference listing.)

The format of the cross-reference listing under VS COBOL II is different from that of OS/VS COBOL, but it provides basically the same information. However, there is one new feature. In the references column of the cross-reference of data names, an *M* is placed before a line number if the data item is

```
000204        PROCEDURE DIVISION.
000205    *
000206        000-PREPARE-INVESTMENT-LISTING.
000207    *
000208            OPEN INPUT  INVMAST
000209                 OUTPUT INVLIST.
000210            PERFORM 100-FORMAT-REPORT-HEADING.
000211            PERFORM 300-PREPARE-INVESTMENT-LINE
000212                UNTIL INVMASTEOF.

==000212==>  IGYPS2121-S    < INVMAST-EOF > WAS NOT DEFINED AS A DATA-NAME.  THE STATEMENT WAS DISCARDED.

==000212==>  IGYPS2096-S    AN INCOMPLETE SINGLE CONDITION WAS FOUND IN A CONDITIONAL EXPRESSION.
                            THE OPERAND(S) WAS DISCARDED.

000213            PERFORM 500-PRINT-TOTAL-LINES.
000214            CLOSE INVMAST
000215                  INVLIST.
000216            STOP RUN.
000217    *
000218    *
000219        100-FORMAT-REPORT-HEADING.
000220    *
000221            ACCEPT PRESENT-DATE FROM DATE.
000222            MOVE PRESENT-MONTH TO TODAYS-MONTH.
000223            MOVE PRESENT-DAY   TO TODAYS-DAY.
000224            MOVE PRESENT-YEAR  TO TODAYS-YEAR.
000225            MOVE TODAYS-DATE   TO HDG1-DATE.
000226            ACCEPT PRESENT-TIME FROM TIME.
000227            IF PRESENT-HOURS < 1
000228                MOVE 12 TO HDG2-HOURS
000229            ELSE
000230                IF PRESENT-HOURS < 13
000231                    MOVE PRESENT-HOURS TO HDG2-HOURS
000232                ELSE
000233                    SUBTRACT 12 FROM PRESENT-HOURS
000234                        GIVING HDG2-HOURS.
000235            MOVE PRESENT-MINUTES TO HDG2-MINUTES.
000236            IF PRESENT-HOURS < 12
000237                MOVE 'AM' TO HDG2-TIME-SUFFIX
000238            ELSE
000239                MOVE 'PM' TO HDG2-TIME-SUFFIX.
       *
...
```

Figure 4-15   A sample source statement listing from Release 2

```
INVENTORY LISTING PROGRAM              INV3520   DATE 06/10/89   TIME 10 16 53    PAGE 3
LINEID  PL SL ----+*A-1-B--+----2----+----3----+----4----+----5----+----6----+----7----+----8 Cross Reference
000204**            PROCEDURE DIVISION.
000205**        *
000206**            000-PREPARE-INVESTMENT-LISTING.
000207**        *
000208**                OPEN INPUT  INVMAST
000209**                     OUTPUT INVLIST.
000210**                PERFORM 100-FORMAT-REPORT-HEADING.
000211**                PERFORM 300-PREPARE-INVESTMENT-LINE
000212**                    UNTIL INVMAST-EOF.
=000212==> IGYPS2121-S   "INVMAST-EOF" WAS NOT DEFINED AS A DATA-NAME. THE STATEMENT WAS DISCARDED.

=000212==> IGYPS2096-S   AN INCOMPLETE SINGLE CONDITION WAS FOUND IN A CONDITIONAL EXPRESSION. THE
                         OPERAND(S) WAS DISCARDED.

000213**                PERFORM 500-PRINT-TOTAL-LINES.
000214**                CLOSE INVMAST
000215**                      INVLIST.
000216**                STOP RUN.
000217**        *
000218**            100-FORMAT-REPORT-HEADING.
000219**        *
000220**                ACCEPT PRESENT-DATE FROM DATE.
000221**                MOVE PRESENT-MONTH TO TODAYS-MONTH.
000222**                MOVE PRESENT-DAY   TO TODAYS-DAY.
000223**                MOVE PRESENT-YEAR  TO TODAYS-YEAR.
000224**                MOVE TODAYS-DATE   TO HDG1-DATE.
000225**                ACCEPT PRESENT-TIME FROM TIME.
000226**                IF PRESENT-HOURS < 1
000227**        1           MOVE 12 TO HDG2-HOURS
000228**                ELSE
000229**        1           IF PRESENT-HOURS < 13
000230**        2               MOVE PRESENT-HOURS TO HDG2-HOURS
000231**        1           ELSE
000232**        2               SUBTRACT 12 FROM PRESENT-HOURS
000233**        2                   GIVING HDG2-HOURS.
000234**                MOVE PRESENT-MINUTES TO HDG2-MINUTES.
000235**                IF PRESENT-HOURS < 12
000236**        1           MOVE 'AM' TO HDG2-TIME-SUFFIX
000237**                ELSE
000238**        1           MOVE 'PM' TO HDG2-TIME-SUFFIX.
                            .
                            .
                            .
```

Figure 4-16   A sample source statement listing from Release 3

modified in the referenced line. And, in the cross-reference of procedures, a code is placed before each line number to indicate what COBOL statement references the procedure. These codes and their meanings are listed at the beginning of the cross-reference of procedure names. The code you'll probably see most often is *P* for PERFORM.

The portions of the cross-reference listing shown in figure 4-17 illustrate these features. (This listing was generated by Release 2. The Release 3 listing is almost identical, so I won't present it here.) In the cross-reference of data names, for example, you can see that the data name HDG1-DATE is modified on line 224. And, in the cross-reference of procedure names, the procedure named 100-FORMAT-REPORT-HEADING is called by a PERFORM statement in line 210.

The imbedded cross reference

If you specify the XREF compiler option under Release 3 of VS COBOL II, you also get a cross reference imbedded in the source listing. Figure 4-18 shows an example of an *imbedded cross reference*. As you can see, the cross-reference information is included in the rightmost column of the listing.

.The numbers in the cross-reference column identify the lines in which the data names and procedure names in each line are defined and referred to. This column can also contain the special definition symbols, UND, DUP, IMP, EXT, and *. UND means that the data name or procedure name is undefined. DUP means that the data name or procedure name is defined more than once. IMP means that the data name is defined implicitly. For example, special registers and figurative constants are implicitly defined. EXT means that the name is defined externally. And an asterisk (*) means that the program name is unresolved because the NOCOMPILE option is in effect.

The Data Division listing

A *Data Division listing* is a map of all the names used in the Data Division, including file names and FILLER. You request the Data Division listing by specifying the MAP compiler option. This is equivalent to specifying the DMAP option of OS/VS COBOL.

The first page of a sample Data Division listing from Release 2 is presented in figure 4-19. This listing contains some information not provided by OS/VS COBOL. First, the line number where each data item is defined is included in the listing. This makes it easier to locate a data item definition if you don't request a cross-reference listing. Second, indentation is used to show the

```
INVENTORY LISTING PROGRAM              INV3520   DATE 12/10/87  TIME 12.35.21    PAGE     6
AN "M" PRECEDING A DATA-NAME REFERENCE INDICATES THAT THE DATA-NAME IS MODIFIED BY THIS REFERENCE.

   DEFINED      CROSS-REFERENCE OF DATA NAMES    REFERENCES

       89      CALCULATED-FIELDS
       84      COUNT-FIELDS
       66      DATE-AND-TIME-FIELDS
      102      HDG1-DATE. . . . . . . . . .   M224
      108      HDG1-PAGE-NO . . . . . . . .   M302
      115      HDG2-HOURS . . . . . . . . .   M227 M230 M232
      117      HDG2-MINUTES . . . . . . . .   M234
      121      HDG2-REPORT-NUMBER
      113      HDG2-TIME-DATA
      119      HDG2-TIME-SUFFIX . . . . . .   M236 M238
       99      HEADING-LINE-1 . . . . . . .   303
      111      HEADING-LINE-2 . . . . . . .   305
      123      HEADING-LINE-3 . . . . . . .   308
      133      HEADING-LINE-4 . . . . . . .   310
      143      HEADING-LINE-5 . . . . . . .   313
      168      IL-INVESTMENT-AMOUNT . . . . .  169 M287
      169      IL-INVESTMENT-AMT-MESSAGE. . .  M291
      157      IL-ITEM-DESC . . . . . . . .   M280
      155      IL-ITEM-NO . . . . . . . . .   M279
      165      IL-LAST-MONTH-SALES. . . . .   M284
      163      IL-LAST-ORDER-DATE . . . . .   M283




THE LETTER PRECEDING A PROCEDURE-NAME REFERENCE INDICATES THE CONTEXT IN WHICH THE
PROCEDURE-NAME IS USED.
THESE LETTERS AND THEIR MEANINGS ARE:
    A = ALTER (PROCEDURE-NAME)
    D = GO TO (PROCEDURE-NAME) DEPENDING ON
    E = END OF RANGE OF (PERFORM) THRU (PROCEDURE-NAME)
    G = GO TO (PROCEDURE-NAME)
    P = PERFORM (PROCEDURE-NAME)
    T = (ALTER) TO PROCEED TO (PROCEDURE-NAME)
    U = USE FOR DEBUGGING (PROCEDURE-NAME)


   DEFINED   CROSS-REFERENCE OF PROCEDURES    REFERENCES

      206      DUMMY-SECTION
      206      000-PREPARE-INVESTMENT-LISTING
      218      100-FORMAT-REPORT-HEADING. . .  P210
      240      300-PREPARE-INVESTMENT-LINE. .  P211
      254      310-READ-INVENTORY-RECORD
      262      320-COMPUTE-INVENTORY-FIELDS .  P251
      275      330-PRINT-INVESTMENT-LINE. . .  P252
      299      340-PRINT-HEADING-LINES. . . .  P278
      318      350-WRITE-PAGE-TOP-LINE. . . .  P304
      324      360-WRITE-REPORT-LINE. . . . .  P295 P307 P309 P312 P315 P342 P346
      330      500-PRINT-TOTAL-LINES. . . . .  P213
```

Figure 4-17   A sample cross-reference listing

```
LINEID  PL SL ---+--*A-1-B--+----2----+----3----+----4----+----5----+----6----+----7-|--+----8 Cross Reference

000204**           PROCEDURE DIVISION
000205**           *
000206**           000-PREPARE-INVESTMENT-LISTING
000207**           *
000208**               OPEN INPUT  INVMAST                                        19 214 256
000209**                    OUTPUT INVLIST.                                       44 215
000210**               PERFORM 100-FORMAT-REPORT-HEADING.                         218
000211**               PERFORM 300-PREPARE-INVESTMENT-LINE                        240
000212**                   UNTIL INVMAST-EOF.                                     55
000213**               PERFORM 500-PRINT-TOTAL-LINES.                             330
000214**               CLOSE INVMAST                                             19 208 256
000215**                     INVLIST.                                            44 208
000216**               STOP RUN
000217**           *
000218**           100-FORMAT-REPORT-HEADING
000219**           *
000220**               ACCEPT PRESENT-DATE FROM DATE.                            68 69 IMP
000221**               MOVE PRESENT-MONTH TO TODAYS-MONTH.                       71 75
000222**               MOVE PRESENT-DAY   TO TODAYS-DAY.                         72 76
000223**               MOVE PRESENT-YEAR  TO TODAYS-YEAR.                        70 77
000224**               MOVE TODAYS-DATE   TO HDG1-DATE.                          73 74 102
000225**               ACCEPT PRESENT-TIME FROM TIME.                            78 79 IMP
000226**               IF PRESENT-HOURS < 1                                      80 229 230 232 235
000227**   1               MOVE 12 TO HDG2-HOURS                                 115 230 232
000228**   1           ELSE
000229**   1               IF PRESENT-HOURS < 13                                 80 226 230 232 235
000230**   2                   MOVE PRESENT-HOURS TO HDG2-HOURS                  80 226 229 232 235 115 227 232
000231**   1               ELSE
000232**   2                   SUBTRACT 12 FROM PRESENT-HOURS                    80 226 229 230 235
000233**   2                       GIVING HDG2-HOURS.                            115 227 230
000234**               MOVE PRESENT-MINUTES TO HDG2-MINUTES.                     81 117
000235**               IF PRESENT-HOURS < 12                                     80 226 229 230 232
000236**   1               MOVE 'AM' TO HDG2-TIME-SUFFIX                         119 238
000237**   1           ELSE
000238**   1               MOVE 'PM' TO HDG2-TIME-SUFFIX.                        119 236
```

Figure 4-18 A sample source statement listing with imbedded cross reference

```
INVENTORY LISTING PROGRAM                    INV3520   DATE 12/10/87   TIME 12.35.21   PAGE   9

DATA DIVISION MAP
LINE  LEVEL NUMBER AND SOURCE NAME      BASE      DISPL  STRCT DISP   DEFINITION   USAGE      R O D F
  19  FD INVMAST . . . . . . . . .                                                QSAM
  23  01 INVENTORY-MASTER-RECORD .      BLF=0000  000                 DS 0CL80    GROUP
  25  02 IM-DESCRIPTIVE-DATA . . .      BLF=0000  000   0 000 000     DS 0CL35    GROUP
  26  03 IM-ITEM-NO. . . . . . .        BLF=0000  000   0 000 005     DS 5C       DISP-NUM
  27  03 IM-ITEM-DESC. . . . . .        BLF=0000  005   0 000 020     DS 20C      DISPLAY
  28  03 IM-UNIT-COST. . . . . .        BLF=0000  019   0 000 019     DS 5C       DISP-NUM
  29  03 IM-UNIT-PRICE . . . . .        BLF=0000  01E   0 000 01E     DS 5C       DISP-NUM
  30  02 IM-INVENTORY-DATA . . . .      BLF=0000  023   0 000 023     DS 0CL15    GROUP
  31  03 IM-REORDER-POINT. . . .        BLF=0000  023   0 000 023     DS 5C       DISP-NUM
  32  03 IM-ON-HAND. . . . . . .        BLF=0000  028   0 000 028     DS 5C       DISP-NUM
  33  03 IM-ON-ORDER . . . . . .        BLF=0000  02D   0 000 02D     DS 5C       DISP-NUM
  34  02 IM-SALES-DATA . . . . . .      BLF=0000  032   0 000 032     DS 0CL22    GROUP
  35  03 IM-LAST-ORDER-DATE. . .        BLF=0000  032   0 000 032     DS 6C       DISP-NUM
  36  03 IM-LAST-ORDER-DATE-R. .        BLF=0000  032   0 000 032     DS 0CL6     GROUP       R
  37  04 IM-LAST-ORDER-MONTH .          BLF=0000  032   0 000 034     DS 2C       DISP-NUM
  38  04 IM-LAST-ORDER-DAY . .          BLF=0000  034   0 000 036     DS 2C       DISP-NUM
  39  04 IM-LAST-ORDER-YEAR. .          BLF=0000  036   0 000 038     DS 2C       DISP-NUM
  40  03 IM-LAST-MONTH-SALES . .        BLF=0000  038   0 000 03F     DS 7C       DISP-NUM
  41  03 IM-LAST-YEAR-SALES. . .        BLF=0000  03F   0 000 048     DS 9C       DISP-NUM
  42  02 FILLER. . . . . . . . . .      BLF=0000  048                 DS 8C       DISPLAY
  44  FD INVLIST . . . . . . . . .                                                QSAM
  48  01 PRINT-AREA. . . . . . . .      BLF=0001  000                 DS 132C     DISPLAY
  52  01 SWITCHES. . . . . . . . .      BLW=0000  000   0 000 000     DS 0CL2     GROUP
  54  02 INVMST-EOF-SWITCH . . . .      BLW=0000  000   0 000 000     DS 1C       DISPLAY
  55  88 INVMST-EOF. . . . . . .        BLW=0000  000
  56  02 INVESTMENT-SIZE-ERROR-SWITCH.  BLW=0000  001   0 000 001     DS 1C       DISPLAY
  57  88 INVESTMENT-SIZE-ERROR .        BLW=0000  001
  59  01 PRINT-FIELDS. . . . . . .      BLW=0000  008   0 000 008     DS 0CL7     GROUP
  61  02 SPACE-CONTROL . . . . . .      BLW=0000  008   0 000 000     DS 1P       COMP-3
  62  02 LINES-ON-PAGE . . . . . .      BLW=0000  009   0 000 002     DS 2P       COMP-3
  63  02 LINE-COUNT. . . . . . . .      BLW=0000  00B   0 000 003     DS 2P       COMP-3
  64  02 PAGE-COUNT. . . . . . . .      BLW=0000  00D   0 000 005     DS 2P       COMP-3
  66  01 DATE-AND-TIME-FIELDS. . .      BLW=0000  010   0 000 000     DS 0CL20    GROUP
  68  02 PRESENT-DATE. . . . . . .      BLW=0000  010   0 000 000     DS 6C       DISP-NUM
  69  02 PRESENT-DATE-R. . . . . .      BLW=0000  010   0 000 000     DS 0CL6     GROUP       R
  70  03 PRESENT-YEAR. . . . . .        BLW=0000  010   0 000 002     DS 2C       DISP-NUM
  71  03 PRESENT-MONTH . . . . .        BLW=0000  012   0 000 004     DS 2C       DISP-NUM
  72  03 PRESENT-DAY . . . . . .        BLW=0000  014   0 000 006     DS 2C       DISP-NUM
  73  02 TODAYS-DATE . . . . . . .      BLW=0000  016   0 000 006     DS 6C       DISP-NUM
  74  02 TODAYS-DATE-R . . . . . .      BLW=0000  016   0 000 008     DS 0CL6     GROUP       R
  75  03 TODAYS-MONTH. . . . . .        BLW=0000  018   0 000 008     DS 2C       DISP-NUM
  76  03 TODAYS-DAY. . . . . . .        BLW=0000  01A   0 000 00A     DS 2C       DISP-NUM
  77  03 TODAYS-YEAR . . . . . .        BLW=0000  01C   0 000 00C     DS 2C       DISP-NUM
  78  02 PRESENT-TIME. . . . . . .      BLW=0000  01C   0 000 00C     DS 8C       DISP-NUM
  79  02 PRESENT-TIME-R. . . . . .      BLW=0000  01C   0 000 00C     DS 0CL8     GROUP       R
  80  03 PRESENT-HOURS . . . . .        BLW=0000  01E   0 000 00E     DS 2C       DISP-NUM
  81  03 PRESENT-MINUTES . . . .        BLW=0000  020   0 000 010     DS 2C       DISP-NUM
  82  02 FILLER. . . . . . . . . .      BLW=0000  028                 DS 4C       DISPLAY
  84  01 COUNT-FIELDS. . . . . . .      BLW=0000  028                 DS 0CL6     GROUP
```

Figure 4-19   A sample Data Division listing from Release 2

subordination of data items. This makes the data grouping more apparent, which makes the listing more readable. Finally, the column labeled STRCT DISP shows how far the data item is from the beginning of the group. In addition to this new information, you should notice that the internal names for the data items are no longer included in the Data Division listing. But since these names are used most frequently with Report Writer, they are rarely necessary.

Figure 4-20 presents a sample Data Division listing from Release 3. Although all the information it contains is the same as in Release 2, some of the headings have been changed. In addition, an explanation of the codes that can appear in the column labeled "Data Def Attributes" is included at the beginning of the listing.

The nested program listing

When you specify the MAP compiler option under Release 3 of VS COBOL II, in addition to a Data Division listing, you'll get a *nested program listing* if your program contains nested programs. Figure 4-21 presents an example of a nested program listing. In general, this listing isn't very useful for anything except as documentation, so I'll describe it only briefly here.

The first column in the listing tells you the line number where each program is defined; in other words, it tells you the line number of the PROGRAM-ID paragraph. The second column tells you the level of each nested program. For example, the program called CALCDATE is called from the main program, so it's nested at level 1; the program named CONVDATE is called from CALCDATE, so it's nested at level 2. The third column contains the name of the program. This is extracted from the PROGRAM-ID paragraph. And the fourth column contains codes that identify certain attributes of the program. These codes are defined at the beginning of the listing. The C code indicates a common program; an I code indicates an initial program; and a U code indicates that the USING phrase is included on the Procedure Division header in that program, which indicates that data is passed to the program from the calling program.

The diagnostics message listing

A *diagnostics message listing* is a listing of the errors detected when a program is compiled. You can request that this listing be printed by specifying the FLAG compiler option or by letting it default. The new format of the FLAG compiler option was presented earlier in this chapter.

```
INVENTORY LISTING PROGRAM                                 INV3520   DATE 12/10/87  TIME 12.35.21   PAGE   9
DATA DIVISION MAP

DATA DEFINITION ATTRIBUTE CODES (RIGHTMOST COLUMN) HAVE THE FOLLOWING MEANINGS:
  D = OBJECT OF OCCURS DEPENDING    G = GLOBAL                          S = SPANNED FILE
  E = EXTERNAL                      O = HAS OCCURS CLAUSE               U = UNDEFINED FORMAT FILE
  F = FIXED LENGTH FILE             OG= GROUP HAS OWN LENGTH DEFINITION V = VARIABLE LENGTH FILE
  FB= FIXED LENGTH BLOCKED FILE     R = REDEFINES                      VB= VARIABLE LENGTH BLOCKED FILE

SOURCE  HIERARCHY AND                              BASE      HEX-DISPLACEMENT  ASMBLR DATA              DATA DEF
LINEID  DATA NAME                                  LOCATOR   BLK   STRUCTURE   DEFINITION  DATA TYPE    ATTRIBUTES

 19     FD INVMAST · · · · · · · · · · · · · · ·                                            QSAM         F
 23     01 INVENTORY-MASTER-RECORD · · · · · ·    BLF=0000  001  0 000 000   DS 0CL80   GROUP
 25     02 IM-DESCRIPTIVE-DATA · · · · · · · ·    BLF=0000  000  0 000 000   DS 0CL35   GROUP
 26     03 IM-ITEM-NO. · · · · · · · · · · · ·    BLF=0000  000  0 000 005   DS 5C      DISP-NUM
 27     03 IM-ITEM-DESC. · · · · · · · · · · ·    BLF=0000  005  0 000 019   DS 20C     DISPLAY
 28     03 IM-UNIT-COST. · · · · · · · · · · ·    BLF=0000  019  0 000 01E   DS 5C      DISP-NUM
 29     03 IM-UNIT-PRICE. · · · · · · · · · · ·   BLF=0000  01E  0 000 023   DS 5C      DISP-NUM
 30     02 IM-INVENTORY-DATA · · · · · · · · ·    BLF=0000  023  0 000 023   DS 0CL15   GROUP
 31     03 IM-REORDER-POINT. · · · · · · · · ·    BLF=0000  023  0 000 028   DS 5C      DISP-NUM
 32     03 IM-ON-HAND. · · · · · · · · · · · ·    BLF=0000  028  0 000 02D   DS 5C      DISP-NUM
 33     03 IM-ON-ORDER · · · · · · · · · · · ·    BLF=0000  02D  0 000 032   DS 5C      DISP-NUM
 34     02 IM-SALES-DATA · · · · · · · · · · ·    BLF=0000  032  0 000 032   DS 0CL22   GROUP
 35     03 IM-LAST-ORDER-DATE. · · · · · · · ·    BLF=0000  032  0 000 032   DS 6C      DISP-NUM
 36     03 IM-LAST-ORDER-DATE-R. · · · · · · ·    BLF=0000  032  0 000 032   DS 0CL6    GROUP        R
 37     04 IM-LAST-ORDER-MONTH · · · · · · · ·    BLF=0000  032  0 000 034   DS 2C      DISP-NUM
 38     04 IM-LAST-ORDER-DAY. · · · · · · · · ·   BLF=0000  034  0 000 036   DS 2C      DISP-NUM
 39     04 IM-LAST-ORDER-YEAR. · · · · · · · ·    BLF=0000  036  0 000 038   DS 2C      DISP-NUM
 40     03 IM-LAST-MONTH-SALES. · · · · · · · ·   BLF=0000  038  0 000 03F   DS 7C      DISP-NUM
 41     03 IM-LAST-YEAR-SALES. · · · · · · · ·    BLF=0000  03F  0 000 048   DS 9C      DISP-NUM
 42     02 FILLER. · · · · · · · · · · · · · ·    BLF=0000  048                          DISPLAY

 44     FD INVLIST · · · · · · · · · · · · · ·              001                          QSAM         F
 48     01 PRINT-AREA. · · · · · · · · · · · ·    BLW=0001  000  0 000 000   DS 132C    DISPLAY
 52     01 SWITCHES. · · · · · · · · · · · · ·    BLW=0000  000  0 000 000   DS 0CL2    GROUP
 54     02 INVMST-EOF-SWITCH. · · · · · · · · ·   BLW=0000  000  0 000 001   DS 1C      DISPLAY
 55     88 INVMST-EOF. · · · · · · · · · · · ·
 56     02 INVESTMENT-SIZE-ERROR-SWITCH. · · ·    BLW=0000  001  0 000 001   DS 1C      DISPLAY
 57     88 INVESTMENT-SIZE-ERROR · · · · · · ·
 59     01 PRINT-FIELDS. · · · · · · · · · · ·    BLW=0000  008  0 000 001              GROUP
 61     02 SPACE-CONTROL · · · · · · · · · · ·    BLW=0000  008  0 000 000   DS 0CL7    PACKED-DEC
 62     02 LINES-ON-PAGE · · · · · · · · · · ·    BLW=0000  009  0 000 001   DS 1P      PACKED-DEC
 63     02 LINE-COUNT. · · · · · · · · · · · ·    BLW=0000  00B  0 000 003   DS 2P      PACKED-DEC
 64     02 PAGE-COUNT. · · · · · · · · · · · ·    BLW=0000  00D  0 000 005   DS 2P      PACKED-DEC
 66     01 DATE-AND-TIME-FIELDS. · · · · · · ·    BLW=0000  010  0 000 000   DS 2P      GROUP
 68     02 PRESENT-DATE. · · · · · · · · · · ·    BLW=0000  010  0 000 000   DS 0CL20   DISP-NUM
 69     02 PRESENT-DATE-R. · · · · · · · · · ·    BLW=0000  010  0 000 000   DS 6C      GROUP        R
 70     03 PRESENT-YEAR. · · · · · · · · · · ·    BLW=0000  010  0 000 002   DS 0CL6    DISP-NUM
 71     03 PRESENT-MONTH · · · · · · · · · · ·    BLW=0000  012  0 000 002   DS 2C      DISP-NUM
 72     03 PRESENT-DAY. · · · · · · · · · · · ·   BLW=0000  014  0 000 004   DS 2C      DISP-NUM
 73     02 TODAYS-DATE. · · · · · · · · · · · ·   BLW=0000  016  0 000 006   DS 6C      DISP-NUM
 74     02 TODAYS-DATE-R. · · · · · · · · · · ·   BLW=0000  016  0 000 006   DS 0CL6    GROUP        R
          · · ·
```

Figure 4-20   A sample Data Division listing from Release 3

Figure 4-22 presents a diagnostics message listing from Release 2 of VS COBOL II. (There are only minor differences in the Release 3 listing, so I won't present it here.) There are several things you should notice about this listing. First, even if the same error occurs more than once, the diagnostic message is printed for only the first occurrence. Then, the other program lines on which the error occurred are printed on the following line of the listing. For example, in figure 4-22, you can see that the error detected on line 212 also occurred on lines 243, 258, and 259. Grouping the messages this way keeps the listing from getting too cluttered. And it's appropriate since only one programming error caused all the diagnostics.

You should also notice the asterisks (*) before some of the message codes in the diagnostics listing. As I mentioned earlier in this chapter, an asterisk indicates that the diagnostic was imbedded in the source statement listing.

RUN-TIME OPTIONS

Run-time options control the way a program runs. They are coded in the PARM parameter of the EXEC statement that starts the execution of your program. There are several run-time options provided by VS COBOL II. Figure 4-23 contains the three I'll present here: NOSSRANGE, NOSTAE, and SPOUT. There are two other options available with Release 2 of VS COBOL II that I won't present here: LIBKEEP and RTEREUS. And there are three other options available with Release 3 I won't present: SIMVRD, WSCLEAR, and MIXRES. These options are complicated and you'll probably never have to use them. If you want to find out about these options, you can refer to the *VS COBOL II Application Programming Guide*. A complete list of run-time options is given in appendix B of this book.

The NOSSRANGE option

Earlier in this chapter, I presented the SSRANGE compiler option. You'll remember that you specify this option if you want to check for out-of-range conditions. The NOSSRANGE run-time option can be used to turn this option off when a program is executed. Since out-of-range testing requires additional overhead, you might want to use this option once you've thoroughly tested a program that was originally compiled with the SSRANGE compiler option.

```
NESTED PROGRAM MAP
PROGRAM ATTRIBUTE CODES (RIGHTMOST COLUMN) HAVE THE FOLLOWING MEANINGS:
   C = COMMON
   I = INITIAL
   U = PROCEDURE DIVISION USING...

SOURCE NESTING                                                              PROGRAM
LINEID LEVEL    PROGRAM NAME FROM PROGRAM-ID PARAGRAPH                      ATTRIBUTES
    2            AP2520. . . . . . . . . . . . . . . . . . . . . . . . . . . . . .
  451     1         CALCDATE. . . . . . . . . . . . . . . . . . . . . . . . . . .
  503     2            CONVDATE. . . . . . . . . . . . . . . . . . . . . . . . . C
  548     1         DATEDIT . . . . . . . . . . . . . . . . . . . . . . . . . . I
```

Figure 4-21   A sample nested program listing

The NOSTAE option

The NOSTAE option specifies that the run-time environment is not to intercept a program abend. If this option is specified, the compiler does not issue abend information, release resources acquired during program execution, or print dumps. You'll probably never have an occasion to use this option since you'll always want the compiler to provide abend processing.

The SPOUT option

If the SPOUT option is specified, the compiler issues a message that describes the amount of storage that was allocated during program execution. This information can then be used to improve space management. If your installation uses space-management tuning tables, you may be required to code this option.

DISCUSSION

The intent of this chapter is to familiarize you with the new features of VS COBOL II that affect the way you compile and execute your programs. You'll use some of these features frequently. Others, you may never use. But if you understand what these features are and follow the recommendations I make for their use as well as your installation's standards, you should have no trouble using them when you need to.

```
INVENTORY LISTING PROGRAM                          INV3520    DATE 12/10/87   TIME 12.35.21    PAGE    12

LINEID  MESSAGE CODE  MESSAGE TEXT ( IMBEDDED MESSAGES MAY BE IDENTIFIED BY THE <*> PRECEDING THE MESSAGE CODE )

        IGYDS0015-I   DIAGNOSTIC MESSAGES WERE ISSUED DURING PROCESSING OF COMPILER OPTIONS. THESE MESSAGES ARE LOCATED
                      AT THE BEGINNING OF THE LISTING.

     1  IGYDS0040-I   PRINTING OF THE SOURCE CODE HAS BEEN SUPPRESSED.

    19  IGYGR1216-I   A "RECORDING MODE" OF < F > WAS ASSUMED FOR FILE < INVMAST >.

    44  IGYGR1216-I   A "RECORDING MODE" OF < F > WAS ASSUMED FOR FILE < INVLIST >.

   212 *IGYPS2121-S   < INVMAST-EOF > WAS NOT DEFINED AS A DATA-NAME. THE STATEMENT WAS DISCARDED.

                      SAME MESSAGE ON LINE:    243    258    259

   212 *IGYPS2096-S   AN INCOMPLETE SINGLE CONDITION WAS FOUND IN A CONDITIONAL EXPRESSION. THE OPERAND(S) WAS DISCARDED.

                      SAME MESSAGE ON LINE:    243    259

   242  IGYPA3007-S   PROCEDURE-NAME < 301-READ-INVENTORY-RECORD > WAS NOT DEFINED. THE STATEMENT WAS DISCARDED.

   254 *IGYPS2008-E   A PERIOD WAS REQUIRED BEFORE PROCEDURE-NAME < 310-READ-INVENTORY-RECORD >. A PERIOD WAS ASSUMED
                      BEFORE < 310-READ-INVENTORY-RECORD >.

TOTAL  MESSAGES     INFORMATIONAL     WARNING     ERROR     SEVERE     TERMINATING

   14                    5                           1          8

* STATISTICS FOR COBOL PROGRAM INV3520 :
*     SOURCE RECORDS = 346
*     DATA DIVISION STATEMENTS = 83
*     PROCEDURE DIVISION STATEMENTS = 92
```

Figure 4-22   A sample diagnostics message listing

VS COBOL II Option	Description
<u>SSRANGE</u> NOSSRANGE	Causes out-of-range conditions to be checked during program execution. The SSRANGE compiler option must be specified for range checking to occur. SSRANGE is the default.
<u>STAE</u> NOSTAE	Causes the run-time environment to intercept an abend. The default is STAE.
SPOUT <u>NOSPOUT</u>	Causes a message indicating the amount of storage used during the execution of a COBOL program to be issued. The default is NOSPOUT.

Figure 4-23 Three run-time options available with VS COBOL II

Terminology

COBOL prompter
command procedure
CLIST
program module
Systems Application Architecture
SAA
normalized level number
source statement listing
cross-reference listing
imbedded cross reference
Data Division listing
nested program listing
diagnostics message listing

Objectives

1. Use MVS JCL, TSO commands, or CMS commands to compile, link-edit, and execute your programs.

2. Use the compiler options presented in this chapter, when appropriate, to compile your COBOL programs.

3. Use the TITLE, *CBL, and *CONTROL compiler-directing statements in your COBOL programs.

4. Use the NOSSRANGE, NOSTAE, and SPOUT run-time options, when appropriate, to execute your COBOL programs.

Chapter
five

Debugging programs using VS COBOL II
Debug

If you've used OS/VS COBOL in an interactive environment, you're probably familiar with OS COBOL Interactive Debug. It's a separately licensed program that helps you test and debug programs interactively. VS COBOL II provides a similar debugging tool called VS COBOL II Debug, or COBTEST.

VS COBOL II Debug is part of VS COBOL II and provides a number of new functions in addition to those of OS COBOL Interactive Debug. The most significant change is that VS COBOL II Debug can be used in either batch or interactive mode. And interactive mode provides for both line and full-screen mode. (Full-screen mode isn't available with VS COBOL II Release 1.)

In this chapter, I'll describe how to use COBTEST. In topic 1, I'll describe some of its basic functions. In topic 2, I'll go on to more advanced functions. And in topic 3, I'll describe the features of COBTEST that can be used only in full-screen mode.

Most of the commands presented in topics 1 and 2 can be used in batch, interactive line, and interactive full-screen mode. However, there are a few exceptions that I'll point out as we come to them. So unless I mention otherwise, you can assume that a command can be used in any of the three modes.

Before I go on, I want to point out that I will not try to teach you *how* to debug COBOL programs in this chapter; that's beyond the scope of this book. Instead, I'll teach you how to use COBTEST so you'll be able to debug your programs more easily.

Topic 1 | Basic functions of VS COBOL II Debug

In this topic, you'll learn the features of VS COBOL II Debug you'll use most often. First, you'll learn how to invoke COBTEST in each of its three modes. Then, you'll learn how to use it to monitor your program's execution and manage its data. Finally, you'll see how to terminate COBTEST.

HOW TO INVOKE COBTEST

The method you use to invoke COBTEST depends on the debugging mode you're using. As a result, I've divided this section into three parts—one on batch mode, one on interactive line mode, and one on interactive full-screen mode.

No matter which mode you're using, you must be sure that the program you're debugging has been compiled with the TEST option. The TEST option produces the symbolic data necessary for a program to be used with COBTEST. It also forces the RESIDENT option, which requests the COBOL Library Management Facility. You should also be aware that the FDUMP option cannot be used for a program compiled with the TEST option. If you need to print a dump for a program you're testing using COBTEST, you use COBTEST's DUMP command. I'll cover the DUMP command later in this topic.

How to invoke COBTEST in batch mode

The specific procedure for invoking COBTEST in batch mode differs from system to system. In this section, I'll present the procedures for invoking COBTEST under MVS and CMS and show an example of each. If you're working in a different environment, be sure to find out the specific requirements for your system.

In general, you have to do three things to invoke COBTEST in batch mode. You have to enter the debug commands, you have to allocate the files required by COBTEST and by the program you're debugging, and you have to execute COBTEST.

Entering COBTEST commands   The commands you want to execute during debug processing must be placed in a data set that's associated with the SYSDBIN data name. Under MVS, this can be either a DASD data set or an in-stream data set that's included in the job stream that executes COBTEST.

Under CMS, the file must be a disk file. In any case, the data set must consist of 80-character records. Since commands can consist of up to 32,763 bytes, a command can be continued by placing a plus sign (+), a minus sign (-), or a comma (,) in the last position of a record.

When you code your COBTEST commands, they must be in a particular order. The first command must be

```
COBTEST program-name
```

where *program-name* is the name of the load module you want to execute.

After the COBTEST command, you can specify the RECORD/NO-RECORD command. This command determines whether the debugging session is logged. I'll have more to say about this command in topic 2 of this chapter.

The next command must be

```
QUALIFY program-name
```

where *program-name* is the name used in the PROGRAM-ID statement of the program you want to debug. This command tells COBTEST the program to which the COBTEST commands that follow it refer. In other words, if you coded the command

```
QUALIFY INV3520
```

any COBTEST commands that followed would refer to INV3520.

The program name specified in a QUALIFY command (abbreviated Q) does not have to be the same as the program name specified in the COBTEST command. For example, if you're debugging a subprogram, you could specify the name of the main program on the COBTEST command and the name of the subprogram on the QUALIFY command.

You can also code multiple QUALIFY commands. For example, if you're debugging both a main program and a subprogram, you can code two QUALIFY commands, one for the main program and one for the subprogram. I'll have more to say about this when I show you how to debug subprograms in topic 2 of this chapter.

After the QUALIFY command, you can code any of the COBTEST commands that are valid for batch processing. When you enter the commands, however, you should be aware that all of them are processed before your COBOL program is executed. So you'll need to plan them carefully and consider when each of them will take effect. As I present the COBTEST commands in this chapter, I'll show you how they can be used effectively in batch mode.

Allocating data sets   After you create the input command file, you need to allocate a data set associated with SYSDBIN. Under MVS, you do that by coding a DD statement in the job stream that executes COBTEST. Under CMS, you code a FILEDEF command.

You'll also need to allocate an output data set and associate it with SYSDBOUT. The SYSDBOUT data set must be defined with records of at least 121 characters. In topic 2, I'll show you how you can control what's written to the output data set.

Finally, you'll need to allocate any data sets used by the program you're debugging. Again, under MVS, you do this by coding DD statements in your job stream, and under CMS, you do this by issuing FILEDEF commands. You'll see an example of these data set allocations in a minute.

Executing COBTEST   Now, you're ready to execute COBTEST. If you're working directly under MVS, you execute the batch debugger by submitting a job with the following JCL statement:

```
EXEC PGM=COBDBG
```

Here, COBDBG is the name of the COBTEST program. If you're working under CMS, you use the following form of the COBTEST command to invoke the debugger:

```
COBTEST program-name [PARM(?)] BATCH
```

Here, *program-name* is the name of the program that will be given control by COBTEST. (This should be the same name coded on the COBTEST command in the SYSDBIN data set.) In most cases, it's the name of the program you want to debug. This program must be a TEXT file or a member in a TXTLIB or LOADLIB. You use the PARM(?) parameter to pass parameters to the program specified by program-name when it's invoked. You use the BATCH parameter to indicate that COBTEST is to be executed in batch mode.

Examples of invoking COBTEST in batch mode   To give you a complete picture, figure 5-1 presents the JCL for invoking COBTEST under MVS and CMS. In the MVS job, I've included a step that compiles and link-edits the program you're debugging, since this will probably be the method you'll use most often. Notice that the output from the linkage editor is stored in a data set in a temporary library. That temporary library is then allocated as the step library in the step that executes COBTEST. Also notice that the source program, the data set that's used as input to the program that's being debugged, and the file containing the COBTEST commands, are all

```
MVS JCL

//DLOWE2A  JOB  USER=DLOWE2,PASSWORD=MMAPW3
//         EXEC COB2UCL,PARM.COB2='APOST,OBJECT,TEST',REGION.LKED=
//COB2.SYSIN DD *
                .
                . Source program
                .
/*
//LKED.SYSLMOD  DD DSN=&&TCLOAD(INV3520),
//              UNIT=3330V,VOL=SER=MPS8BV,
//              SPACE=(CYL,(1,1,1)),DISP=(NEW,PASS)
//DEBUG    EXEC PGM=COBDBG
//STEPLIB  DD   DSN=&&TCLOAD(INV3520),DISP=(SHR,PASS)
//INVMAST  DD   *
                .
                . Input data
                .
/*
//INVLIST  DD   SYSOUT=A
//SYSOUT   DD   SYSOUT=A
//SYSDBOUT DD   SYSOUT=A
//SYSDBIN  DD   *
COBTEST INV3520
QUALIFY INV3520
AT 238 (IF (INVESTMENT-AMOUNT LE 1000),
(LIST (IM-ITEM-NO,INVESTMENT-AMOUNT)))
/*


CMS commands

FILEDEF SYSDBIN DISK INV3520 SYSDBIN A
FILEDEF SYSDBOUT PRINTER INV3520 SYSDBOUT A (LRECL 121 RECFM F
FILEDEF INVMAST DISK INVMAST DATA A
FILEDEF INVLIST PRINTER INVLIST PRINT A
COBTEST INV3520 BATCH
```

Figure 5-1   Invoking COBTEST in batch mode

coded as in-stream data sets. Obviously, the DD statements coded for these data sets would be different if any of them were coded as DASD data sets. (Don't worry about the AT command included in this figure. I'll present its syntax later in this topic.)

In the bottom part of figure 5-1, four FILEDEF commands are used to define the input and output to COBTEST and the program that's being debugged. These files are SYSDBIN, SYSDBOUT, INVMAST, and

INVLIST. Once these files have been allocated, COBTEST is invoked by entering the COBTEST command. Then, the file specified on the COBTEST command, in this case INV3520, is loaded and executed along with the COBTEST commands in the SYSDBIN file.

How to invoke COBTEST in interactive line mode

Invoking the debugger in interactive line mode is simpler than invoking it in batch mode. That's because you enter the COBTEST commands interactively as your program executes rather than storing them in a data set before execution. Before executing COBTEST, then, all you need to do is allocate the required data sets.

Allocating data sets   If you plan to create printed output during your debugging session, you'll need to allocate a data set associated with SYSDBOUT. Again, the way you do that depends on the system you're using.

Under CMS, a default file definition is provided if SYSDBOUT is used, so you need to allocate a data set for SYSDBOUT only if you want to change that default. The default file definition is

```
FILEDEF SYSDBOUT PRINTER SYSDBOUT FILE A (LRECL 121 RECFM F
```

To change this definition, you simply issue a different FILEDEF command. In addition, you'll need to issue FILEDEF commands for any files required by the program you're debugging.

Under TSO, you enter an ALLOCATE command to allocate SYSDBOUT. In addition, if the program you're debugging is stored in a private library that isn't allocated in your logon procedure, you'll need to issue an ALLOCATE command for that library. And, you'll need to issue ALLOCATE commands for the files used by the program you're debugging. I'll show you examples of the FILEDEF and ALLOCATE commands in a minute.

Executing COBTEST   To execute COBTEST in interactive line mode, you issue the COBTEST command. Its format depends on the system you're using. The formats for TSO and CMS are given in figure 5-2.

For TSO, you specify the name of the load module, followed by an optional parameter string. As you can see, the load module can be specified in one of two ways. You can specify it just as you do for batch processing by simply entering the load module name, or you can specify it using the LOAD format. You use the LOAD format when the load module you're debugging is in a private library that isn't allocated in your logon procedure. The ddname

---

The COBTEST command under TSO

```
COBTEST {LOAD(load-module-name:ddname)}  [PARM('parameter-string')]
        {load-module-name              }
```

Explanation

load-module-name   The name of the load module to be executed by COBTEST.

ddname   The ddname associated with the partitioned data set of which load-module-name is a member. Must be specified if the load module is in a private library not allocated in your logon procedure.

'parameter-string'   A list of run-time options and parameters that are passed to the load module.

The COBTEST command under CMS

```
COBTEST program-name [PARM(?)]
```

Explanation

program-name   A TEXT file or a member of a TXTLIB or LOADLIB to be executed by COBTEST.

PARM(?)   Indicates that run-time parameters are to be entered.

Figure 5-2   The COBTEST command used in interactive line mode

parameter specifies the name of that private library, which is concatenated with the STEPLIB by COBTEST.

The PARM parameter is optional. It's used to pass run-time options and parameters to your COBOL program. If it is specified, the parameters must be enclosed in single quotes. If the parameter string contains run-time options, they must be specified first, followed by a slash (/) and any run-time parameters. The run-time parameters specified must be separated by commas; blanks are not allowed. The maximum length of the parameter string is 100 characters.

The format of the COBTEST command used under CMS is similar. First, you specify the name of the program to be executed. This program must be a TEXT file or a member of a TXTLIB or LOADLIB. The program name can be followed by the PARM(?) parameter, which is optional. If you specify the PARM(?) parameter, you will be prompted to enter a parameter string. This parameter string can contain both run-time options and parameters. If run-time options are specified, they must be specified first, followed by a slash (/). Then you can code a list of run-time parameters of up to 100 characters, with the parameters separated by commas. If no run-time options are specified, the parameter string can be up to 130 characters.

If you use the PARM option to specify run-time parameters under either TSO or CMS, you should realize that the debugger adds a two-byte length field in front of the parameter string when it's passed to the COBOL program. Therefore, you need to be sure that two additional bytes are defined at the beginning of the Linkage Section of your program. Otherwise, the parameters won't be passed properly. But, since most COBOL programs don't use run-time parameters, you won't use the PARM parameter often.

Examples of invoking COBTEST in interactive line mode   Figure 5-3 presents examples of the procedures for invoking COBTEST in line mode under TSO and CMS. In the TSO example in the top of figure 5-3, four ALLOCATE commands are issued. The data sets that are allocated are the output file for COBTEST (SYSDBOUT), the library containing the program to be debugged (MMA2.COBOL2.LOAD), and the two files used by the program being debugged (INVMAST and INVLIST). After these data sets are allocated, the COBTEST command is issued. Notice that the COBTEST command is coded with the LOAD operand. This operand specifies that the module INV3520 is located in the partitioned data set associated with the ddname LIB1. (LIB1 is the ddname that was specified in the ALLOCATE command for MMA2.COBOL2.LOAD.) Because the PARM operand isn't coded, no parameters are passed to the program.

In the CMS example in the bottom of figure 5-3, only two FILEDEF commands are issued. They are for the two files (INVMAST and INVLIST) used by the program that's being debugged. Because I didn't code a FILEDEF command for SYSDBOUT, the default file definition will be used if any output is generated. The COBTEST command specifies that the CMS file named INV3520 is to be executed.

After you invoke COBTEST from either TSO or CMS, a message is displayed indicating that COBTEST is active. This message is followed by the name of the program you're debugging and the line number in the program that contains the first verb. (I'll show you the exact format COBTEST uses to refer to program statements in just a minute.) The last line displayed is this:

```
COBTEST
```

Once this line is displayed, you can enter any of the commands I'll present in the first two topics of this chapter.

TSO commands

```
ALLOCATE DDNAME(SYSDBOUT) SYSOUT(A)
ALLOCATE DSNAME('MMA2.COBOL2.LOAD') DDNAME(LIB1) SHR
ALLOCATE DSNAME('MMA2.COBOL2.INVMAST') DDNAME(INVMAST)
ALLOCATE DDNAME(INVLIST) SYSOUT(A)
COBTEST LOAD(INV3520:LIB1)
```

CMS commands

```
FILEDEF INVMAST DISK INVMAST DATA A
FILEDEF INVLIST PRINTER INVLIST PRINT A
COBTEST INV3520
```

Figure 5-3   Invoking COBTEST in interactive line mode

How to invoke COBTEST in interactive full-screen mode

If you're using ISPF Version 2 or later under TSO or VM/SP CMS, you can use the full-screen mode of COBTEST. Usually, when VS COBOL II is installed for use with ISPF, it's set up so you can debug a program using standard ISPF procedures. As I present the procedure for invoking COBTEST in full-screen mode, I'll assume that it has been installed in this manner. If it isn't installed that way on your system, you'll have to check with your supervisor to find out how to invoke it.

Before you invoke COBTEST, you need to be sure you've allocated any data sets required by the program you're debugging. However, you don't have to allocate a SYSDBOUT data set. COBTEST does that for you.

When you first invoke ISPF, you'll want to select the FOREGROUND option from the Primary Option Menu. The Foreground Selection Panel should include a selection for VS COBOL II Debug. When you make that selection, the full-screen debug invocation panel will appear. The actual format of the panel and the entries required to invoke COBTEST depend on whether you're in a TSO or CMS environment. In either case, note that you do *not* use the COBTEST command to invoke COBTEST. This command is invalid in full-screen mode.

Invoking the full-screen debugger under TSO   Figure 5-4 shows the panel that appears when you select the full-screen debugger under TSO. On this panel, you specify the name of the program to be debugged and its run-time parameters. If you're familiar with TSO and ISPF panels, you should have no problem understanding the required entries.

```
- - - - - - - - - - - - - - - - - - - - - - - VS COBOL II DEBUG INVOCATION - - - - - - - - - - - - - - - - - - - - - -
COMMAND ===>

ISPF LIBRARY:
    PROJECT ===> MMA2
    GROUP   ===> COBOL2
    TYPE    ===> LOAD
    MEMBER  ===> INV3520              (Blank for member selection list)

OTHER PARTITIONED DATA SET:
    DATASET NAME  ===>

PASSWORD ===>                    MIXED MODE ===> NO  (YES or NO)

VS COBOL II PROGRAM PARAMETERS:
    ===>
    ===>

LOG      ===> NO  (Yes or No)
LOG DSN ===>
RESTART ===> NO  (Yes or No)
RESTART DSN ===>
```

Figure 5-4   The COBTEST full-screen invocation panel under TSO

In the command area, you can enter an ISPF command. Under ISPF LIBRARY, you enter the fully qualified name of the program or run unit you want to execute if you're using ISPF naming conventions. (A run unit is a group of object modules that function together as a single entity at execution time.) If you're using TSO naming conventions, you provide the data set name under OTHER PARTITIONED DATA SET. If the program you're using is password protected, be sure to enter the password. And, if you'll be using characters from the Double Byte Character Set in the debugging session, specify YES under MIXED MODE.

Run-time options and parameters can be specified in the area labeled VS COBOL II PROGRAM PARAMETERS. They're coded the same way as in line mode.

The LOG, LOG DSN, RESTART, and RESTART DSN entries provide for two optional debugging files. The first one is created during your debugging session and contains any COBTEST commands you enter as well as any output that's sent to your terminal. If you want to log your debugging session, specify YES under LOG and the name of the data set you want created to contain the log under LOG DSN. This data set will consist of fixed-length, 80-character records.

The second file allows you to restart a debugging session at a specific point. In most cases, you'll use it to restart a session at the point at which it was previously terminated. To do that, you specify YES under RESTART and the name of the restart data set under RESTART DSN. The restart data set is an existing file that contains the commands that were entered before the program was terminated. Then, when the debugger is invoked, those commands are re-executed, returning you to the previous termination point. From there, you can continue by entering additional debugging commands.

Although you can create a restart file from scratch with the ISPF source file editor, it's much easier to use the log file created during the previous execution of a debugging session as the restart file. Then, all you have to do is specify the name of the log file under RESTART DSN, and the input commands in the log file are executed. (If you want, you can also edit the log file before using it as a restart file.) The restart data set must have fixed-length, 80-character records, which is the default for a log file.

Under Release 3 of VS COBOL II, an additional option, DDNAME, is available. This option appears on the full-screen invocation panel just above the LOG, LOG DSN, RESTART, and RESTART DSN options. In this field, you can enter the name of a data set that's been previously allocated. If you do, the data set you specify is concatenated to the data set where the program you're debugging resides.

After you make the required entries on the full-screen panel to invoke COBTEST, the full-screen debugging panel appears. From this panel, you can enter COBTEST commands and view the execution of the debugging session. I'll show you how to use this panel in topic 3 of this chapter.

Invoking the full-screen debugger under CMS   Figure 5-5 presents the CMS full-screen invocation panel. As you can see, it's very similar to the panel that's displayed under TSO, so I'll describe only the differences.

The program to be executed can be specified using ISPF or CMS naming conventions. If you specify a CMS file that's located on a virtual machine not linked to your own, you'll also need to provide some link information (OWNER'S ID, DEVICE ADDR., and LINK ACCESS MODE) so COBTEST can locate the file.

The only other difference is the last entry on the panel, USER TXTLIB. In this area, you can enter up to four TEXT libraries. Any TXTLIBs specified are concatenated with the TXTLIBs used by COBTEST.

```
-------------------------- VS/COBOL II DEBUG INVOCATION ------------------------
COMMAND ===>

ISPF LIBRARY:
   PROJECT  ===>
   GROUP    ===>
   TYPE     ===>
   MEMBER   ===>                    (Blank for member selection list)

CMS FILE:
   FILE ID   ===>  INV3520  (File type test assumed)

   IF NOT LINKED, SPECIFY:
   OWNER'S ID ===>             DEVICE ADDR. ===>       LINK ACCESS MODE ===>

READ   PASSWORD ===>            MIXED MODE   ===>  NO  (YES or NO)

VS COBOL II PROGRAM PARAMETERS:
   ===>
   ===>

LOG     ===>  NO   (YES or NO)  LOG FILE ID     ===>
RESTART ===>  NO   (YES or NO)  RESTART FILE ID ===>

USER TXTLIB ===>            ===>            ===>            ===>
```

Figure 5-5   The COBTEST full-screen invocation panel under CMS

HOW TO MONITOR YOUR PROGRAM'S EXECUTION

COBTEST lets you monitor your program's execution in two ways. First, you can establish *breakpoints* at one or more statements in your program. Whenever your program comes to a breakpoint, it stops executing temporarily. As a result, using breakpoints allows you to look at your program at specific times during its execution. The second way to monitor program execution is to use a *trace*. A trace displays information about your program's execution without actually interrupting the program.

Before I go on, I want you to understand how COBTEST refers to individual statements in your program. COBTEST follows this format when it refers to a particular Procedure Division statement:

```
program-id.line-number.verb-number
```

Program-id identifies the program that contains the statement. Normally, this will be the name of the program you're executing. However, if your program calls subprograms, program-id will name the subprogram if that's where the interrupt occurs.

Line-number identifies the line containing the Procedure Division state-ment that was *about* to execute when the interrupt occurred. This number corresponds to the compiler-generated line number that appears in the source listing.

Verb-number is only significant when you code more than one COBOL verb on a single line. It indicates which verb was about to execute when the interrupt occurred: if it's one, the first verb on the line was about to execute; if it's two, the second verb was about to execute; and so on. Of course, it's a good practice to limit yourself to one COBOL verb on each line of your Procedure Division. If you do that, the verb number will always be one.

To illustrate the statement-referral notation, consider this message:

```
INV3520.000201.1
```

This refers to the first verb on line 201 in the program named INV3520.

Now that you know how COBTEST refers to Procedure Division state-ments, I'll show you how to use its commands to start or resume a program's execution, to use breakpoints, and to establish a program trace.

How to start or resume your program's execution

In batch mode, your program will automatically begin executing after the commands in the input file (SYSDBIN) are processed. In interactive mode, however, once COBTEST is invoked, you must enter a command to tell it what to do. Here, you can set a breakpoint, establish a trace, or just start your program executing.

There are three commands for starting your program's execution. They are presented in figure 5-6. The command most commonly used to start program execution is GO (abbreviated G). If you simply specify the word GO, your program begins executing and continues until a breakpoint occurs, an abend occurs, or your program executes a STOP RUN statement.

The RUN command (abbreviated R) is like the GO command except that it ignores any breakpoints you established. So the RUN command causes your program to execute to its completion—either an abend or a STOP RUN.

You can also use the RUN or GO command to resume your program's execution after it's been interrupted by a breakpoint. Usually, when an inter-rupt occurs, you'll issue other COBTEST commands to find out what's happening in your program or to set additional breakpoints. Then you'll issue a RUN or GO command to continue execution. Once your program ends by executing a STOP RUN, however, you can't resume it with a RUN or GO command.

The GO command

```
GO [statement-number]
```

The RUN command

```
RUN [statement-number]
```

The RESTART command

```
RESTART
```

Explanation

GO	Start or resume program execution. Can be abbreviated G.
RUN	Start or resume program execution, ignoring active breakpoints. Can be abbreviated R.
RESTART	Delete and reload the executing program. Can be abbreviated RESTA.
statement-number	A statement number in the COBOL source program. Must be in the form [program-id.] line-number [.verb-number].

Figure 5-6   COBTEST commands used to start or resume program execution

---

When a breakpoint occurs in batch mode, control is automatically returned to your program after the specified processing takes place. Therefore, the RUN and GO commands aren't necessary. However, they can be useful in command lists, which I'll present in the next topic.

If you specify a statement number on a RUN or GO command, program execution starts at the specified statement. For example, if you enter

```
GO INV3520.000236.1
```

execution begins at the first verb in line 236 of INV3520. You can achieve the same result like this (assuming INV3520 is the program that's been executing):

```
GO 236
```

Here, the first verb in line 236 is assumed because you omitted the verb number. And INV3520 is the program that will be executed since you omitted the program-id.

Coding a statement number on a RUN or GO command is the same as issuing a GO TO statement in a COBOL program. You'll use this feature most when you're testing a single section of code repeatedly, perhaps changing the value of a data field between each execution.

If you're using VS COBOL II Release 2 or 3, you can also use the RESTART command (abbreviated RESTA) to start program execution. When the RESTART command is issued, the previous version of the program invoked by the debugger is deleted and the program is reloaded. In the process, all program variables are initialized. However, all debug tool settings, such as breakpoints, remain unchanged. The RESTART command makes it easy to test a program several times without having to get out of COBTEST. For example, you might want to restart a program after an abend occurs.

Like the RUN and GO commands, the RESTART command cannot be used in batch mode. However, if you're using VS COBOL II Release 2 or 3, you can simulate the RESTART command in batch mode by coding multiple QUALIFY commands for the main program. Then, the main program is reloaded each time another QUALIFY command is encountered. (Remember, VS COBOL II Release 1 doesn't let you specify multiple QUALIFY commands for the same program in batch mode.)

How to use breakpoints

One of the most powerful features of COBTEST is its ability to use breakpoints. Basically, a breakpoint is a specific point in your program where you want to temporarily interrupt program execution. Once the program is stopped, you can use other COBTEST commands to inspect data fields, display the status of files, or perform other debugging functions.

COBTEST provides four types of breakpoints. A *NEXT breakpoint* lets you execute your program one statement at a time by setting a breakpoint at the next statement that's executed. A *STEP breakpoint* lets you step through your program, executing a specified number of verbs at a time. An *unconditional breakpoint* sets a breakpoint at a specific statement number you supply, so your program is interrupted whenever that statement is about to execute. And a *conditional breakpoint* interrupts your program whenever a condition you specify occurs—for example, whenever a particular field's value changes.

After I present the commands for using breakpoints, I'll present two more commands that are used frequently with breakpoints: the LISTBRKS and WHERE commands. Then, I'll discuss how to use breakpoints most effectively in batch mode.

The NEXT command

```
NEXT [command-list]
```

Explanation

NEXT   Set a temporary breakpoint at the next verb to be executed. Can be
                              abbreviated N.

command-list   A series of VS COBOL II Debug commands, separated by semicolons, that
                              are automatically executed when the specified breakpoint occurs. The entire
                              list is enclosed in parentheses.

Figure 5-7   The NEXT command

How to use a NEXT breakpoint   The NEXT command (abbreviated N)
establishes a breakpoint at the next statement that's executed. Its format is
presented in figure 5-7. To set a NEXT breakpoint, you just issue the NEXT
command with no operands, like this:

```
NEXT
```

Then, when program execution continues, only one statement of your program
is executed before the next breakpoint is taken.

As you can see in figure 5-7, you can also specify a command list on a
NEXT command. A *command list* is a list of commands that is executed when
a specified condition occurs. When you code a command list, each command
is separated by semicolons and the entire list is enclosed in parentheses. The
commands in the list are executed before control returns to your terminal
(interactive mode) or before the next COBTEST command is executed (batch
mode). I'll describe command lists in more detail later in this topic when I
discuss using breakpoints in batch mode, and in the next topic when I present
the IF command.

There are two situations in which a NEXT breakpoint is particularly useful.
The first is when your program reaches a decision point, such as an IF
statement, and you want to see which statement of your program is executed
next. By setting a NEXT breakpoint, you cause your program to be interrupted
after the next statement executes, even though you don't know in advance
which statement that will be.

The second situation where a NEXT breakpoint is helpful is when you first
enter COBTEST in interactive mode. Before you begin the execution of your
program, you cannot use certain COBTEST commands, including the ones

---

The STEP command

```
STEP [number]
```

Explanation

STEP	Execute the specified number of verbs, then take a breakpoint. Can be abbreviated ST.
number	The number of verbs to be executed before the next breakpoint is taken. One is the default.

Figure 5-8   The STEP command

---

you use to examine and change your program's data. That's because COBTEST doesn't actually load your program into storage until you issue a GO or RUN command. But if you enter a NEXT command followed by a GO command, COBTEST loads your program and interrupts it *before* the first statement executes. Then, you can enter any COBTEST command you wish.

How to use a STEP breakpoint   The STEP command (abbreviated ST) was introduced with VS COBOL II Release 2. Its format is presented in figure 5-8. This command causes a specified number of verbs to be executed before the next breakpoint is taken. For example, if you specify

```
STEP 5
```

five verbs are executed.

The STEP command is probably most useful for executing one verb at a time in full-screen mode. Then, the STEP function can be assigned to a PF key so that each time the PF key is pressed one verb is executed. To execute one verb at a time, you can code the STEP command

```
STEP 1
```

or just

```
STEP
```

since one is the default. Notice that this is *not* the same as issuing a NEXT command. The NEXT command simply establishes a breakpoint. The STEP command establishes a breakpoint and causes your program to continue execution.

How to use an unconditional breakpoint   An unconditional breakpoint causes your program to be interrupted whenever a particular statement is about to be executed. To use unconditional breakpoints, you need to know about two debugging commands: AT and OFF. Figure 5-9 gives the formats of these commands.

You use the AT command (abbreviated A) to establish one or more breakpoints in your program. As you can see, there are two different formats. In the first format, AT ENTRY, you specify the name of one or more programs or ALL. ALL includes all programs in the run unit for which COBTEST can be used. Then, COBTEST will stop before it executes the first verb in each program specified.

The AT ENTRY format is available only with VS COBOL II Releases 2 and 3. With Release 1, COBTEST automatically stops at the entry to each program in the debugging session. But with Releases 2 and 3, COBTEST stops only at the first entry to the first program. If you want it to stop at the entry to any other programs or at a subsequent entry to the first program, you have to use the AT ENTRY command.

This form of the AT command is particularly useful for debugging subprograms. For example, suppose you want to stop program execution when a subprogram called DATEDIT is first entered. Then, all you do is enter this command:

```
AT ENTRY DATEDIT
```

COBTEST will then stop program execution before the first verb in the subprogram is executed.

In the second format of the AT command, you provide one or more statement numbers at which program execution is to be interrupted. To set one breakpoint, you simply code AT followed by the statement number for the breakpoint you wish to set. For example, if you enter the command

```
AT 236
```

a breakpoint is established at statement 236.

To specify more than one statement number in an AT command, you separate the numbers with commas and enclose the entire list in parentheses. For example, the command

```
AT (236,243,258)
```

The AT command

```
AT ENTRY  {program-name}
          {ALL        }

AT statement-list [command-list] [COUNT(n[,m][,k])]

  [{NOTIFY  }] [DEFER]
   {NONOTIFY}
```

The OFF command

```
OFF [statement-list]
```

Explanation

AT ENTRY	Set a breakpoint at the first verb of the specified program. The breakpoint is taken for the first entry into the program only. Can be abbreviated A ENTRY.
AT	Set a breakpoint at the specified statement. Can be abbreviated A.
OFF	Remove the specified breakpoints.
program-name	The name of the COBOL program for which the breakpoint applies. Multiple programs can be specified by separating them with commas and enclosing them in parentheses.
ALL	Apply the breakpoint to all programs in the run unit.
statement-list	One or more statements in the form [program-id.] line-number [.verb-number] where statement-number is specified as: (1) a single number; (2) several numbers separated by commas and enclosed in parentheses; or (3) a range of numbers separated by a colon. If no statements are specified in an OFF command, all unconditional breakpoints are deleted.
command-list	A series of VS COBOL II Debug commands, separated by semicolons, that are automatically executed when the specified breakpoint occurs. The entire list is enclosed in parentheses.
COUNT(n,m,k)	Take the breakpoint on the specified occurrences: n specifies the first occurrence of the breakpoint; m specifies each occurrence after the first occurrence; k specifies the maximum number of breakpoints to be taken.
NOTIFY NONOTIFY	Print (NOTIFY) or do not print (NONOTIFY) a message each time a breakpoint is taken. NOTIFY is the default.
DEFER	The program referenced by *program-name* is not currently in storage.

Figure 5-9   COBTEST commands used for unconditional breakpoints

sets three breakpoints at lines 236, 243, and 258. You can also specify a range of statement numbers in an AT command, like this:

```
AT 236:258
```

Here, a breakpoint is established at every statement between (and including) lines 236 and 258. This form of the AT command is useful when you want to "single-step" a segment of your program to locate an elusive program bug.

In the statement-list form of the AT command, you can also specify a list of commands to be executed automatically when the breakpoint occurs just as you can for the NEXT command. In addition, you can specify: (1) when to take a breakpoint for a statement that's executed more than once in a program (COUNT); (2) whether a message is to be printed every time a breakpoint is taken (NOTIFY/NONOTIFY); and (3) whether the breakpoint occurs in a program not currently in storage (DEFER).

The COUNT operand lets you specify three things: the occurrence of the statement for which the first breakpoint will be taken (n), the occurrence of the statement for which the breakpoint will be taken following the first occurrence (m), and the maximum number of times the breakpoint is to be taken for the statement (k). For example, if you want to set a breakpoint at the first execution of statement 236 and at every tenth execution of that statement thereafter up to ten breakpoints, you code the AT command like this:

```
AT 236 COUNT(1,10,10)
```

As a default, COBTEST prints an identifying message every time an AT breakpoint is taken. If you don't want these messages to be printed, you can specify the NONOTIFY operand on the AT command. However, I don't recommend you do that unless you have only one AT breakpoint set. Otherwise, you won't know where the breakpoint occurred.

If you're using VS COBOL II Release 2 or 3, you can set a breakpoint for a program that's not in storage by specifying the DEFER operand. In this case, you must include the program-id in the statement-list operand. The specified break will then be taken if and when the program is called into storage. A program is in storage if it is currently executing or if it has been referenced by an AT ENTRY, QUALIFY, or previous AT DEFER command.

You use the OFF command to remove one or more breakpoints you've previously set using the AT command. In an OFF command, you specify statement numbers just as in an AT command. For instance, you can specify a single statement number like this:

```
OFF 236
```

Here, the breakpoint at line 236 is removed. Or, you can specify more than one statement number by separating them with commas and enclosing the entire list in parentheses, like this:

```
OFF (236,243,258)
```

Here, the three breakpoints at lines 236, 243, and 258 are removed. Or, you can specify a range of statements, like this:

```
OFF 236:258
```

Here, all of the breakpoints between (and including) lines 236 and 258 are removed. Finally, you can specify an OFF command with no operands. In that case, all of your unconditional breakpoints are deleted.

Special forms of the AT and OFF commands can be used in full-screen mode. Their formats are simply

```
AT number
```

and

```
OFF number
```

where *number* is a value between one and seven that specifies a relative verb number. A breakpoint is then set or removed at the specified verb. For example, if you enter

```
AT 2
```

a breakpoint is taken at the second verb on the line on which the AT command is specified. If you enter

```
OFF 2
```

on the same line, the breakpoint is removed. (Incidentally, these commands can be entered only in the prefix area of the full-screen debugging panel. You'll learn more about the prefix area when I discuss the special features of full-screen debugging in topic 3 of this chapter.)

How to use a conditional breakpoint   A conditional breakpoint interrupts your program based on the contents of a particular data field. As a result, conditional breakpoints let you monitor the contents of specific data fields to see when they are changed or when they attain a particular value.

The WHEN command

```
WHEN character-string {identifier  } [command-list]
                      {(expression)}
```

The OFFWN command

```
OFFWN character-string
```

Explanation

WHEN	Establish a condition that tells when to take a breakpoint, which is checked before the execution of each verb. Can be abbreviated WN.
OFFWN	Remove breakpoints established by WHEN commands. Can be abbreviated OFFW.
character-string	A one- to four-character string that uniquely identifies a conditional breakpoint. For an OFFWN command, you can specify more than one character string by separating them with commas and enclosing the list in parentheses. If no character strings are specified in an OFFWN command, all conditional breakpoints are deleted.
identifier	If you specify an identifier, the breakpoint is taken whenever the content of that identifier changes.
expression	A relational condition in this form: identifier operator value where *operator* is a relational operator selected from the list in figure 5-11 and *value* is another identifier or literal value. A breakpoint is taken when the expression is true.
command-list	A series of VS COBOL II Debug commands, separated by semicolons, that are automatically executed when the specified breakpoint occurs. The entire list is enclosed in parentheses.

Figure 5-10 COBTEST commands used for conditional breakpoints

You use two commands for conditional breakpoints. The WHEN command establishes a conditional breakpoint. And the OFFWN command removes one or more conditional breakpoints. These commands are shown in figure 5-10.

Operator	Meaning
EQ =	Equal to
GT >	Greater than
LT <	Less than
NE ¬=	Not equal to
GE >=	Greater than or equal to
LE <=	Less than or equal to

Figure 5-11   Relational operators for conditions

For the WHEN command (abbreviated WN), you must specify a one- to four-character string. You use this character string later to remove the breakpoint. As a result, the character string must be unique during a debugging session.

After the character string, you specify either a single identifier or an expression. If you specify just an identifier, it is evaluated each time a program statement is executed. Whenever the identifier's value changes, your program is interrupted. For example, suppose you enter this WHEN command:

```
WHEN ITNO IM-ITEM-NO
```

Then, your program is interrupted whenever the value of IM-ITEM-NO changes. ITNO is the character string associated with this conditional breakpoint.

You can test an identifier for a specific value by coding an expression that compares the identifier with another identifier or a literal. To do this, you use one of the operators shown in figure 5-11. For example, suppose you code this WHEN command:

```
WHEN HIT (INVESTMENT-AMOUNT > 1000)
```

Then, your program is interrupted whenever the value of INVESTMENT-AMOUNT is greater than 1000. Notice that the expression must be enclosed in parentheses. Even so, complex or compound conditions are not allowed.

You can also specify a command list on the WHEN command just as you can on the NEXT and AT commands. I'll describe the use of command lists in more detail later.

To remove one or more conditional breakpoints, you specify one or more character strings from WHEN commands in an OFFWN command (abbreviated OFFW). For example, if you enter the OFFWN command

```
OFFWN ITNO
```

the ITNO conditional breakpoint is removed. To specify more than one conditional breakpoint, you enclose the list in parentheses, like this:

```
OFFWN (ITNO,HIT)
```

Here, two conditional breakpoints are removed. And, if you enter the OFFWN command without any character strings, all the conditional breakpoints you've set are removed.

How to display active breakpoints   The LISTBRKS command (abbreviated LISTB) displays all of your active breakpoints set with AT, NEXT, and WHEN commands. In addition, the LISTBRKS command tells you if a program trace, a program flow, or frequency tallying is in effect. I'll cover the commands associated with these functions later in this chapter.

As you can see in figure 5-12, the only operand of the LISTBRKS command is PRINT. If you specify PRINT during an interactive debugging session, the list of active breakpoints will be written to a print file instead of to the terminal. The print file is either the file associated with SYSDBOUT or the file specified in a PRINTDD command. (I'll cover the PRINTDD command in the next topic.) PRINT is the default for batch mode.

How to display the current statement number   The WHERE command (abbreviated WHER) displays the current statement number in your program where execution has been suspended by a breakpoint or an attention interrupt. (You cause an attention interrupt by pressing the ATTN key or its equivalent.) Its only operand is PRINT, which causes the output to be written to a print file instead of to the terminal during an interactive debugging session. The print file is either the file associated with SYSDBOUT or the file specified in a PRINTDD command. You can see the syntax of this command in figure 5-12.

The LISTBRKS command

```
LISTBREAKS [PRINT]
```

The WHERE command

```
WHERE [PRINT]
```

Explanation

LISTBRKS   List all breakpoints that are currently set in the program. Can be abbreviated LISTB.

WHERE   Display the statement number of the next verb to be executed. Can be abbreviated WHER.

PRINT   Direct the output to a print file instead of to the terminal.

Figure 5-12   The LISTBRKS and WHERE commands

When a breakpoint is taken, the default is for the line number of the next statement to be executed to be displayed at the terminal if you're in interactive mode, or printed on the output listing if you're in batch mode. So in most cases, there's no reason to use the WHERE command. However, if you specify the NONOTIFY operand on an AT command, the line number is *not* displayed or listed when the breakpoint is taken. So, the WHERE command can be useful in that instance. It's also useful if you need to redisplay a breakpoint that no longer appears on the screen. (In full-screen mode, you can also scroll backwards to redisplay a breakpoint. I'll tell you more about that in topic 3.)

How to use breakpoints in batch mode   If they're used properly, breakpoints can be effective in batch mode. But they should only be used when they specify command lists. Otherwise, they will have no apparent effect on your program. Let me explain why this is so.

When you set a breakpoint in interactive mode, control is returned to your terminal so that you can enter additional COBTEST commands. Your program does not continue execution until you enter a GO, RUN, or RESTART command. In batch mode, however, program execution continues immediately after the breakpoint command is executed. So, if you don't specify a command list on the command that establishes the breakpoint, the breakpoint has no effect.

Because the STEP command doesn't provide for a command list, you probably won't use it in batch mode. However, you will use the NEXT, AT, and WHEN commands. To illustrate, suppose you want to list the contents of a field named IM-ITEM-NO each time statement 236 is executed. Then, you can enter this command:

```
AT 236 (LIST IM-ITEM-NO)
```

When this command is processed by COBTEST, the breakpoint is established. (Remember, all COBTEST commands in the SYSDBIN data set are processed before your program is executed.) Then, when the program is executed, the contents of IM-ITEM-NO are listed each time statement 236 is reached. (I'll cover the LIST command, as well as a number of other commands you might want to use, later in this chapter.)

How to trace program flow

Figure 5-13 gives the format of the TRACE command (abbreviated T). You use the TRACE command to initiate or terminate a program trace. A program trace helps you track your program's execution by providing information about the program as it executes. If you specify PRINT, the output is routed to the print file associated with SYSDBOUT or the print file specified in a PRINTDD command instead of being displayed on your terminal. PRINT is the default for batch mode debugging.

The ENTRY operand starts a trace of programs and subprograms. Each time a program transfers control to another program via a CALL statement, the new program's name (taken from the PROGRAM-ID paragraph) is listed. When control returns to the calling program, the calling program's name is listed. This type of trace helps you check that your subprograms are being invoked in the correct sequence.

The PARA and NAME operands both trace the execution of the logical groups of statements in your program. By a logical group of statements, I mean a paragraph or any sequence of statements that can cause a change in the program logic. For example, an IF-THEN-ELSE statement and an EVALUATE statement are both considered logical groups.

If you say PARA, the statement number of the first statement in a logical group of statements is listed whenever that group is about to be executed. If you say NAME, the name of the paragraph containing the logical group is listed in addition to the statement number. Since the output created by NAME is much easier to follow than that created by PARA, I recommend you use

---

The TRACE command

TRACE [$\left\{ \begin{array}{l} \text{ENTRY} \\ \underline{\text{PARA}} \\ \text{NAME} \\ \text{OFF} \end{array} \right\}$] [PRINT]

Explanation

TRACE	Display the flow of program execution. Can be abbreviated T.
ENTRY	List each program's program-id as it is entered via a CALL or EXIT PROGRAM statement.
PARA	List the statement number corresponding to each logical group of statements as it is entered. (PARA is the default.)
NAME	List the paragraph name of each logical group of statements as it is entered.
OFF	Deactivate any previous TRACE command.
PRINT	Direct the output to the print file specified by SYSDBOUT or by a PRINTDD command.

Figure 5-13 The TRACE command

Since PARA is the default, you'll normally enter the TRACE command like this:

```
TRACE NAME
```

To stop a program trace, you enter the TRACE command with the OFF operand, like this:

```
TRACE OFF
```

Figure 5-14 shows output typical of that generated by the TRACE command. (This output was generated running COBTEST in batch mode under MVS.) As you can see, the list of paragraph names makes it easy to follow the execution of the program.

```
IGZ100I PP - 5668-958 VS COBOL II DEBUG FACILITY -- REL 2.0
IGZ100I (C) COPYRIGHT IBM CORPORATION 1986
IGZ102I INV3520.000201.1
IGZ106I TRACING INV3520
IGZ109I 000213.1 100-FORMAT-REPORT-HEADING
IGZ109I 000222.1
IGZ109I 000225.1
IGZ109I 000227.1
IGZ109I 000231.1
IGZ109I 000235.1 300-PREPARE-INVESTMENT-LINE
IGZ109I 000243.1 310-READ-INVENTORY-RECORD
IGZ109I 000246.1
IGZ109I 000247.1
IGZ109I 000237.1
IGZ109I 000251.1 320-COMPUTE-INVENTORY-FIELDS
IGZ109I 000256.1
IGZ109I 000257.1
IGZ109I 000239.1
IGZ109I 000270.1 330-PRINT-INVESTMENT-LINE
IGZ109I 000271.1
IGZ109I 000294.1 340-PRINT-HEADING-LINES
IGZ109I 000313.1 350-WRITE-PAGE-TOP-LINE
IGZ109I 000319.1 360-WRITE-REPORT-LINE
IGZ109I 000319.1 360-WRITE-REPORT-LINE
IGZ109I 000319.1 360-WRITE-REPORT-LINE
IGZ109I 000319.1 360-WRITE-REPORT-LINE
IGZ109I 000272.1
IGZ109I 000239.1
IGZ109I 000287.1
IGZ109I 000319.1 360-WRITE-REPORT-LINE
IGZ109I 000235.1 300-PREPARE-INVESTMENT-LINE
IGZ109I 000243.1 310-READ-INVENTORY-RECORD
IGZ109I 000246.1
IGZ109I 000247.1
IGZ109I 000237.1
IGZ109I 000251.1 320-COMPUTE-INVENTORY-FIELDS
IGZ109I 000256.1
IGZ109I 000257.1
IGZ109I 000258.1
     .
     .
     .
IGZ109I 000319.1 360-WRITE-REPORT-LINE
IGZ109I 000319.1 360-WRITE-REPORT-LINE
IGZ256I COBTEST ENDED ABNORMALLY, SYSTEM CODE 0C4
LAST PSW BEFORE ABEND 078D20008001C89A
IGZ350I ******** END OF COBTEST ********
```

Figure 5-14   Sample TRACE output

HOW TO MANAGE YOUR PROGRAM'S DATA

Besides monitoring your program's statements as they execute, COBTEST lets you manage your program's data. You use the LIST command to display the contents of one or more data fields. You use the SET command to change the contents of data fields. And because COBOL data names can be cumbersome to type repeatedly, the EQUATE and DROP commands let you substitute a short name for a longer one.

How to list data fields

Figure 5-15 shows the format of the LIST command, which is used to list the contents of one or more data fields. In a LIST command (abbreviated L), you specify one or more identifiers. Each identifier can be an FD name, a data name, an index name, or one of several COBOL special registers.

You specify the identifiers much as you specify statement numbers in an AT command. You can specify just one identifier, like this:

```
LIST IM-ITEM-NUMBER
```

Here, the value of the field named IM-ITEM-NUMBER is listed. Or, you can specify several identifiers separated by commas and enclosed in parentheses, like this:

```
LIST (IM-ITEM-NUMBER,IM-ON-HAND,IM-UNIT-PRICE)
```

Here, the contents of three fields are listed. Finally, you can specify a range of identifiers, like this:

```
LIST IM-ITEM-NUMBER:IM-UNIT-PRICE
```

Here, the value of each data field coded in the record description between and including IM-ITEM-NUMBER and IM-UNIT-PRICE is listed.

If you specify ALL on a LIST command, all of your program's data is listed. That includes all FD names, index names, data names, and pointer data items, but COBOL special registers are not included. You probably won't use the ALL operand often, though, because it can result in a large quantity of output. It's usually better to specify the field or fields you want to list.

The remaining operands determine how the fields specified in the LIST command are presented. If you code GROUP, the fields are presented as elementary items whether they are part of a group item or not. If you omit GROUP, fields are displayed with their normalized level numbers. The

---

The LIST command

```
       (identifier-list)              (DISPLAY)
LIST  {literal         } [GROUP] [{HEX    }] [PRINT]
       (ALL            )              (BOTH   )
```

Explanation

LIST	Display or print the specified data. Can be abbreviated L.
identifier-list	One or more identifiers specified as: (1) a single data name; (2) several data names separated by commas and enclosed in parentheses; or (3) a range of data names separated by a colon. An identifier can be a COBOL FD name, a data name, an index name, or one of several special registers.
literal	Any literal value enclosed in quotes.
ALL	List all of the program's FD names, data names, index names, and pointer data items.
GROUP	List each identifier at the highest level possible.
DISPLAY	List the data in EBCDIC format.
HEX	List the data in hexadecimal format.
BOTH	List the data in both EBCDIC and hexadecimal format.
PRINT	List the data on the print file specified by SYSDBOUT or by the PRINTDD command.

Figure 5-15   The LIST command

PLAY, HEX, and BOTH operands determine whether the data is presented in EBCDIC format, hex format, or both formats. DISPLAY is the default. If you code the PRINT operand, the data is written to a print file instead of being displayed on the terminal. PRINT is assumed for batch debugging.

Each item listed by the LIST command is labeled by its statement number, normalized level number, name, and type code. The type code says how the field is defined in the COBOL program—whether it's alphanumeric, packed decimal, or some other data type. Figure 5-16 shows the type codes along with their meanings.

The LIST output is formatted according to how the field is defined in the COBOL program. Alphabetic and alphanumeric items are presented in stand-

Type code	Meaning
CMP3	Numeric packed decimal
COMP	Numeric binary
DISP	Alphabetic, alphanumeric, alphanumeric-edited, unsigned numeric, numeric-edited
DSL	Numeric (overpunch sign leading)
DSLS	Numeric (separate sign leading)
DSP1	Double-byte character
DSPF	External floating point
DSTS	Numeric (separate sign trailing)

Figure 5-16   LIST type codes

```
list im-inventory-data
000026 02 INV3520.IM-INVENTORY-DATA              AN-GR
000027 03 INV3520.IM-REORDER-POINT               S9(5)
       DISP    ===>+00010
000028 03 INV3520.IM-ON-HAND                     S9(5)
       DISP    ===>+00015
000029 03 INV3520.IM-ON-ORDER                    S9(5)
       DISP    ===>+00000
```

Figure 5-17   Sample LIST output

ard character format. Numeric items, whether they're zoned decimal or packed decimal, are presented as decimal values. If you specify a group item, the elementary items that make up the group are listed on separate lines. If a field is subscripted, each occurrence is presented on a separate line, preceded by its subscript value. If you specify an index name, the type code and occurrence number corresponding to the index name's value are presented. And if you specify an FD or SD name, the statement number, type code, information obtained from the file's control blocks, and a list of the records associated with the FD or SD are presented.

Figure 5-17 shows output typical of the LIST command. Here, I entered this command:

```
LIST IM-INVENTORY-DATA
```

The SET command

$$\text{SET identifier-1} = \begin{Bmatrix} \text{identifier-2} \\ \text{literal} \end{Bmatrix}$$

Explanation

SET	Initialize or change the value of the specified item. Can be abbreviated S.
identifier-1	The data name, index name, or special register whose value is to be changed.
identifier-2	The data name, index name, or special register whose value is moved to identifier-1.
literal	A literal value that's moved to identifier-1.

Figure 5-18   The SET command

In batch mode, the LIST command is generally used in a command list. Then, it will be executed only when a specified condition occurs.

How to change a data field

Figure 5-18 shows the format of the SET command, which is used to change the contents of a data field. The operation of the SET command (abbreviated S) is simple: the contents of identifier-1 are replaced by the contents of identifier-2 or the literal. For example, consider this SET command:

```
SET IM-ITEM-NO = 100
```

Here, the value of IM-ITEM-NO is changed to 100.

If the lengths or types of the sending and receiving fields differ, the SET command follows the rules for a standard COBOL MOVE statement. Thus, values are truncated or padded with spaces as necessary, and data is converted from one form to another, just as when you code a MOVE statement in your COBOL program. And, of course, certain combinations of sending and receiving fields aren't valid. For example, you can't move an alphanumeric value to a numeric packed decimal field.

Here, the value of IM-ITEM-NO is changed to 100.

If the lengths or types of the sending and receiving fields differ, the SET command follows the rules for a standard COBOL MOVE statement. Thus, values are truncated or padded with spaces as necessary, and data is converted from one form to another, just as when you code a MOVE statement in your COBOL program. And, of course, certain combinations of sending and receiving fields aren't valid. For example, you can't move an alphanumeric value to a numeric packed decimal field.

Because the rules for certain types of moves are obscure, it's a good idea to check the results of your SET command by following it with a LIST command. That way, you'll know if your SET command worked as you intended.

In batch mode, you'll probably use the SET command most often in a command list. Then, you can use it to set variables when certain conditions occur.

How to shorten data names

I strongly recommend that you use data names that are meaningful in your COBOL programs. For example, a data name like INVESTMENT-AMOUNT is much more meaningful than X or INVAMT. Since one of the primary goals of program development is to create programs that are easy to read and maintain, I can't stress this point too much.

Still, longer data names can be an irritation during a debugging session. That's why COBTEST provides three commands that make it easy for you to substitute a shorter name for a longer one. These three commands (EQUATE, DROP, and LISTEQ) are shown in figure 5-19.

The EQUATE command (abbreviated EQ) lets you assign a *symbol* to a data name, file name, index name, or special register. For example, consider this EQUATE command:

```
EQUATE ITEM IM-ITEM-NO
```

Once you've entered this command, you can use the symbol ITEM instead of the data name IM-ITEM-NO throughout your debugging session.

The DROP command (abbreviated DR) lets you remove a previously defined symbol. So if you enter

```
DROP ITEM
```

The EQUATE command

```
EQUATE symbol [program-name.] identifier
```

The DROP command

```
DROP [symbol]
```

The LISTEQ command

```
LISTEQ [PRINT]
```

Explanation

EQUATE   Establish a symbol, or synonym, for the specified item. Can be abbreviated EQ.

DROP   Delete the specified symbols. Can be abbreviated DR.

LISTEQ   List all active symbols established with the EQUATE command. Can be abbreviated LISTE.

symbol   A character string that follows the rules for forming a COBOL data name. Usually shorter than the actual data name it will stand for. For a DROP command, you can specify more than one symbol by separating them with commas and enclosing the entire list in parentheses. If no symbols are specified in a DROP command, all symbols are deleted.

program-name   The name of a COBOL program currently resident in storage. The default is the program currently executing or referenced by a QUALIFY command.

identifier   The data name, file name, index name, or special register that the specified symbol represents.

PRINT   Direct the output to the print file specified by SYSDBOUT or by a PRINTDD command.

Figure 5-19   The EQUATE, DROP, and LISTEQ commands

you can no longer use ITEM to refer to IM-ITEM-NO. You can specify several symbols in a single DROP command, like this:

```
DROP (ITEM,COST,DESCR)
```

Here, three symbols are deleted. If you enter DROP with no symbols, all of your symbols are deleted.

The LISTEQ command (abbreviated LISTE) lists all symbols that have been assigned using the EQUATE command during the current debugging session. To write this list to an output file instead of to the terminal, you can specify the PRINT operand. Then, the output is written to the file associated with SYSDBOUT or to the file specified in a PRINTDD command. PRINT is the default for batch mode debugging.

Of course, you probably won't use the EQUATE, DROP, and LISTEQ commands in batch mode. They're more useful in interactive mode where the debugging sessions are generally more complex.

HOW TO TERMINATE COBTEST

In batch mode, COBTEST is terminated automatically when a STOP RUN statement is executed or an abend occurs and there are no additional QUALIFY commands in the SYSDBIN data set. In interactive mode, however, you have to exit from COBTEST explicitly.

Normally, under VS COBOL II Releases 2 and 3, you issue a QUIT command (abbreviated QUI) like this:

```
QUIT
```

Control is then returned to the system from which you invoked COBTEST. If you're using VS COBOL II Release 1, however, you should realize that the QUIT command isn't supported. Instead, the END command is used to terminate COBTEST.

The DUMP command (abbreviated DU) can also be used to terminate COBTEST. Besides terminating COBTEST, it produces a dump of your program's storage areas (not including register information). If you're operating under CMS, the dump output is routed to your virtual printer. But, if you're operating under MVS, the output goes to the data set associated with SYSABOUT. So be sure that data set is allocated before issuing a DUMP command. In full-screen mode, the SYSABOUT data set is allocated automatically.

DISCUSSION

In this topic, I've presented the COBTEST commands that you'll use most often in your debugging sessions. However, there are many more functions provided by COBTEST that you should know about. I'll present the most important of those functions in the next two topics.

Terminology

breakpoint
trace
NEXT breakpoint
STEP breakpoint
unconditional breakpoint
conditional breakpoint
command list
symbol

Objectives

1. Invoke COBTEST to debug a COBOL program on your system using batch, interactive line, or interactive full-screen mode.

2. Use the following COBTEST features in your debugging sessions:

    a. NEXT breakpoint
    b. STEP breakpoint
    c. unconditional breakpoint
    d. conditional breakpoint
    e. program trace

3. Use COBTEST commands to examine and change the contents of data fields during your debugging sessions.

Topic 2 Advanced functions of VS COBOL II Debug

This topic presents a variety of VS COBOL II Debug functions. You'll use some of these functions, such as debugging a subprogram and simulating a called program, only under specific circumstances. But other functions, such as logging a debugging session, monitoring verb frequencies, and using a command list, provide you with greater flexibility than the commands you learned in the last topic. Although you won't use all of the commands presented in this topic every day, you will probably use them all at one time or another.

How to log a debugging session

Sometimes when you're debugging a program, it's helpful to know what commands you issued in previous sessions and what output resulted from them. By keeping a record of all debugging sessions, you'll be less likely to repeat the same testing. And you can review your sessions to determine if additional testing is needed or if a different approach should be taken. There are two COBTEST commands that allow you to keep a log of your debugging sessions: RECORD and PRINTDD. The format of these commands is presented in figure 5-20.

How to create a log file   The RECORD command (abbreviated RE) tells COBTEST that you want to keep a record of your debugging session. If you specify RECORD, any COBTEST commands you issue and any output from COBTEST are written to a print file. The print file is either the one associated with SYSDBOUT or the file specified on a PRINTDD command, if one was issued. Since NORECORD (abbreviated NORE) is the default, you'll need to issue a RECORD command each time you want to log a debugging session.

If you're using VS COBOL II Release 1, you can't use the RECORD command in batch mode. If you're using Release 2 or 3, you can use the RECORD command in batch mode, but you can't specify it in a command list. In other words, in batch mode, you can use it only to turn logging on or off for an entire debugging session.

In interactive mode, you can use the RECORD/NORECORD command to log specific parts of a session. For example, you might want to start logging a debugging session if a particular condition occurs. If you have a breakpoint set for that condition, you can issue the RECORD command when the

---

The RECORD command

```
⎧RECORD  ⎫
⎨NORECORD⎬
⎩        ⎭
```

The PRINTDD command

```
PRINTDD ddname
```

Explanation

RECORD NORECORD	Activate or deactivate the logging of a debugging session. Can be abbreviated as RE or NORE.
PRINTDD	Direct print output to the specified file. Can be abbreviated PRI.
ddname	The name of the previously defined file that output is to be written to.

Figure 5-20   The RECORD and PRINTDD commands

---

breakpoint occurs. As you can see in figure 5-20, the RECORD command has no operands. So, you simply code it like this:

```
RECORD
```

If you want to stop the logging of a session, you can issue the command

```
NORECORD
```

Then, no more logging is done until another RECORD command is issued.

You'll probably find the RECORD command most useful when you're using the interactive debugger. That's because it's difficult to remember or keep track of the specific testing you do in each debugging session if you don't keep a log of it. (Remember, in full-screen mode, you can also log a debugging session by specifying the appropriate parameters on the invocation panel. So if you want to debug an entire session, you don't need to use the RECORD command at all.) In contrast, the RECORD command isn't nearly as useful in batch mode since you already have an input file containing the commands being issued to COBTEST and a print file containing output from COBTEST.

In full-screen mode, you can also use the RECORD command to restart a program. To do this, you simply specify the name of a log file created during a previous debugging session as the restart file on the ISPF panel for COBTEST. (This panel is illustrated in figure 5-4 for TSO and figure 5-5 for CMS.) Then, the same commands that were executed in the previous session are executed again. This can be extremely useful for testing the effect of programming changes. (The debugger is able to ignore the output records in the log and process only the input records because the input records have a ">" placed in front of them when they are written to the log file.)

How to specify a log file   If you want to specify that log records be written to a file other than the one associated with SYSDBOUT, you'll need to use the PRINTDD command (abbreviated PRI). As you can see in figure 5-20, the only operand of the PRINTDD command is *ddname*, which is the name of a file previously defined as an output file. So, if you want to direct output to a file defined as TESTOUT, you code

```
PRINTDD TESTOUT
```

When the PRINTDD command is used in interactive mode, any file referenced in a previous PRINTDD command is closed. In batch mode, the file specified in the PRINTDD command replaces the file currently associated with SYSDBOUT.

In full-screen mode, you can also specify a log file by coding the appropriate parameters on the invocation panel as described in topic 1 of this chapter (LOG and LOG DSN for TSO, LOG and LOG FILE ID for CMS). However, if you forget to code these parameters, or if you want to change the name of the log file during the debugging session, you can use the PRINTDD command.

You should be aware that the PRINTDD command will redirect output from *any* command that allows the PRINT option, such as TRACE, LIST, and LISTEQ. You need to be very careful, then, when you use the PRINTDD command in interactive mode so that output from different sources doesn't get mixed. I recommend that you use only one command with the PRINT option in each debugging session. That way, you can route specific output, such as output from the RECORD command, to the PRINTDD file and all other output to the terminal.

The FLOW command

```
          (ON         )
          )OFF        (
FLOW  [ { PRINT       } ]
          (n) [PRINT])
```

Explanation

FLOW	Activate tracing of program flow. If you issue this command without any operands, it will list the information that's been accumulated in the flow table. Can be abbreviated FL.
ON	Accumulate statement numbers in the flow table.
OFF	Stop accumulating statement numbers in the flow table and clear all table entries.
PRINT	Direct the output to the print file specified by SYSDBOUT or by a PRINTDD command.
n	List *n* entries. The default is for all entries to be listed.

Figure 5-21   The FLOW command

How to trace the flow of selected portions of your program

In topic 1 of this chapter, I showed you how to use the TRACE command to trace the flow of your programs. The FLOW command (abbreviated FL) provides a similar function except that trace information is saved in a table, which can then be displayed or listed upon request. You use the FLOW command to trace specific parts of your program.

Figure 5-21 shows the format of the FLOW command. To begin a trace, you issue the command

```
FLOW ON
```

Then, each time there is a possible change in program flow, the statement number at the beginning of the logical group of statements is saved in a table entry. To list the entries accumulated in the table, you issue the command without any operands, like this:

```
FLOW
```

Then, the entire table is listed, with the most recently executed statement first. If you want to list only part of the table, you issue the command

```
FLOW (n)
```

where *n* is a number between 1 and 255 that indicates the number of entries to be listed. (255 is the maximum number of entries that can be saved in the table.)

If you're using COBTEST in interactive mode, the default is to display the table on your terminal. If you want to write the table to an output file, you issue the command

```
FLOW PRINT
```

or

```
FLOW (n) PRINT
```

Then, the output is written to the file associated with SYSDBOUT or the file specified in a PRINTDD command. In the first example, the entire table is printed. In the second example, only *n* entries are printed. The default for batch mode is PRINT.

Finally, if you want to turn the trace off, you issue the command

```
FLOW OFF
```

Then, the flow table is cleared and no more entries are accumulated until another FLOW command with the ON operand is issued.

In batch mode, you'll use the FLOW command most often in a command list. Then, you can start, stop, and list the trace when certain conditions occur. However, you might code the FLOW command outside of a command list to start a trace at the beginning of your program.

One advantage of using the FLOW command instead of the TRACE command is that flow output isn't mixed with other output. In other words, the flow output is listed in one block, which makes it easier to follow. Of course, the TRACE command can accomplish the same thing if other COBTEST commands aren't used in the same session.

One distinct *dis*advantage of the FLOW command is that it lists only statement numbers. It doesn't provide paragraph names like the TRACE command can. This makes the program flow a little more difficult to follow. And, of course, it provides only for a maximum of 255 statements at one time. For that reason, you'll probably use it for tracing blocks of code rather than entire programs.

How to monitor verb frequencies

In some cases, it's helpful to know how many times particular verbs are executed in your program or in parts of your program. If you're using VS COBOL II Release 2 or 3, COBTEST gives you two commands that provide this information: FREQ and LISTFREQ. The formats of these commands are shown in figure 5-22. (These commands aren't available with VS COBOL II Release 1.)

How to keep track of verb frequencies: The FREQ command   The FREQ command (abbreviated FR) is used to keep track of the number of times the verbs in a program are executed. Figure 5-23 lists the verbs for which a tally is kept. If you issue the command

```
FREQ ALL
```

frequency tallying is started for every program in the run unit. Since ALL is the default, the same thing can be accomplished by issuing the command

```
FREQ
```

If the FREQ command is issued with the ALL operand or with no operands and frequency tallying is already on, the tallies are reset to zero and tallying is restarted.

To keep a tally of only the verbs in a specific program, you issue the command

```
FREQ program-name
```

You can also turn tallying on for several programs by listing the program names in parentheses and separating them with commas.

To turn tallying off for every program in the run unit, you code

```
FREQ ALL OFF
```

To turn tallying off for a specific program, you code

```
FREQ program-name OFF
```

The FREQ command

$$FREQ \quad [\begin{Bmatrix} ALL \\ program-name \end{Bmatrix}] \quad [OFF]$$

The LISTFREQ command

$$LISTFREQ \quad [\begin{Bmatrix} ALL \\ program-name \end{Bmatrix}] \quad [ZEROFREQ] \quad [PRINT]$$

Explanation

FREQ	Activate frequency tallying. Can be abbreviated FR.
LISTFREQ	List the results of frequency tallying. Can be abbreviated LISTF.
ALL	Keep or list frequency tallies for all programs.
program-name	Keep or list frequency tallies for the specified program. Multiple programs can be specified by separating them with commas and enclosing the list in parentheses.
OFF	Turn frequency tallying off and zero all existing tallies.
ZEROFREQ	List only those verbs that have *not* been executed.
PRINT	Direct the output to the print file specified by SYSDBOUT or by a PRINTDD command.

Figure 5-22   The FREQ and LISTFREQ commands

Note that the ALL operand must be specified to turn all tallying off; it is not the default. A group of programs can also be specified when using the OFF operand.

One thing I want to make clear is that when you use frequency tallying, each verb in the program is tallied separately. In other words, if there are 50 PERFORM statements in the program, a separate count is kept for each of them. You should also realize that if tallying is turned off for a program by specifying the program name (instead of ALL), tallying can be restarted for that program only by using the program-name format. It will not be restarted by issuing a FREQ command with the ALL operand.

```
ACCEPT              ADD                 ALTER               CALL
CANCEL              CLOSE               COMPUTE             CONTINUE
DELETE              DISPLAY             DIVIDE              ENTRY
EVALUATE            EXIT                GO TO               GOBACK
IF                  INITIALIZE          INSPECT             MERGE
MOVE                MULTIPLY            NEXT                OPEN
PERFORM             READ                RELEASE             RETURN
REWRITE             SEARCH              SET                 SORT
START               STOP                STRING              SUBTRACT
UNSTRING            WRITE
```

Figure 5-23   Verbs for which frequencies are tallied

How to list verb frequencies: The LISTFREQ command   If you use
FREQ, you'll want to use LISTFREQ (abbreviated LISTF) to list the results.
Depending on the format of the command you use, you can list the frequencies
for the verbs in specified programs, or you can list the verbs for which the
frequency is zero. For example, if you want to list the frequencies for the verbs
in all programs for which tallies were kept, you issue the command

        LISTFREQ ALL

or just

        LISTFREQ

If you want to list the frequencies only for specific programs, you code a
program name or a group of program names instead of ALL. But, if you want
to list those verbs that were never executed, you issue the command

        LISTFREQ ALL ZEROFREQ

or

        LISTFREQ program-name ZEROFREQ

Note that when you code the ZEROFREQ operand, ALL is *not* the default;
it must be specified explicitly. The same is true when the PRINT operand is
specified. The PRINT operand causes output to be written to a print file.

In batch mode, you'll use the FREQ and LISTFREQ commands most often
in a command list. That way, you can turn frequency tallying on and off and
list frequencies when certain conditions occur.

The IF command

```
IF (expression) ⎧(command-list)⎫
                ⎨HALT         ⎬
                ⎩GO           ⎭
```

Explanation

IF	Evaluate the specified condition; if the condition is met, perform the specified commands. Can be abbreviated I.
expression	A relational condition in the form
	data-item operator value
	where *operator* is a relational operator selected from the list in figure 5-11 and *value* is another data item or literal value.
command-list	A series of COBTEST commands separated by semicolons that are automatically executed when the specified condition occurs.
HALT	In interactive mode, return control to the terminal. In batch mode, resume program execution.
GO	Resume program execution.

Figure 5-24   The IF command

Usually, when you use the FREQ and LISTFREQ commands, it will be to list verbs that are not executed; in other words, those with zero frequencies. There just aren't many circumstances in which you'll want to know how many times a verb is executed.

How to use the IF command in a command list

Although there are many possible uses for coding a command list, the most common is to list the contents of one or more data fields and then resume program execution. In some cases, however, you'll want to resume program execution only under certain circumstances. The IF command, whose format is shown in figure 5-24, lets you do just that. Although you can enter an IF command by itself, it's normally used in a command list.

On an IF command (abbreviated I), you specify an expression that is tested when the command is executed. The format of the expression is the same as for a WHEN command, so you can review that command if you need to. After the expression, you specify either HALT, GO, or a command list to tell COBTEST what to do if the expression is true. If you say GO, your program's execution is resumed. If you say HALT, control is returned to your terminal in interactive mode and your program's execution is resumed in batch mode. If you code a command list, the commands in the list are executed. If the expression specified by the IF command is false, control returns to the command in the list that follows the IF command. If there are no more commands in the list, control is returned to the terminal in interactive mode, and your program's execution is resumed in batch mode.

To illustrate, consider this AT command entered in interactive mode:

```
AT 243 (IF (INVESTMENT-AMOUNT > 1000) HALT;GO)
```

Here, the IF command is executed each time the breakpoint at line 243 is taken. Then, INVESTMENT-AMOUNT is compared with 1000. If the expression is true—that is, if INVESTMENT-AMOUNT is greater than 1000—the program is halted and control returns to the terminal. Otherwise, the next command in the list is executed. In this case, the next command is GO, so the program continues.

Suppose you entered this AT command in interactive mode:

```
AT 243 (IF (INVESTMENT-AMOUNT <= 1000) GO)
```

Here, program execution continues if INVESTMENT-AMOUNT is less than or equal to 1000. Otherwise, control is returned to the terminal, since there are no more commands in the list to be executed. If you compare this command list with the previous one, you'll see that they both have the same effect: the program continues executing until INVESTMENT-AMOUNT is greater than 1000.

You usually won't use HALT and GO in batch mode since they both cause your program to resume execution, which is the default action. Instead, you'll code a command list. For example, consider this AT command entered in batch mode:

```
AT 243 (IF (INVESTMENT-AMOUNT > 1000) (LIST INVESTMENT-AMOUNT))
```

Here, if INVESTMENT-AMOUNT is greater than 1000, the contents of INVESTMENT-AMOUNT are listed and the program continues. Otherwise, the program continues immediately.

The ONABEND command

```
ONABEND [(command-list)]
```

Explanation

ONABEND   Establish the commands to be executed if a program abend occurs. Can
                 be abbreviated ONAB.

command-list   A series of COBTEST commands separated by semicolons that are auto-
                 matically executed when a program abend occurs.

Figure 5-25   The ONABEND command

As you can imagine, if you use IF commands within command lists, you can code quite complicated commands. You can even nest IF commands by coding them within the command list of another IF command. However, there shouldn't be too many occasions on which you'll need to code anything much more complicated than what I've presented here.

How to handle a program abend: The ONABEND command

The ONABEND command (abbreviated ONAB) tells COBTEST what to do if a program abends. Its format is given in figure 5-25. As you can see, its only operand is a command list. If an ONABEND command is issued without a command list, control is returned to the terminal in interactive mode. In batch mode, ONABEND has no effect without a command list.

To illustrate the use of ONABEND, suppose you want to print a dump when your program abends. Then, you can issue this command:

```
ONABEND (DUMP)
```

Or, you might want to list the values of certain fields to determine the cause of the abend. Then, you could issue a command like this:

```
ONABEND (LIST (IM-ON-HAND,IM-UNIT-PRICE))
```

How to debug a subprogram

Throughout most of this chapter, I've assumed you're debugging a main program. But COBTEST provides features that make it easy to debug subprograms as well. You already know how to use the ENTRY operand of the TRACE command to trace subprogram execution. In addition, you need to know how to qualify the operands of your COBTEST commands so they refer to your subprogram and how to simulate calling and called programs.

How to qualify operands of COBTEST commands   In topic 1 of this chapter, I showed you how to code a QUALIFY command in batch mode to indicate the program to which the COBTEST commands that follow it refer. So, if you're debugging a subprogram, you can code a QUALIFY command for the subprogram. Then, any commands that follow will refer to that subprogram until a QUALIFY command for another program is encountered. This type of reference to a program is called *implicit qualification*. And the commands that refer to a program in this way are called a *QUALIFY set*. The QUALIFY set for a subprogram is executed each time the subprogram is invoked.

You can run into a problem here, though. If you want to do further testing of the main program after you've qualified the subprogram, you can't simply issue a QUALIFY command for the main program. If you do, the main program is restarted; it doesn't continue from the point where it regained control from the subprogram like you want it to. In this case, you have to use *explicit qualification* for the main program. That means you must include the program-id in each subsequent command that refers to the main program.

Another way around this problem is to qualify the main program using a QUALIFY command and to then qualify each command issued for the subprogram explicitly. For example, if you want to take a breakpoint at line 320 in a subprogram named DATEDIT that's called from a program named INV3520, you can code the following commands:

```
QUALIFY INV3520
AT DATEDIT.320
```

Then, a breakpoint is taken when statement 320 of the DATEDIT subprogram is reached. The method you use for handling main program and subprogram qualification depends on the requirements of the particular debugging session.

Although you can also use the QUALIFY command in interactive mode, there are other ways to establish qualification. You can issue a command for the program that is currently executing, in which case that command refers implicitly to that program. Or, if you want to refer to a program that's not

---

The LINK command

```
LINK [USING] data-name
```

Explanation

LINK	Simulate the Linkage Section of a nonexistent calling program. Can be abbreviated LIN.
USING	Coded for conformity with a COBOL CALL statement.
data-name	A data name specified at the 01 or 77 level in the Linkage Section of the subprogram being tested. Multiple data names can be specified by separating them with commas and enclosing the list in parentheses.

Figure 5-26   The LINK command

---

currently executing, you can use explicit qualification. Explicit qualification works the same in interactive mode as in batch mode.

If you do issue a QUALIFY command in interactive mode, you should realize that it is in effect only during the current breakpoint. Once program execution is resumed, any command that is entered without qualification implicitly refers to the currently executing program. It does not refer to the program qualified by the previous QUALIFY command.

To illustrate, suppose a breakpoint is taken during the execution of the program INV3520. If you want to refer to a statement in a subprogram called DATEDIT that's called from INV3520, you can issue the command

```
QUALIFY DATEDIT
```

Then, any command you enter at that breakpoint will refer to DATEDIT. If you continue program execution and the next breakpoint is again taken in INV3520, you have to issue another QUALIFY command or use explicit qualification to refer to DATEDIT.

How to simulate a calling program: The LINK command   Sometimes, it's desirable or necessary to test a subprogram before its calling program is completed. If you're using VS COBOL Release 2 or 3, COBTEST provides a way to do that by simulating the calling program. The LINK command, shown in figure 5-26, is used for that purpose. (The LINK command isn't available with VS COBOL II Release 1.)

To use the LINK command (abbreviated LIN), you simply specify a list of the fields used in the Linkage Section of the subprogram you want to test. For example, suppose you are testing a subprogram named DATEDIT that receives a date field from the calling program, edits the date, and returns a switch to the main program that indicates if the date is valid. In this case, the Linkage Section of the subprogram would look something like this:

```
LINKAGE SECTION.
*
01   EDIT-DATE.
     05   EDIT-MONTH        PIC 99.
     05   EDIT-DAY          PIC 99.
     05   EDIT-YEAR         PIC 99.
*
01   VALID-DATE-SW         PIC X.
     88   VALID-DATE        VALUE 'Y'.
```

Then, to test the subprogram, you would issue the following LINK command:

```
LINK (EDIT-DATE,VALID-DATE-SW)
```

This command must be coded before any of the specified data names are referred to. Usually, you'll code it at the beginning of the debugging session. In batch mode, you'll specify the LINK command in a command list associated with the AT command. Then, the LINK command isn't executed until the specified line is reached.

Once the link is established, you can initialize the linkage fields using SET commands. For example, if you want to initialize EDIT-DATE, you issue a command like

```
SET EDIT-DATE = '023187'
```

Then, you can set breakpoints and execute the subprogram just as if it were a main program.

There are several other things you should know if you use the LINK command. First, the subprogram you're debugging must be compiled and linked as if it were a main program. Also, when you code the LINK command, you don't have to specify every field that's used in the Linkage Section of the subprogram. However, if you don't specify a field, you cannot refer to it during the debugging session in either the COBTEST commands or the subprogram itself. Also, the LINK command can be issued only once for any program during a debugging session. Finally, if you're using batch mode, be sure you code a QUALIFY command for the subprogram you're linking to.

The PROC command

```
PROC program-name [(command-list)]
```

Explanation

PROC	Trap all calls to the specified programs and execute the specified commands. Can be abbreviated PRO.
program-name	The name of the program for which you want all calls to be trapped. Multiple program names can be specified by separating them with commas and enclosing them in parentheses.
command-list	A series of COBTEST commands separated by semicolons that are automatically executed when a call to the specified program is trapped.

Figure 5-27   The PROC command

How to simulate a called program: The PROC command   Just as you may want to test a subprogram before its calling program is completed, you may want to test a main program before one or more of its called programs are completed. If you're using VS COBOL II Release 2 or 3, you can do that using the PROC command. Its format is given in figure 5-27. (The PROC command isn't available with VS COBOL II Release 1.)

Before I show you how to use the PROC command, you need to know about some internal counters that are kept by COBTEST. These counters, which have the symbolic name $PCTR, are used to determine the number of times that subprograms are called. Each time a subprogram is called, the $PCTR counter for that subprogram is incremented by one. I'll show you how to use these counters in a minute.

The PROC command (abbreviated PRO) is used to trap a call to a specified program and return values to the main program as if the subprogram call had been executed. To use the PROC command, you specify the name of the subprogram whose calls are to be trapped and a command list that's to be executed each time a call is trapped. For example, suppose the DATEDIT subprogram referred to previously was not completed, but you wanted to test the main program to be sure that it properly processed the VALID-DATE-SW field returned from the subprogram. Then, you might issue this command:

```
PROC DATEDIT (IF ($PCTR = 1) (SET VALID-DATE-SW = 'Y');
              IF ($PCTR = 2) (SET VALID-DATE-SW = 'N'))
```

Here, the $PCTR counter is used to determine which occurrence of the call is being trapped. If it's the first occurrence, 'Y' is moved to VALID-DATE-SW. If it's the second occurrence, 'N' is moved to VALID-DATE-SW. In either case, the main program continues using the assigned value as if it had been returned from the subprogram.

In interactive mode, you can also issue the PROC command without a command list, in which case control is returned to your terminal. Then, you can issue any COBTEST commands you want, including commands to set the variables that will be returned from the subprogram. Using the same example as above, if you issue the command

```
PROC DATEDIT
```

when a call to DATEDIT is intercepted by COBTEST, COBTEST waits for you to enter additional commands at your terminal. Then, the first time a trap occurs, you might enter these commands:

```
SET VALID-DATE-SW = 'Y'
GO
```

At the second trap, you might enter these commands:

```
SET VALID-DATE-SW = 'N'
GO
```

This would accomplish the same thing as the command list described above.

How to display information on COBTEST commands in line mode

Occasionally, you may have a question about how a particular COBTEST command works or what's required to perform a particular function. In interactive line mode, you may be able to find many of the answers to your questions by accessing the TSO or CMS help facilities. To do that, you use the HELP command of COBTEST. The format of this command is given in figure 5-28. (If you're using VS COBOL Release 1, the HELP command is not available in the CMS environment.)

If you issue the HELP command (abbreviated H) without any operands, the main menu of the help facility is displayed. From there, you simply make the appropriate selections to display the information you need. The exact procedure depends on what system you're using.

The HELP command

```
                            (ALL                          )
                            )FUNCTION                      )
HELP [[command-name] [)OPERANDS   [(operand-list)])]]
                            (SYNTAX                        )
```

Explanation

HELP	Display information on Debug commands. Can be abbreviated H.
command-name	The COBTEST command for which you want to display information.
ALL	Display information on the function, syntax, and operands of the specified command.
FUNCTION	Display information on the function of the specified command.
OPERANDS	Display information on the operands of the specified command.
operand-list	A list of the operands for which you want information. Operands must be separated by one or more blanks or a comma. Valid only under TSO.
SYNTAX	Display information on the syntax of the specified command.

Figure 5-28   The HELP command

If you want to display all the information on a specific COBTEST command, you issue a command like this:

```
HELP command-name ALL
```

Then, a description of the function, syntax, and operands of the command is displayed. The same thing can be accomplished without specifying ALL, since it's the default.

If you want to display only the function, syntax, or operands of a command, you specify FUNCTION, SYNTAX, or OPERANDS following the command name. If you're using TSO, you can also specify a particular operand or list of operands on the OPERANDS parameter. If you specify a list of operands, they must be separated by commas or blanks and enclosed in parentheses.

Discussion

If you're using COBTEST in batch or interactive line mode, the commands and concepts presented in the last two topics should be everything you need to know to debug your programs effectively. Although there are a few intricacies that I haven't presented here, they are things that you will probably never need to use. But, if you should need more information on any of the COBTEST commands, be sure to consult the IBM manual *VS COBOL II Application Programming: Debugging.*

If you're using full-screen mode, however, there are some additional commands you should be familiar with. I'll present these commands in the next topic.

Terminology

implicit qualification
QUALIFY set
explicit qualification

Objective

Use COBTEST commands to perform the following functions:

1. log a debugging session
2. trace the flow of selected portions of your program
3. monitor verb frequencies
4. code IF in a command list
5. handle program abends
6. simulate a calling program
7. simulate a called program
8. display information on COBTEST commands (interactive line mode only)

Topic 3 Full-screen functions of VS COBOL II Debug

In the last two topics, I presented all of the VS COBOL II Debug commands and concepts you'll need to know if you're using COBTEST in batch or interactive line mode. But there are some additional commands you'll need to know if you're using it in full-screen mode. I'll present those full-screen commands in this topic. Before I do that though, I want to familiarize you with the main full-screen panel of COBTEST.

How to use the full-screen panel

Once you invoke the full-screen debugger as described in topic 1 of this chapter, the main debugging panel is displayed. From this panel, illustrated in figure 5-29, you can enter COBTEST commands and view the execution of the debugging session.

Areas of the full-screen panel The top of the debugging panel contains some heading information. In the upper left-hand corner is the name of the debug tool, COBTEST. Then, after the heading QUALIFY: is the *qualify field*, which contains the name of the currently qualified program. In figure 5-29, the currently qualified program is INV3520. After the heading WHERE: is the statement number of the next statement to be executed. When the debugging panel is first displayed, the statement number specified will always be the first executable statement of the program, since COBTEST doesn't automatically begin executing your program when you invoke it in interactive mode. In figure 5-29, the first executable statement is number 201.

At the beginning of the second line of the screen is the *command area*, indicated by the heading COMMAND ===>. This is where you'll enter most of your COBTEST commands as well as any ISPF, TSO, or CMS commands. At the end of the second line is an area headed SCROLL ===>. This is where you indicate how far the screen is to be scrolled when you issue an ISPF scrolling command. In figure 5-29, PAGE is indicated, so one full screen will be scrolled.

The rest of the screen consists of the log area, source area, and auto monitoring area. The *log area* is where the COBTEST commands you issue during your debugging session are displayed (excluding full-screen commands) as well as any output from COBTEST that's routed to your terminal. The log area always occupies the part of the screen not allocated to

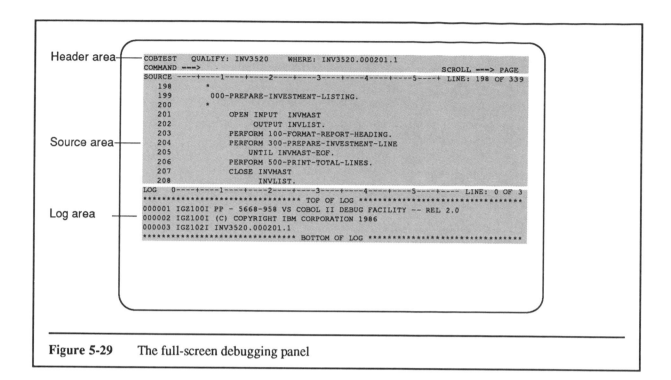

Header area

Source area

Log area

```
COBTEST    QUALIFY: INV3520    WHERE: INV3520.000201.1
COMMAND ===>                                          SCROLL ===> PAGE
SOURCE ----+----1----+----2----+----3----+----4----+----5----+ LINE: 198 OF 339
    198      *
    199          000-PREPARE-INVESTMENT-LISTING.
    200      *
    201              OPEN INPUT   INVMAST
    202                   OUTPUT INVLIST.
    203              PERFORM 100-FORMAT-REPORT-HEADING.
    204              PERFORM 300-PREPARE-INVESTMENT-LINE
    205                  UNTIL INVMAST-EOF.
    206              PERFORM 500-PRINT-TOTAL-LINES.
    207              CLOSE INVMAST
    208                    INVLIST.
LOG    0----+----1----+----2----+----3----+----4----+----5----+---- LINE: 0 OF 3
******************************* TOP OF LOG *********************************
000001 IGZ100I PP - 5668-958 VS COBOL II DEBUG FACILITY -- REL 2.0
000002 IGZ100I (C) COPYRIGHT IBM CORPORATION 1986
000003 IGZ102I INV3520.000201.1
****************************** BOTTOM OF LOG *******************************
```

Figure 5-29   The full-screen debugging panel

the source and auto monitoring areas. Lines similar to those in the log area in figure 5-29 will always appear when you first invoke the debugger. Here, the first two lines identify the software and the third line indicates the breakpoint taken before the first executable statement of the program.

The *source area* is where you can display your source programs. The default is for the source area to consist of 12 lines of 80 characters each, including a heading line. As you can see, that's what's displayed in figure 5-29. You can change the size of the source area using the PROFILE or SOURCE command. With the SOURCE command, you can also change the program that's displayed in the source area. I'll discuss these commands later in this topic.

In the *auto monitoring area*, you can display the value of specific fields in your program. The fields to be displayed are established by issuing the AUTO command. In figure 5-29, I haven't issued an AUTO command, so the auto area isn't displayed. I'll discuss the AUTO command later in this topic.

A header line appears at the beginning of the log, source, and auto monitoring areas. This line consists of the name of the area, a scale indicating the column numbers, and a line counter that indicates the line number of the first line of the display and the total number of lines in the area. In figure 5-29,

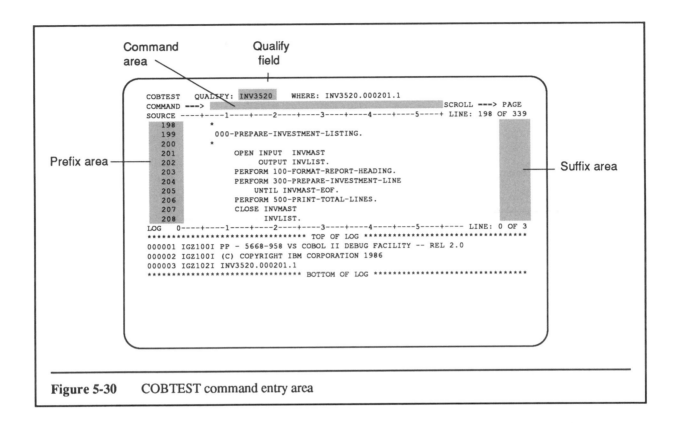

Figure 5-30 COBTEST command entry area

you can see that all three lines of the log area are displayed. In the source area, the first line displayed is line 198 and there are 339 lines in the source listing.

Entering commands on the full-screen panel There are four areas in which you can enter COBTEST commands on the full-screen panel. These areas are shown in figure 5-30.

In the qualify field, you can enter the name of a source statement listing you want to display. Of course, the source listing must be available to COBTEST. Note that entering a program name here changes the qualified program only during the current program interruption. Once program execution is continued, the program that's actually executing will again be displayed in the source area at the next program interrupt.

As I've already mentioned, you'll enter most of your COBTEST commands in the command area. Any COBTEST command is valid here except for COBTEST, which isn't valid in full-screen mode. You can enter commands in the command area either by typing them directly, or by retrieving any line in the log area that's marked with an asterisk (*). The asterisk identifies the line as a COBTEST command.

The lines marked with an asterisk in the log area are COBTEST commands

```
COBTEST   QUALIFY: INV3520    WHERE: INV3520.000236.1
COMMAND ===>                                              SCROLL ===> PAGE
SOURCE ----+----1----+----2----+----3----+----4----+----5----+ LINE: 235 OF 339
    235              PERFORM 310-READ-INVENTORY-RECORD.
AT                   IF NOT INVMAST-EOF
    237                  MOVE 'N' TO INVESTMENT-SIZE-ERROR-SWITCH
    238                  COMPUTE INVESTMENT-AMOUNT = IM-ON-HAND * IM-UNIT-PRICE
    239                     ON SIZE ERROR
LOG    0----+----1----+----2----+----3----+----4----+----5----+--- LINE: 0 OF 11
***************************** TOP OF LOG *********************************
000001 IGZ100I PP - 5668-958 VS COBOL II DEBUG FACILITY -- REL 2.0
000002 IGZ100I (C) COPYRIGHT IBM CORPORATION 1986
000003 IGZ102I INV3520.000201.1
000004 * AT 236
000005 * GO
000006 IGZ105I AT INV3520.000236.1
000007 * LIST IM-ITEM-NO
000008 000022 03 INV3520.IM-ITEM-NO                    9(5)
000009        DISP    ===>00001
000010 * GO
000011 IGZ105I AT INV3520.000236.1
***************************** BOTTOM OF LOG *****************************
```

Figure 5-31   Retrieving input lines from the log area (part 1 of 3)

To retrieve a line from the log area, you move the cursor to the line you want to use, delete the asterisk, make any required modifications, and press enter. The command will then appear on the command line where you can modify it further before issuing the command.

This technique is illustrated in figure 5-31. (Note that the source area consists of only six lines in this figure.) In part 1 of the figure, you can see that several COBTEST commands have been issued. First, I entered an AT command to set a breakpoint at line 236. Then, I entered a GO command to start program execution. When the first breakpoint at line 236 was taken, I entered a LIST command to list the contents of IM-ITEM-NO. Then, I issued another GO command to resume program execution.

When the second breakpoint at line 236 was taken, instead of entering another LIST command to list the contents of IM-ITEM-NO, I retrieved the one I had already entered from the log area. In part 2 of figure 5-31, you can see that I removed the asterisk from that line in the log area (the cursor location is shaded). Then, when I pressed the enter key, the log line was duplicated on the command line. This is illustrated in part 3 of figure 5-31.

To retrieve a command from the log area, move the cursor to the desired command, delete the leading asterisk, and make any other modifications you want

```
COBTEST    QUALIFY:  INV3520    WHERE: INV3520.000236.1
COMMAND --->                                                SCROLL ---> PAGE
SOURCE ----+----1----+----2----+----3----+----4----+----5----+ LINE: 235 OF 339
    235              PERFORM 310-READ-INVENTORY-RECORD.
AT                   IF NOT INVMAST-EOF
    237                  MOVE 'N' TO INVESTMENT-SIZE-ERROR-SWITCH
    238                  COMPUTE INVESTMENT-AMOUNT = IM-ON-HAND * IM-UNIT-PRICE
    239                  ON SIZE ERROR
LOG    0----+----1----+----2----+----3----+----4----+----5----+--- LINE: 0 OF 11
****************************** TOP OF LOG ******************************
000001 IGZ100I PP - 5668-958 VS COBOL II DEBUG FACILITY -- REL 2.0
000002 IGZ100I (C) COPYRIGHT IBM CORPORATION 1986
000003 IGZ102I INV3520.000201.1
000004 * AT 236
000005 * GO
000006 IGZ105I AT INV3520.000236.1
000007 ▌LIST IM-ITEM-NO
000008 000022 03 INV3520.IM-ITEM-NO                          9(5)
000009        DISP    --->00001
000010 * GO
000011 IGZ105I AT INV3520.000236.1
****************************** BOTTOM OF LOC ******************************
```

Figure 5-31   Retrieving input lines from the log area (part 2 of 3)

If you want to retrieve commands from the log area that aren't currently displayed on the screen, you'll need to use the ISPF scrolling commands. These commands—UP, DOWN, LEFT, and RIGHT—are usually associated with PF keys. If not, they can be entered on the command line.

There are some COBTEST commands you can enter in the *prefix area* or *suffix area* of the source listing display. The commands you can enter in the prefix area are AT, OFF, and PEEK. The AT and OFF commands were discussed in topic 1. The PEEK command (abbreviated P) is used to display a line number that has been obscured by the feedback of a previous AT command, as in figure 5-32. From here, you'd type PEEK right over AT, press the enter key, and line number 236 would reappear in the prefix area. As for the suffix area, the only command you can issue there is SELECT. I'll discuss it later in this topic.

Commands should be entered in only one panel area at a time. If commands are entered in more than one area, the areas are recognized in the following order: (1) qualify field, (2) prefix and suffix areas, (3) log area, and (4) command line. Only the first command recognized is executed; all others are ignored. If more than one command is entered in the same area, only the first

When you press the enter key, the command is duplicated on the command line
where you can modify if further or issue it as is

```
COBTEST    QUALIFY: INV3520     WHERE: INV3520.000236.1
COMMAND ---> LIST IM-ITEM-NO                                        SCROLL ---> PAGE
SOURCE ----+----1----+----2----+----3----+----4----+----5----+ LINE: 235 OF 339
   235                PERFORM 310-READ-INVENTORY-RECORD.
AT                    IF NOT INVMAST-EOF
   237                    MOVE 'N' TO INVESTMENT-SIZE-ERROR-SWITCH
   238                    COMPUTE INVESTMENT-AMOUNT = IM-ON-HAND * IM-UNIT-PRICE
   239                        ON SIZE ERROR
LOG    0----+----1----+----2----+----3----+----4----+----5----+--- LINE: 0 OF 11
****************************** TOP OF LOG ********************************
000001 IGZ100I PP - 5668-958 VS COBOL II DEBUG FACILITY -- REL 2.0
000002 IGZ100I (C) COPYRIGHT IBM CORPORATION 1986
000003 IGZ102I INV3520.000201.1
000004 * AT 236
000005 * GO
000006 IGZ105I AT INV3520.000236.1
000007 * LIST IM-ITEM-NO
000008 000022 03 INV3520.IM-ITEM-NO                          9(5)
000009       DISP    --->00001
000010 * GO
000011 IGZ105I AT INV3520.000236.1
****************************** BOTTOM OF LOG ****************************
```

Figure 5-31   Retrieving input lines from the log area (part 3 of 3)

one is executed, except on the command line. On the command line, you can
enter multiple commands by separating them with semicolons, and they will
all be executed. In addition, you can use command lists just as you do for batch
and line mode. In a command list, you can include any COBTEST commands
that are valid in line mode, except COBTEST. You can also include ISPF
commands and TSO or CMS commands. However, you cannot use any
full-screen commands in a command list.

The maximum length of a command is 32,763 bytes. Commands can be
continued by placing a plus (+), minus (-), or comma (,) at the end of a line.
After a continued line is entered, only input from the command line is accepted
until the command is completed. However, input can still be retrieved from
the log area and placed on the command line.

How to handle terminal I/O from your program   If you're testing an
interactive program using full-screen mode, you'll need to know how
COBTEST handles terminal I/O from your program. When output is sent to
the terminal, it's intercepted by COBTEST and displayed in the log area. If an
ACCEPT statement is issued from your program, COBTEST changes to input

```
COBTEST   QUALIFY: INV3520    WHERE: INV3520.000236.1
COMMAND ===>                                              SCROLL ===> PAGE
SOURCE ----+----1----+----2----+----3----+----4----+----5----+ LINE: 233 OF 339
     233       300-PREPARE-INVESTMENT-LINE.
     234       *
     235           PERFORM 310-READ-INVENTORY-RECORD.
AT               IF NOT INVMAST-EOF
     237              MOVE 'N' TO INVESTMENT-SIZE-ERROR-SWITCH
     238              COMPUTE INVESTMENT-AMOUNT = IM-ON-HAND * IM-UNIT-PRICE
     239                  ON SIZE ERROR
     240                      MOVE 9999999.99 TO INVESTMENT-AMOUNT
     241                      SET INVESTMENT-SIZE-ERROR TO TRUE
     242              END-COMPUTE
     243              IF INVESTMENT-AMOUNT > 1000
LOG    0----+----1----+----2----+----3----+----4----+----5----+---- LINE: 0 OF 6
****************************** TOP OF LOG *********************************
000001 IGZ100I PP - 5668-958 VS COBOL II DEBUG FACILITY -- REL 2.0
000002 IGZ100I (C) COPYRIGHT IBM CORPORATION 1986
000003 IGZ102I INV3520.000201.1
000004 * AT 236
000005 * GO
000006 IGZ105I AT INV3520.000236.1
***************************** BOTTOM OF LOG *******************************
```

Figure 5-32   Feedback in the source area from an AT command

mode, indicated by the word INPUT in the command line prompt. To send input to your program, you simply enter the data, preceded by a percent sign (%) in the command line. If you want to perform more debugging before you send the input to your program, you can enter COBTEST commands in input mode as usual. However, GO, RUN, STEP, and VTRACE commands cannot be executed until the required input has been entered. (I'll cover the VTRACE command later in this topic.)

How to set screen parameters: The PROFILE command

I mentioned earlier in this topic that the default for the size of the source area is 12 lines. This default, along with other settings that affect the way the full-screen debugger works, can be changed using the PROFILE command (abbreviated PROF). When you enter the PROFILE command, which has no operands, the panel shown in figure 5-33 is displayed.

The first five settings on the profile panel should be self-explanatory. You specify the size of the source area with the "source area columns" and "source area rows" settings. You specify the number of lines in the auto area with the

```
                    VS COBOL II DEBUG PROFILE PANEL
        COMMAND --->


                             CURRENT SETTING
                             ---------------
        Source area columns          80          (8 to screen width)
        Source area rows             12          (0 to screen depth)
        Auto area rows               6           (0 to screen depth)
        Auto line numbers            YES         (yes or no)
        Log line numbers             YES         (yes or no)
        Default listings             YES         (yes or no)
        Refresh screen               NO          (yes or no)
        VTRACE delay                 50          (0 to 99999, 1 unit= .01 second)


        Enter:
          SAVE      to save your profile settings.
          DEFAULT   to restore default profile settings.
          END       to return to the debug session with current profile settings
                    in effect.
```

Figure 5-33   The COBTEST profile panel

"auto area rows" setting. (The auto area is always 80 columns wide.) You specify whether you want line numbers displayed in the auto and log areas with the "auto line numbers" and "log line numbers" settings.

The "default listings" setting is used to determine where the source listings that are to be displayed in the source area are located. If you specify YES, COBTEST looks for each listing by a default name as the program is executed. For TSO, the default name is *userid.program-name*.LIST. For CMS, it's *program-name* LISTING *. If you specify NO, you must identify each listing explicitly using the LISTINGS command. I'll show you how to use that command in a minute.

The "refresh screen" setting determines whether the entire screen is transmitted for each display. In most cases, you won't need for the screen to be refreshed every time. However, if you're testing a program that performs full-screen I/O without ISPF services, the screen may not be cleared properly unless you specify YES for the "refresh screen" setting. You shouldn't use this setting unless absolutely necessary, however, since it dramatically increases response time.

The last setting, "VTRACE delay," specifies the time delay between program statements when you execute your program dynamically using the VTRACE command. I'll show you how to use VTRACE later in this topic.

The profile settings can be changed at any time during a debugging session. To change the settings, you simply type over the old values and enter the END command. The settings will then remain in effect until the end of the debugging session. If you want to save the values you enter as your new default settings, you enter the SAVE command before entering the END command. Then, the settings will remain in effect from one debugging session to another. Finally, if you want to restore the default settings after making modifications, you enter the DEFAULT command. The settings will then be restored to the last settings that were saved.

How to use cursor-oriented commands

A *cursor-oriented command* is one whose execution depends on the location of the cursor. For example, the ISPF scrolling commands are cursor-oriented when used with COBTEST. If the cursor is located in the source area when one of these commands is issued, the source listing is scrolled. If the cursor is located in the auto area, the auto listing is scrolled. And if the cursor is located anywhere outside the source and auto areas, the log listing is scrolled.

Some of the COBTEST commands are cursor-oriented as well. For example, the LIST command, which was discussed in topic 1, can be cursor-oriented. If you want to list the contents of a variable in the source listing, you enter the LIST command on the command line, place the cursor under the field you want to display, and press enter. That saves you having to enter the field name on the LIST command.

The other full-screen COBTEST commands that are cursor-oriented are AUTO, MOVECURS, POSITION, SEARCH, and SOURCE. Before each of these commands is issued, the cursor must be positioned at the appropriate location. I'll discuss all of these commands in detail later in this topic.

How to display source listings

Although the source area is optional, you'll almost always use it. When you do, you will need to know how to use the three commands presented in figure 5-34: SOURCE, LISTINGS, and RESTORE.

The SOURCE command   Earlier in this topic, I showed you how you can control the size of the source area using the settings in the profile panel. But

The SOURCE command

```
SOURCE [ {LISTING program-name}
         {OFF                  }  ]
         {ON                   }
```

The LISTINGS command

```
LISTINGS
```

The RESTORE command

```
RESTORE
```

Explanation

SOURCE   Open, close, or change the size of the source area. Can be abbreviated
                                SO.

LISTINGS   Invoke the listing panel to specify the location of source listings to be
                                displayed during the debugging session. Can be abbreviated LI.

RESTORE   Position the source area so that the last executed statement is displayed.
                                Can be abbreviated RESTO.

LISTING program-name   Change the listing displayed in the source area to *program-name*.

OFF   Close the source area.

ON   Open the source area using the defualt size settings on the profile panel.

Figure 5-34   The SOURCE, LISTINGS, and RESTORE commands

unless you're changing the default, you probably won't change the size this
way. Instead, you'll use the SOURCE command (abbreviated SO).

To change the size of the source area, you type the SOURCE command
without any operands in the command line, place the cursor where you want
the bottom left corner of the source area to be, and press enter. The area will
extend from the top right corner of the source area to the cursor position. Figure
5-35 illustrates this use of the SOURCE command. In part 1, I placed the cursor
so the source area would consist of 10 lines of 40 columns. Then, I issued the
SOURCE command. The results are illustrated in part 2 of figure 5-35. If you

To change the size of the source area, position the cursor where you want the bottom left corner to be, and enter the SOURCE command

```
COBTEST   QUALIFY: INV3520    WHERE: INV3520.000201.1
COMMAND ---> SOURCE                                        SCROLL ---> PAGE
SOURCE ----+----1----+----2----+----3----+----4----+----5----+ LINE: 198 OF 339
    198        *
    199           000-PREPARE-INVESTMENT-LISTING.
    200        *
    201             OPEN INPUT  INVMAST
    202                  OUTPUT INVLIST.
    203             PERFORM 100-FORMAT-REPORT-HEADING.
    204             PERFORM 300-PREPARE-INVESTMENT-LINE
    205                 UNTIL INVMAST-EOF.
    206             PERFORM 500-PRINT-TOTAL-LINES.
    207             CLOSE INVMAST
    208                   INVLIST.
LOG    0----+----1----+----2----+----3----+----4----+----5----+---- LINE: 0 OF 3
****************************** TOP OF LOG ******************************
000001 IGZ100I PP - 5668-958 VS COBOL II DEBUG FACILITY -- REL 2.0
000002 IGZ100I (C) COPYRIGHT IBM CORPORATION 1986
000003 IGZ102I INV3520.000201.1
***************************** BOTTOM OF LOG *****************************
```

Figure 5-35   Using the SOURCE command to define the size of the source area (part 1 of 2)

change the size of the source area frequently, you'll probably want to assign the SOURCE command to a PF key.

If you want to close the source area completely, you issue the command

    SOURCE OFF

To reopen the source area, you have to position the cursor and reissue the SOURCE command or issue the command

    SOURCE ON

If you use the ON operand, the size of the source area is determined by the defaults specified on the profile panel. One point to be aware of here: If you use the SOURCE command to determine the size of the source area, the defaults on the profile panel are automatically changed to the indicated size.

You can also use the SOURCE command to select a different listing to be displayed. You do that by using the LISTING *program-name* operand. For

When you press the enter key, the source area is changed to the indicated size

```
COBTEST   QUALIFY: INV3520    WHERE: INV3520.000201.1
COMMAND ===>                                       SCROLL ===> PAGE
LOG   0----+----1----+---- LINE: 0 OF 3+   SOURCE ----+----1---- LINE: 198 OF 339
************* TOP OF LOG *************+     198    *
000001 IGZ100I PP - 5668-958 VS COBOL I+   199       000-PREPARE-INVESTMENT-L
000002 IGZ100I (C) COPYRIGHT IBM CORPOR+   200    *
000003 IGZ102I INV3520.000201.1        +   201          OPEN INPUT   INVMAST
*********** BOTTOM OF LOG ***********+      202               OUTPUT INVLIST.
                                     +     203          PERFORM 100-FORMAT-R
                                     +     204          PERFORM 300-PREPARE-
                                     +     205              UNTIL INVMAST-EO
                                     +     206          PERFORM 500-PRINT-TO
                                     +
```

Figure 5-35   Using the SOURCE command to define the size of the source area (part 2 of 2)

example, if a subprogram named DATEDIT was called by the currently executing program, I could display its source listing by issuing the command

```
SOURCE LISTING DATEDIT
```

The effect is the same as entering DATEDIT in the qualify field.

The LISTINGS command   If you specify NO for default listings on the profile panel, you have to explicitly identify the source listings you want to display during the debugging session. You do that using the LISTINGS command (abbreviated LI), which has no operands. When you issue this command, the listing panel shown in figure 5-36 is displayed. (This is the panel for TSO, but the panel for CMS is similar.) You can also access this panel by entering a question mark (?) in the first character of the qualify field.

To identify a source listing, you simply enter the program name and the name of the data set containing the source listing for the program. You also need to specify if you want the source listing to display when the program is executed. If you specify NO, you will have to issue a SOURCE command or

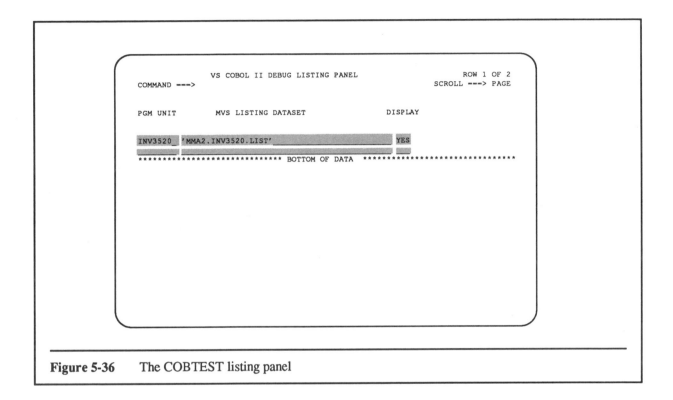

```
                     VS COBOL II DEBUG LISTING PANEL                    ROW 1 OF 2
        COMMAND --->                                        SCROLL ---> PAGE


        PGM UNIT       MVS LISTING DATASET              DISPLAY

        INV3520_  'MMA2.INV3520.LIST'_____   YES
        _____   _____
        **************************** BOTTOM OF DATA ********************************
```

Figure 5-36   The COBTEST listing panel

specify the name of the program in the qualify field in order to display the listing. To exit from this screen, you enter END.

The RESTORE command   Sometimes during a debugging session, you'll need to scroll the source listing of the currently executing program or display the source listing for a program other than the one that's executing. When you do one of those things, you lose the display of the line that's currently executing. To restore the display to the currently executing line, you issue the RESTORE command (abbreviated RESTO). The RESTORE command has no operands.

How to use the auto monitoring area: The AUTO command

The auto monitoring area is used to display the values of variables in your program as the program executes. The area is optional and, by default, is not displayed. To open the auto monitoring area and list program variables, you use the AUTO command (abbreviated AU). Its format is presented in figure 5-37.

The AUTO command

```
          ⎧List-command⎫
AUTO  [ ⎨ON          ⎬]
          ⎩OFF         ⎭
```

Explanation

AUTO	Control automatic monitoring of program variables. Can be abbreviated AU.
list–command	Any valid LIST command. (See figure 5-15 for the LIST command syntax.)
ON	Open the auto monitoring area using the default size settings on the profile panel.
OFF	Close the auto monitoring area and temporarily stop monitoring any variables on the AUTO LIST command.

Figure 5-37   The AUTO command

You can open the auto monitoring area in two ways. First, you can issue the command

```
AUTO ON
```

Then, the size of the area defaults to the setting on the profile panel. Second, you can place the cursor at the desired depth on the screen and issue the AUTO command without any operands. Either way, the area is displayed immediately below the command line and takes up the full width of the screen. However, you should realize that the auto monitoring area is not displayed at all unless you have specified variables to be listed.

You specify these variables by using the LIST form of the AUTO command. The LIST operand has the same form and follows the same rules as the LIST command. For example, if I want to list the value of a field named RECORD-COUNT, I issue this command:

```
AUTO LIST RECORD-COUNT
```

Then, the value of RECORD-COUNT is displayed in the auto area each time a breakpoint is taken. Output from this command is illustrated in figure 5-38. Here, I displayed the field RECORD-COUNT after the program had completed execution.

```
COBTEST   QUALIFY: INV3520   WHERE: INV3520.000209.1   PROGRAM ENDED NORMALLY
COMMAND --->                                           SCROLL ---> PAGE
AUTO  0----+----1----+----2----+----3----+----4----+----5----+--- LINE: 1 OF 2
000001 000082 02 INV3520.RECORD-COUNT                  S9(5)
000002        COMP    --->+00005
**************************** BOTTOM OF AUTO ********************************


SOURCE ----+----1----+----2----+----3----+----4----+----5----+ LINE: 206 OF 339
   206            PERFORM 500-PRINT-TOTAL-LINES.
   207            CLOSE INVMAST
   208                 INVLIST.
   209            STOP RUN.
   210       *
   211        100-FORMAT-REPORT-HEADING.
   212       *
   213            ACCEPT PRESENT-DATE FROM DATE.
   214            MOVE PRESENT-MONTH TO TODAYS-MONTH.
   215            MOVE PRESENT-DAY   TO TODAYS-DAY.
   216            MOVE PRESENT-YEAR  TO TODAYS-YEAR.
LOG   0----+----1----+----2----+----3----+----4----+----5----+-- LINE: 10 OF 12
000010 IGZ105I AT INV3520.000236.1
000011 * RUN
000012 IGZ129I PROGRAM UNDER COBTEST ENDED NORMALLY
```

Figure 5-38   Display output from the AUTO LIST command

You can temporarily stop the monitoring of program variables by issuing the command

    AUTO OFF

However, the variables specified on the previous AUTO LIST command are saved and monitoring can be restored by issuing the command

    AUTO ON

To change the variables that are being monitored, a new AUTO LIST command must be issued.

How to search panel areas: The POSITION and SEARCH commands

To locate specific information in a screen display, you can search panel areas in one of two ways. First, you can search a panel area for a particular line number using the POSITION command. Second, you can search for a partic-

---

The POSITION command

```
POSITION line-number
```

The SEARCH command

```
SEARCH [delimiter character-string [delimiter]]
```

Explanation

POSITION	Move the specified line in the source area, log area, or auto monitoring area to the top of its respective area. Can be abbreviated POS.
SEARCH	Search the source listing area, the log area, or the auto monitoring area for a given character string. Can be abbreviated SEA.
line-number	The line number POSITION will search for.
delimiter	Any non-blank character not in the string. The second delimiter is optional unless the string has trailing blanks. If used, it must be the same as the first delimiter.
character-string	The character string to be searched for.

Figure 5-39   The POSITION and SEARCH commands

---

ular character string using the SEARCH command. The formats of these commands are presented in figure 5-39.

To use the POSITION command (abbreviated POS), you place the cursor in the area you want to search and issue the command in this format:

```
POSITION line-number
```

For example, in the top part of figure 5-40, I entered the command

```
POSITION 268
```

and placed the cursor in the source area. Then, when I pressed the enter key, the source listing was scrolled so line 268 became the first line displayed in the source area. This is illustrated in the bottom part of figure 5-40. You can also assign the POSITION command to a PF key. Then, you can search a listing

To search for a specific line number in the source area, place the cursor anywhere in the area and enter the POSITION command with the desired line number

```
COBTEST    QUALIFY: INV3520    WHERE: INV3520.000201.1
COMMAND ---> POSITION 268                            SCROLL ---> PAGE
SOURCE ----+----1----+----2----+----3----+----4----+----5----+ LINE: 198 OF 339
    198        *
    199        000-PREPARE-INVESTMENT-LISTING.
    200        *
    201            OPEN INPUT  INVMAST
    202                 OUTPUT INVLIST.
    203            PERFORM 100-FORMAT-REPORT-HEADING.
    204            PERFORM 300-PREPARE-INVESTMENT-LINE
    205                UNTIL INVMAST-EOF.
    206            PERFORM 500-PRINT-TOTAL-LINES.
    207            CLOSE INVMAST
    208                  INVLIST.
LOG    0----+----1----+----2----+----3----+----4----+----5----+---- LINE: 0 OF 3
****************************** TOP OF LOG ******************************
000001 IGZ100I PP - 5668-958 VS COBOL II DEBUG FACILITY -- REL 2.0
000002 IGZ100I (C) COPYRIGHT IBM CORPORATION 1986
000003 IGZ102I INV3520.000201.1
****************************** BOTTOM OF LOG ***************************
```

When you press the enter key, the specified liine is displayed at the top of the source area

```
COBTEST    QUALIFY: INV3520    WHERE: INV3520.000201.1
COMMAND --->                                         SCROLL ---> PAGE
SOURCE ----+----1----+----2----+----3----+----4----+----5----+ LINE: 268 OF 339
    268        330-PRINT-INVESTMENT-LINE.
    269        *
    270            IF LINE-COUNT  LINES-ON-PAGE
    271                PERFORM 340-PRINT-HEADING-LINES.
    272            MOVE IM-ITEM-NO         TO IL-ITEM-NO.
    273            MOVE IM-ITEM-DESC       TO IL-ITEM-DESC.
    274            MOVE IM-UNIT-PRICE      TO IL-UNIT-PRICE.
    275            MOVE IM-ON-HAND         TO IL-ON-HAND.
    276            MOVE IM-LAST-ORDER-DATE TO IL-LAST-ORDER-DATE.
    277            MOVE IM-LAST-MONTH-SALES TO IL-LAST-MONTH-SALES.
    278            ADD IM-LAST-MONTH-SALES  TO SELECTED-LM-SALES-TOTAL.
LOG    0----+----1----+----2----+----3----+----4----+----5----+---- LINE: 0 OF 3
****************************** TOP OF LOG ******************************
000001 IGZ100I PP - 5668-958 VS COBOL II DEBUG FACILITY -- REL 2.0
000002 IGZ100I (C) COPYRIGHT IBM CORPORATION 1986
000003 IGZ102I INV3520.000201.1
****************************** BOTTOM OF LOG ***************************
```

Figure 5-40   Using the POSTION command to search a source listing

by positioning the cursor, entering the line number in the command line, and pressing the appropriate PF key.

To use the SEARCH command (abbreviated SEA), you position the cursor in the area you want to search and issue a command like this:

```
SEARCH delimiter character-string delimiter
```

Here, *delimiter* can be any character not in the character string. The second delimiter isn't required unless the character string contains trailing blanks. If it's used, it must be the same as the first delimiter.

Figure 5-41 shows how to use the SEARCH command to search the source area. In the first screen , I issued the command

```
SEARCH /RECORD-COUNT
```

with the cursor positioned in the source area. The result is illustrated in the second screen in the figure. As you can see, the source listing has been positioned so that the first line displayed is the first line found containing RECORD-COUNT.

You can also issue the SEARCH command without specifying a character string at all. Then, the area is searched for the last character string specified on a SEARCH command. That makes it easy to locate multiple occurrences of a character string.

When a SEARCH command is issued, the search begins at the first line displayed in the area. To search the entire listing, then, the listing must first be positioned at its beginning. You can accomplish this using the ISPF scrolling commands or the POSITION command.

How to position the cursor for command entry: The MOVECURS command

If you ever need to enter several commands consecutively in the source or auto area, the MOVECURS command can be useful. It saves you time by allowing you to go back and forth between the source or auto area and the command line without using the cursor keys. As you can see in figure 5-42, the MOVECURS command has no operands.

The MOVECURS command (abbreviated MOVEC or MC) is used most often with cursor-oriented commands. And, it is almost always assigned to a PF key, although it can also be effective when used in a command list. To illustrate its use, suppose the MOVECURS command is assigned to PF12. Also suppose you want to search your source listing for all occurrences of a

To search for a specific character string in the source area, place the cursor anywhere
in the area and enter the SEARCH command with the desired character

```
COBTEST   QUALIFY: INV3520    WHERE: INV3520.000201.1
COMMAND ===> SEARCH /RECORD-COUNT                            SCROLL ===> PAGE
SOURCE ----+----1----+----2----+----3----+----4----+----5----+ LINE: 198 OF 339
    198        *
    199        000-PREPARE-INVESTMENT-LISTING.
    200        *
    201           OPEN INPUT  INVMAST
    202                OUTPUT INVLIST.
    203           PERFORM 100-FORMAT-REPORT-HEADING.
    204           PERFORM 300-PREPARE-INVESTMENT-LINE
    205                UNTIL INVMAST-EOF.
    206           PERFORM 500-PRINT-TOTAL-LINES.
    207           CLOSE INVMAST
    208                INVLIST.
LOG    0----+----1----+----2----+----3----+----4----+----5----+---- LINE: 0 OF 3
****************************** TOP OF LOG ********************************
000001 IGZ100I PP - 5668-958 VS COBOL II DEBUG FACILITY -- REL 2.0
000002 IGZ100I (C) COPYRIGHT IBM CORPORATION 1986
000003 IGZ102I INV3520.000201.1
****************************** BOTTOM OF LOG *****************************
```

When you press the enter key, the first line containing the specified character is
displayed

```
COBTEST   QUALIFY: INV3520    WHERE: INV3520.000201.1
COMMAND ===>                                                 SCROLL ===> PAGE
SOURCE ----+----1----+----2----+----3----+----4----+----5----+ LINE: 253 OF 339
    253                ADD 1 TO RECORD-COUNT.
    254        *
    255        320-COMPUTE-INVENTORY-FIELDS.
    256        *
    257           IF NOT INVESTMENT-SIZE-ERROR
    258              IF IM-LAST-MONTH-SALES > ZERO
    259                 COMPUTE NO-OF-MONTHS-STOCK ROUNDED =
    260                    INVESTMENT-AMOUNT / IM-LAST-MONTH-SALES
    261                    ON SIZE ERROR
    262                       MOVE 999.9 TO NO-OF-MONTHS-STOCK
    263              ELSE
LOG    0----+----1----+----2----+----3----+----4----+----5----+---- LINE: 0 OF 3
****************************** TOP OF LOG ********************************
000001 IGZ100I PP - 5668-958 VS COBOL II DEBUG FACILITY -- REL 2.0
000002 IGZ100I (C) COPYRIGHT IBM CORPORATION 1986
000003 IGZ102I INV3520.000201.1
****************************** BOTTOM OF LOG *****************************
```

Figure 5-41   Using the SEARCH command to search a source listing

---

The MOVECURS command

MOVECURS

Explanation

MOVECURS   Move the cursor between the last position in the source area or the auto
                            monitoring area and the command area. Can be abbreviated MOVEC or
                            MC.

Figure 5-42   The MOVECURS command

---

particular variable. To do that, you can place the cursor in the source area and
press PF12, which will move the cursor to the command line. Then, you can
type the SEARCH command in the command line, press PF12 again, and the
cursor will return to the same place in the source area that it was before the
first MOVECURS command was entered. To begin the search, you press the
enter key. Then, you can continue to move back and forth between the source
area and the command area by pressing PF12.

How to execute a program dynamically: The VTRACE command

The VTRACE command, shown in figure 5-43, is used to step through your
program one statement at a time. If it's issued without any operands, the entire
program is executed from its last point of interruption. If the VTRACE
command is issued in this format:

VTRACE number

only the number of statements specified by *number* are executed.

The amount of time between the execution of each statement is determined
by the VTRACE delay setting on the profile panel. The default is one half of
a second. During the execution of a VTRACE command, the keyboard is
locked so no additional commands can be issued. However, a previously set
breakpoint or an attention or I/O interrupt will cause the VTRACE command
to be terminated.

After each statement in the program is executed, the debugging screen is
redisplayed. In the source area, the currently executing statement is always
highlighted. If the auto area is open and an AUTO LIST command has been

---

The VTRACE command

```
VTRACE [number]
```

Explanation

VTRACE   Step through the program one statement at a time. Can be abbreviated V.

number   The number of verbs to be executed.

Figure 5-43   The VTRACE command

---

issued, the values of the requested variables are displayed. And, of course, the information in the log area is updated as well.

If you look at the output from a VTRACE command, you'll notice that it's logged as consecutive STEP commands. As a result, dynamic program execution can also be accomplished using the STEP command. The difference is that with the STEP command, you can issue other COBTEST commands between the execution of each statement. If you use the STEP command for dynamic program execution, you'll probably want to assign it to a PF key for efficiency.

How to use the suffix area for frequency tallying

You'll remember from the last topic that you can keep a count of verb frequencies using the FREQ command. In full-screen mode, those frequencies can be displayed in the suffix area within the source area. This is illustrated in figure 5-44. If the suffix area is open, which is the default, the frequencies are displayed automatically when a FREQ command is issued. If the suffix area is closed or you need to display a tally for a verb other than the first on a line, you'll need to know how to use the two commands in figure 5-45: SUFFIX and SELECT.

The SUFFIX command   The SUFFIX command (abbreviated SUF) causes the suffix area within the source area to be opened or closed. To open the suffix area, you issue the SUFFIX command like this:

```
SUFFIX ON
```

```
COBTEST   QUALIFY: INV3520    WHERE: INV3520.000236.1
COMMAND ===>                                           SCROLL ===> PAGE
AUTO  0----+----1----+----2----+----3----+----4----+----5----+---- LINE: 1 OF 2
000001 000082 02 INV3520.RECORD-COUNT               S9(5)
000002        COMP    ===>+00002
**************************** BOTTOM OF AUTO ******************************


SOURCE ----+----1----+----2----+----3----+----4----+----5----+ LINE: 233 OF 339
     233        300-PREPARE-INVESTMENT-LINE.                      ...
     234        *                                                 ...
     235            PERFORM 310-READ-INVENTORY-RECORD.            0002
AT                 IF NOT INVMAST-EOF                             0001
     237                MOVE 'N' TO  INVESTMENT-SIZE-ERROR-SWITCH 0001
     238                COMPUTE INVESTMENT-AMOUNT = IM-ON-HAND * IM-UNIT-PRI 0001
     239                    ON SIZE ERROR                         ...
     240                        MOVE 9999999.99 TO INVESTMENT-AMOUNT 0000
     241                        SET INVESTMENT-SIZE-ERROR TO TRUE 0000
     242                    END-COMPUTE                           ...
     243                    IF INVESTMENT-AMOUNT > 1000           0001
LOG    0----+----1----+----2----+----3----+----4----+----5----+-- LINE: 37 OF 39
000037 IGZ105I AT INV3520.000236.1
000038 * GO
000039 IGZ105I AT INV3520.000236.1
```

Figure 5-44   Verb frequencies displayed in the suffix area of the source area

To close the suffix area, you issue this command:

    SUFFIX OFF

Since the default is for the suffix area to be open, you won't have to issue the SUFFIX ON command unless you've previously issued the SUFFIX OFF command.

The SELECT command   The SELECT command (entered as S) is used to display the frequencies of verbs other than the first on a line. It's entered in the suffix area in the format

    S number

where *number* is the relative number of the verb on the line. For example, if you issued the command

    S 2

The SUFFIX command

$$\text{SUFFIX} \begin{Bmatrix} ON \\ OFF \end{Bmatrix}$$

The SELECT command

S number

Explanation

SUFFIX	Open or close the suffix area within the source area. Can be abbreviated SUF.
S	Allow viewing of a specified frequency count on a line with multiple verbs. Must be entered as S.
ON	Opens the suffix area if the FREQ command has been specified for the currently qualified program.
OFF	Closes the suffix area.
number	Specifies which verb (from left to right) the frequency count is to be shown for. May range from 1 to 7.

Figure 5-45   The SUFFIX and SELECT commands

---

in the suffix area of a line containing two verbs, the frequency of the second verb on the line would be displayed. When program execution continues and the screen is redisplayed, the suffix area will again show the frequency of the first verb on the line.

How to display information on COBTEST commands: The HELP command

If you need information on a particular COBTEST command or task during a debugging session, you can issue the HELP command (abbreviated H) to invoke the ISPF HELP facility. When you do that, the main help panel in figure 5-46 is displayed. (If you're using VS COBOL II Release 1, this facility isn't available for the CMS environment.)

As you can see in figure 5-46, all of the COBTEST commands are listed on this menu. In addition, there are selections for a tutorial, a task menu, and

```
SELECTION --->                                   VS COBOL II INTERACTIVE DEBUG

                            Main Help Menu

         1  Task menu    14  Go          27  Offwn       40  Search
         2  Tutorial     15  Help        28  Onabend     41  Set
         3  Prefix cmds  16  If          29  Position    42  Source
         4  Suffix cmds  17  Link        30  Prevdisp    43  Step
         5  At           18  List        31  Proc        44  Suffix
         6  Auto         19  Listbrks    32  Profile     45  Syscmd
         7  Color        20  Listeq      33  Printdd     46  Trace
         8  Comment      21  Listfreq    34  Qualify     47  Vtrace
         9  Drop         22  Listings    35  Quit        48  When
        10  Dump         23  Movecurs    36  Record      49  Where
        11  Equate       24  Next        37  Restart
        12  Flow         25  Norecord    38  Restore
        13  Freq         26  Off         39  Run


        Select a topic by number. When finished reading a topic
        enter TOP to redisplay this menu.
```

Figure 5-46   The main menu of the HELP command for COBTEST

prefix and suffix commands. To select a topic, you simply enter its corresponding number. To display the task menu, you can either enter 1 or press the enter key. The task menu that's displayed is shown in figure 5-47.

Figure 5-48 shows the first screen that's displayed by HELP for the AT command. To continue to the next screen, you simply press the enter key. When you reach the end of a display, pressing the enter key will return you to the first screen. You can also use the BACK ISPF command to move backward in a display. When you're finished viewing a display, you can enter END to return to the debugging screen. TOP returns you to the main menu.

You should be sure to note the syntax notation that's used in figure 5-48, since it's probably different than what you're used to seeing. This notation seems to be the trend in many of the new IBM manuals. So, although I won't describe it in this book, you should become familiar with it. If you're using Release 1 or 2 of VS COBOL II, only the *Application Programming: Debugging* manual uses this notation, so you can refer to it for an explanation of how to read it. If you're using Release 3, all the manuals use this notation, so you can refer to any of them.

```
 SELECTION --->                              VS COBOL II INTERACTIVE DEBUG

                                 TASK MENU

         1  Setting breakpoints
         2  Removing breakpoints
         3  Resuming execution of suspended programs
         4  Changing the values of variables
         5  Displaying the value of variables
         6  Gathering information about the program's behavior
            during execution
         7  Querying the status of various settings in COBTEST
         8  Creating and deleting alias names
         9  Routing the output of COBTEST to different files (in CMS) or
            data sets (in MVS)
        10  Explicitly referring to other programs in storage

 TOP for main menu
```

Figure 5-47   The task menu of the HELP command for COBTEST

Discussion

In general, the full-screen commands presented in this topic don't provide any debugging functions that aren't already available to you in interactive line mode. They simply provide you with an easier and more efficient means of performing those functions. So if you use these commands during your full-screen debugging sessions, I think you'll find the task of debugging your programs much more enjoyable. And you'll be debugging your programs in the most efficient way possible.

Terminology

qualify field
command area
log area
source area

auto monitoring area
prefix area
suffix area
cursor-oriented command

```
SELECTION --->                              VS COBOL INTERACTIVE DEBUG
AT COMMAND                                              panel 1 of 7

   The AT command establishes breakpoints at one or more COBOL verbs in your
   program.  When an AT breakpoint is reached, the system may print a message
   to identify the program-name, statement number, and verb number of that
   breakpoint.  Execution stops and a command list can be executed.


   >>-+-AT-+-+-statement--------------+-+---------------+-->
      +-A--+ +-stmnt-1:stmnt-2---------+ +-(command list)-+
             +                          +
             +    +--------,-------+    +
             +    V               +    +
             +-(-+-statement------+-)-+
                 +-stmnt-1:stmnt-2-+
   >---+--------------------+--+-----------+--->< 
       +--COUNT(-+-n-----+-)--+  +--NOTIFY----+
                 +-n,m---+        +--NONOTIFY--+
                 +-n,m,k-+


   TOP for main menu                          hit ENTER for next page
```

Figure 5-48   The first HELP screen for the AT command

Objectives

1. Identify each of the COBTEST command entry areas and explain how they are used.

2. Explain how to retrieve COBTEST commands from the log area.

3. Explain how to use cursor-oriented commands.

4. Use COBTEST full-screen commands to perform the following functions:

    a. set screen parameters
    b. display source listings
    c. use the auto monitoring area
    d. search panel areas
    e. position the cursor
    f. execute a program dynamically
    g. use the suffix area for frequency tallying
    h. display information on COBTEST commands

Section

4

Related subjects

In the three previous sections, I presented the information that's essential if you're going to use and understand VS COBOL II. Now, I'll present some related subjects you might be interested in. In chapter 6, I'll explain how VS COBOL II will affect your CICS programming. And in chapter 7, I'll give you some ideas on when and how to convert to VS COBOL II.

Chapter
six

How VS COBOL II affects CICS
programming

If you're using CICS/OS/VS Release 1.7 or later, you can use VS COBOL II for your CICS programs. VS COBOL II provides many of the same advantages under CICS as it does under MVS/XA. For example, under CICS, your programs can use 31-bit addressing, you can request formatted dumps using the FDUMP option, and you can use many of the new language elements. (In general, the language elements you can't use are those related to file handling.) In addition, there are some improvements that are specific to CICS. I'll present those improvements in this chapter.

Before I go on, you should realize that VS COBOL II supports only command level CICS. It does not support macro level CICS. Any macro calls issued in a CICS program that's compiled with VS COBOL II will produce diagnostics.

Using the Linkage Section

Probably the most noticeable change in terms of coding VS COBOL II programs under CICS is in the way you address data areas defined outside of your program. Under OS/VS COBOL, you had to code a series of *Base Locator for Linkage cells* (*BLL cells*) to hold the addresses of these areas. Under VS COBOL II, you simply use the ADDRESS special register.

To illustrate, look at figure 6-1. It compares the coding for addressing areas outside of your CICS program under OS/VS COBOL and VS COBOL II. To be specific, it shows you how fields in the *Common Work Area (CWA)* are addressed. The Common Work Area is an area of storage that's available to all tasks in a CICS system. If you've used CICS under OS/VS COBOL, the coding in the top portion of the figure should look familiar to you.

Under both OS/VS COBOL and VS COBOL II, the CWA must be defined in the Linkage Section. To access the CWA under OS/VS COBOL, you need to define a field in the Linkage Section to hold its address. In figure 6-1, it's the second field defined under BLL-CELLS, BLL-CWA. (The first field under BLL-CELLS holds the address of BLL-CELLS itself.) To load the address of the Common Work Area into BLL-CWA, you issue this command:

```
EXEC CICS
     ADDRESS CWA(BLL-CWA)
END-EXEC.
```

Once the address has been loaded, the fields in the CWA can be accessed.

Under VS COBOL II, the use of BLL cells isn't necessary. In fact, it isn't even allowed. Instead, you use the ADDRESS special register. In chapter 3, I explained that a separate ADDRESS special register is automatically provided for each field in the Linkage Section that's defined at the 01 level. To access the Common Work Area, then, all you need to do is issue an ADDRESS command like this:

```
EXEC CICS
     ADDRESS CWA(ADDRESS OF COMMON-WORK-AREA)
END-EXEC.
```

This is illustrated in the bottom portion of figure 6-1.

Using the ADDRESS special register simplifies coding in other ways, too. First, under OS/VS COBOL, you have to use the SERVICE RELOAD statement to insure addressability to areas defined in the Linkage Section. That means any time you issue a CICS command that modifies a BLL cell, you have to follow it with a SERVICE RELOAD statement. (Actually, SERVICE RELOAD is required only if the COBOL OPTIMIZE option is used; however, it's recommended even if OPTIMIZE isn't used.) In contrast, under VS COBOL II, you don't need the SERVICE RELOAD statement at all since there aren't any BLL cells to worry about.

Second, under OS/VS COBOL, the size of an area addressed by a BLL cell is limited to 4K bytes. So, if an area is larger than 4K bytes, multiple BLL cells have to be used to address the entire area. Replacing BLL cells with the ADDRESS special register eliminates this problem too.

```
OS/VS COBOL

 LINKAGE SECTION.
*
 01   DFHCOMMAREA                 PIC X.
*
 01   BLL-CELLS.
*
      05   FILLER                 PIC S9(8)    COMP.
      05   BLL-CWA                PIC S9(8)    COMP.
*
 01   COMMON-WORK-AREA.
*
      05   CWA-CURRENT-DATE       PIC X(8).
      05   CWA-COMPANY-NAME       PIC X(30).
*
 PROCEDURE DIVISION.
*
        .
        .
      EXEC CICS
          ADDRESS CWA(BLL-CWA)
      END-EXEC.
        .
        .


VS COBOL II

 LINKAGE SECTION.
*
 01   DFHCOMMAREA                 PIC X.
*
 01   COMMON-WORK-AREA.
*
      05   CWA-CURRENT-DATE       PIC X(8).
      05   CWA-COMPANY-NAME       PIC X(30).
*
 PROCEDURE DIVISION.
*
        .
        .
      EXEC CICS
          ADDRESS CWA(ADDRESS OF COMMON-WORK-AREA)
      END-EXEC.
        .
        .
```

Figure 6-1   Addressing areas outside of your CICS program

Unfortunately, eliminating BLL cells with all their programming complications introduces a new, even larger problem: the need for program conversion. Any program now running under CICS with the OS/VS COBOL compiler will *not* run under VS COBOL II if it uses BLL cells. This is a particular problem if the CICS programs in your shop rely on locate-mode I/O, which uses I/O areas in the Linkage Section rather than in the Working-Storage Section. In that case, you have to convert and recompile just about every program on your system. The same is true if you make frequent use of CICS areas like the Common Work Area (CWA), Terminal Control Table User Area (TCTUA), or Transaction Work Area (TWA). Although the conversion is straightforward, it's time-consuming.

Specifying the length of I/O areas

With OS/VS COBOL, you frequently have to code the LENGTH option on CICS I/O commands to indicate the length of the data area the command is to process. For example, when you read a record from a variable-length file, you have to use the LENGTH option to specify the largest record your program can read. After the read operation is completed, CICS places the actual length of the record that was read in the field you specified in the LENGTH option. Similarly, in the WRITE command, the LENGTH option specifies the size of the record to be written. You can omit LENGTH in an OS/VS COBOL program only when the file is fixed-length (for example, when you're processing fixed-length VSAM files or using BMS maps, which have a defined length).

Under VS COBOL II, you normally don't have to code the LENGTH option. Instead, CICS uses a new VS COBOL II facility, the LENGTH special register, to determine the length of the data you want to process. When you omit the LENGTH option from an I/O command, the CICS translator incorporates the LENGTH register into the command, using it to record the length of the data area you specify in the FROM or INTO option. As a result, you have to specify LENGTH only when you want to use less than the currently defined length of the data area.

Figure 6-2 should help you understand how this works. It shows you two versions of a program that reads a record and then rewrites it. In each version, the record is variable-length, consisting of a root segment (8 bytes) and an invoice segment (16 bytes) that occurs up to 10 times, depending on the value of CM-INVOICE-COUNT. Thus, if all 10 invoice segments are used, the total record length is 168 bytes (an 8-byte root segment plus ten 16-byte invoice segments). If only one invoice segment is used, the record has a length of 24 bytes (an 8-byte root segment plus one 16-byte invoice segment).

OS/VS COBOL

```
 WORKING-STORAGE SECTION.
*
 01   WORK-FIELDS.
*
     05   WS-CUSTMAS-LENGTH        PIC S9(4)         COMP        VALUE 158.
*
 01   CUSTOMER-MASTER-RECORD.
*
     05   CM-ROOT-SEQMENT.
          10   CM-CUSTOMER-NO       PIC X(6).
          10   CM-INVOICE-COUNT     PIC S9(3)         COMP-3.
     05   CM-INVOICE-SEGMENT        OCCURS 1 TO 10 TIMES
                                    DEPENDING ON CM-INVOICE-COUNT.
          10   CM-INVOICE-DATE      PIC 9(6).
          10   CM-INVOICE-NO        PIC X(6).
          10   CM-INVOICE-AMOUNT    PIC S9(5)V99      COMP-3.
     .
     .


*
 PROCEDURE DIVISION.
*
 0000-UPDATE-CUSTOMER-RECORD SECTION.
*
       .
       .
*
 1100-READ-CUSTOMER-RECORD SECTION.
*
     MOVE 168 TO WS-CUSTMAS-LENGTH.
     EXEC CICS
         READ DATASET('CUSTMAS')
              INTO(CUSTOMER-MASTER-RECORD)
              LENGTH(WS-CUSTMAS-LENGTH)
              RIDFLD(CM-CUSTOMER-NO)
              UPDATE
     END-EXEC.
     .
     .
*
 1400-REWRITE-CUSTOMER-RECORD SECTION.
*
     COMPUTE WS-CUSTMAS-LENGTH = 8 + CM-INVOICE-COUNT * 16.
     EXEC CICS
         REWRITE DATASET('CUSTMAS')
                 FROM(CUSTOMER-MASTER-RECORD)
                 LENGTH(WS-CUSTMAS-LENGTH)
     END-EXEC.
     .
     .
```

Figure 6-2   Specifying the length of an I/O area (part 1 of 2)

```
VS COBOL II

 WORKING-STORAGE SECTION.
*
 01   CUSTOMER-MASTER-RECORD.
*
     05   CM-ROOT-SEGMENT.
          10   CM-CUSTOMER-NO         PIC X(6).
          10   CM-INVOICE-COUNT       PIC S9(3)        COMP-3.
     05   CM-INVOICE-SEGMENT          OCCURS 1 TO 10 TIMES
                                      DEPENDING ON CM-INVOICE-COUNT.
          10   CM-INVOICE-DATE        PIC 9(6).
          10   CM-INVOICE-NO          PIC X(6).
          10   CM-INVOICE-AMOUNT      PIC S9(5)V99     COMP-3.
     .
     .

*
 PROCEDURE DIVISION.
*
 0000-UPDATE-CUSTOMER-RECORD SECTION.
*
     .
     .
*
 1100-READ-CUSTOMER-RECORD SECTION.
*
     MOVE 10 TO CM-INVOICE-COUNT.
     EXEC CICS
         READ DATASET('CUSTMAS')
              INTO(CUSTOMER-MASTER-RECORD)
              RIDFLD(CM-CUSTOMER-NO)
              UPDATE
     END-EXEC.
     .
     .
*
 1400-REWRITE-CUSTOMER-RECORD SECTION.
*
     EXEC CICS
         REWRITE DATASET('CUSTMAS')
                 FROM(CUSTOMER-MASTER-RECORD)
     END-EXEC.
     .
     .
```

Figure 6-2   Specifying the length of an I/O area (part 2 of 2)

Part 1 of figure 6-2 shows how you would process this record using OS/VS COBOL. Here, I coded a binary halfword field (WS-CUSTMAS-LENGTH) to hold the length of the customer record, and I specified WS-CUSTMAS-LENGTH in the LENGTH option of both the READ and REWRITE commands. In the READ command, WS-CUSTMAS-LENGTH has two functions: first, it specifies the length of the longest record the program will process (168 bytes); second, it holds the length of the record that was actually read. In the REWRITE command, WS-CUSTMAS-LENGTH indicates the length of the record to be rewritten.

The COMPUTE statement in module 1400 calculates the new length of the customer record. It simply multiplies 16 by the number of invoice segments (CM-INVOICE-COUNT) and adds 8 to allow for the root segment. If the COMPUTE statement were omitted, the record would be rewritten using the length of the record that was read, even if the program changed the length by adding or deleting an invoice segment.

Part 2 of figure 6-2 shows that under VS/COBOL II, the LENGTH option isn't required. On the READ command, CICS uses the length of the INTO area (CUSTOMER-MASTER-RECORD) as the maximum the program will accept. And on the REWRITE command, CICS uses the FROM area to determine the length of the record to be rewritten.

The coding in part 2 of figure 6-2 works properly because the length of a working storage field can vary if the OCCURS DEPENDING ON clause is used. Thus, the length of CUSTOMER-MASTER-RECORD depends on the value of CM-INVOICE-COUNT. That length will be at its maximum when the READ command is executed because I initialized CM-INVOICE-COUNT to 10 (the maximum number of occurrences for the invoice segment) before issuing the READ command.

Notice that there's no need to compute a new record length in module 1400 of the VS COBOL II code. That's because CICS uses the LENGTH register to recalculate the record length each time the REWRITE command is issued.

I hope you can appreciate the value of the LENGTH register. It takes the burden of counting data area lengths off the programmer and puts it on the computer, where it belongs. Fortunately, the introduction of the LENGTH register is less painful than that of the ADDRESS register. Since coding the LENGTH option on your CICS commands still works under VS COBOL II, you don't have to convert your existing programs.

**Statements restricted under OS/VS COBOL
that are permitted under VS COBOL II**

Because of the nature of CICS, certain COBOL statements cannot be used in
CICS programs. For example, you can't issue READ or WRITE statements in
a COBOL program that runs under CICS. With VS COBOL II, however, you
can use a few of the statements that you can't use with OS/VS COBOL. These
newly supported statements are the CALL statement, the string handling
statements (INSPECT, STRING, and UNSTRING), and the STOP RUN
statement.

The CALL statement   Under OS/VS COBOL, you can't use the CALL
statement in a CICS program to invoke another CICS program. And, although
you can use a CALL statement to invoke a program that doesn't contain CICS
commands, it causes complications with the linkage editor. So, the CALL
statement isn't generally used.

Under VS COBOL II, however, you can use the CALL statement whether
or not the program it invokes uses CICS commands. There is one restriction,
though: your CALL statement must always pass the addresses of DFHEIBLK
(the *Execute Interface Block*) and DFHCOMMAREA (the *communication
area*) as the first two parameters. (DFHEIBLK is an area that contains
information related to the current task, and DFHCOMMAREA is an area used
to pass data from one program execution to the next.) For example, if you want
to call a subprogram that requires a date and a switch to be passed to it, you
code the CALL statement like this:

```
CALL 'DATEDIT' USING DFHEIBLK
                     DFHCOMMAREA
                     VALID-DATE
                     VALID-DATE-SW.
```

Then, DFHEIBLK and DFHCOMMAREA are automatically added to the
Linkage Section of the subprogram by the CICS translator, and the parameters
are added to the USING phrase of the Procedure Division statement. In other
words, no special coding is required in the subprogram.

String handling statements   Under OS/VS COBOL, the string handling
statements INSPECT, STRING, and UNSTRING are not allowed in CICS
programs. You can use them under VS COBOL II, however, because VS
COBOL II implements them differently. Although you probably won't use
these statements in many programs, there are situations in which you'll find
them useful.

The STOP RUN statement   The STOP RUN statement has long been notorious for crashing CICS systems. In brief, if your program issues a STOP RUN under CICS, it doesn't just end your program; it terminates the entire CICS system! The proper way to end a CICS program, then, is to use a CICS RETURN command, not a STOP RUN statement.

Most CICS installations quickly learn that even if you don't code a STOP RUN statement, the compiler generates one for you at the end of your program. That way, if control inadvertently falls out of the back of your program, the STOP RUN is executed. That's great for a batch program, but disastrous for a CICS program. More than one CICS system has been crashed because of a program that let its control fall through to the compiler-generated STOP RUN statement.

With VS COBOL II, STOP RUN doesn't bring down the entire system; instead, it works just like the CICS RETURN command. However, I still recommend you never use STOP RUN. That way, if you ever find yourself working on a system that doesn't support VS COBOL II, you won't cause CICS to crash by coding a STOP RUN statement out of habit.

Discussion

Depending on your shop's situation, converting your CICS applications to VS COBOL II may or may not be difficult. If you make heavy use of Linkage Section coding, you have a major conversion effort on your hands. If you don't, the conversion effort will be much more manageable.

Don't forget that most of the other VS COBOL II enhancements I've described in this book can be used in CICS programs. For example, you can use the END-IF delimiter to make your IF statements more readable. And you can use the EVALUATE statement and inline PERFORM statements. Used properly, these statements and the other new VS COBOL II features can make on-line programs easier to code and maintain.

Finally, many shops are converting from CICS release 1.6 to CICS 1.7 as they convert from OS/VS COBOL to VS COBOL II. If you're in that situation, you should realize that additional programming enhancements are available with CICS 1.7.

Terminology

Base Locator for Linkage cells	CWA
BLL cells	Execute Interface Block
Common Work Area	communication area

Objectives

1. Use the ADDRESS special register in your CICS programs to address data areas defined outside your programs.

2. Explain when you need to use the LENGTH option on an I/O command to specify the length of an I/O area and when you can use the LENGTH special register instead.

3. Describe the COBOL language elements that can be used with CICS under VS COBOL II that weren't allowed under OS/VS COBOL.

Chapter
seven

Converting to VS COBOL II

If you're a manager, you probably have some important decisions to make about VS COBOL II. Not only do you need to decide when your shop will convert to it, you also need to decide how the conversion will be implemented.

If you're a COBOL programmer, chances are you don't have much to say about when and how your shop converts to VS COBOL II. However, you may be involved in the program conversions. If you are, you need to know what programming changes you'll have to make as you move from OS/VS COBOL to VS COBOL II. And you'll need to know how to make them.

In this chapter, I'll start by presenting the conversion requirements. Then, I'll present the conversion aids that are available to you as you convert from OS/VS COBOL to VS COBOL II, and I'll present the conversion alternatives that you have when you install VS COBOL II. I'll finish by presenting the costs and benefits of converting to VS COBOL II so you can decide for yourself when you should install it in your shop.

Conversion requirements

Figure 7-1 summarizes the language elements that have to be changed as you convert from OS/VS COBOL to VS COBOL II. If you study this list, you can see that most of the changes are required because VS COBOL II doesn't support the Report Writer module, the communication module, the debug module, ISAM files, or BDAM files. In addition, VS COBOL II doesn't

---

OS/VS COBOL language element	Required change/Explanation
Identification Division	
REMARKS paragraph	Replace with comment line (* in column 7).
Environment Division	
NOMINAL KEY clause	ISAM not supported; replace with VSAM code.
TRACK-AREA clause	ISAM not supported; replace with VSAM code.
FILE-LIMITS clause	Omit.
PROCESSING MODE clause	Omit.
Report Writer file description entry	Omit or use precompiler; Report Writer module not supported.
REPORT(S) IS (ARE)	Omit or use precompiler; Report Writer module not supported.
Data Division	
Communication Section	Omit; communication module not supported.
Report Section	Omit or use precompiler; Report Writer module not supported.
Procedure Division	
ACCEPT MESSAGE COUNT statement	Omit; communication module not supported.
Debug packets	Replace with USE FOR DEBUGGING declarative.
DISABLE statement	Omit; communication module not supported.
ENABLE statement	Omit; communication module not supported.
EXAMINE statement	Replace with INSPECT statement.
EXHIBIT statement	Replace with DISPLAY statement.
GENERATE statement	Omit or use precompiler; Report Writer module not supported.
INITIATE statement	Omit or use precompiler; Report Writer module not supported.

Figure 7-1   Changes required to convert OS/VS COBOL programs to VS COBOL II (part 1 of 2)

OS/VS COBOL language element	Required change/Explanation
Procedure Division (continued)	
NOTE statement	Replace with comment line (* in column 7).
ON statement	Omit.
READY TRACE statement	Treated as comment.
RECEIVE statement	Omit; communication module not supported.
RESET TRACE statement	Treated as comment.
SEEK statement	Omit.
SEND statement	Omit; communication module not supported.
TERMINATE statement	Omit or use precompiler; Report Writer module not supported.
TRANSFORM statement	Replace with INSPECT statement.
Compiler-directing statements	
USE BEFORE REPORTING statement	Omit or use precompiler; Report Writer module not supported.
USE FOR DEBUGGING statement	Omit any statements that reference communication description entries, identifiers, or file names; level 2 of the debug module not supported.
Special registers	
CURRENT-DATE	Replace with DATE special register and ACCEPT statement.
PAGE-COUNTER	Omit or use precompiler; Report Writer module not supported.
TIME-OF-DAY	Replace with TIME special register and ACCEPT statement.

Figure 7-1   Changes required to convert OS/VS COBOL programs to VS COBOL II (part 2 of 2)

support language that wasn't a part of the 1974 COBOL standards, such as the EXAMINE statement, the TRANSFORM statement, and the CURRENT-DATE register. As a result, if a program doesn't use any of these elements, the conversion process can be an easy one.

Not shown in figure 7-1 are the changes required in programs that use CICS. In particular, you can't use BLL cells in your CICS programs when you use VS COBOL II, so you'll have to remove any statements that manipulate BLL cells and replace any references to BLL cells with the ADDRESS special register. Also, remember that you can use VS COBOL II only if you have CICS Release 1.7 or later installed on your system.

Also not shown in figure 7-1 are the changes that may be required because of the difference in execution of some language elements under Release 3 of VS COBOL II. In particular, you should note that the file status codes have changed under Release 3. So if your program tests file status codes, the codes may need to be changed. Appendix D contains a complete list of the Release 2 and Release 3 file status codes. Refer back to figure 4-11 for a list of all the language elements that execute differently under Release 3.

Conversion aids

To help you convert your programs from OS/VS COBOL to VS COBOL II, IBM offers several conversion aids. To start, if you're using the OS/VS COBOL compiler Release 2.4, you can specify the MIGR option. Then, the compiler will flag any statements that need to be changed when you convert to VS COBOL II. Since this option can be used before VS COBOL II is installed, you might want to start using it right away. Then, you can be sure that the programs you're creating or maintaining are acceptable to VS COBOL II.

When you use the MIGR option, you should realize that the VS COBOL II compiler may catch some syntax errors that are not detected by the OS/VS COBOL compiler. That's because the VS COBOL II compiler applies a stricter interpretation of the syntax rules. As a result, you may still have to change the syntax of some of the statements in your programs when you compile them under VS COBOL II, even though no messages are produced when they're compiled under OS/VS COBOL with the MIGR option.

To automate the conversion process, IBM offers *COBOL Conversion Aids* that do the required coding conversions for you. These aids provide programs that convert both OS/VS COBOL and CICS source programs to VS COBOL II source programs. The conversion programs operate under MVS Release 3.8, MVS/SP Version 1, or MVS/XA. You also need ISPF and ISPF/PDF to process the necessary menus and panels. And you need a sort program that can be used in conjunction with the sort feature of OS/VS COBOL Release 2 for processing the reserved word table and some of the reports.

The COBOL Conversion Aids consist of three components: the *Language Conversion Programs* (*LCPs*), the *LCP compiler*, and the *driver*. Figure 7-2

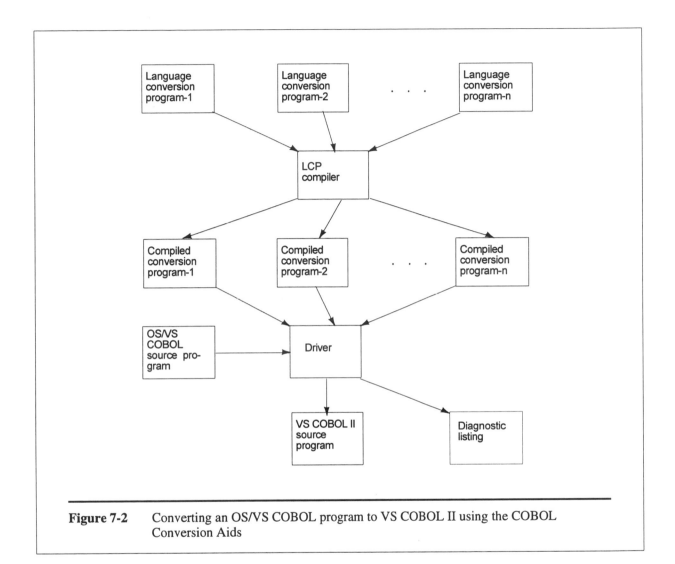

Figure 7-2   Converting an OS/VS COBOL program to VS COBOL II using the COBOL
Conversion Aids

shows schematically how these components are used to convert your source
programs.

The LCPs are source programs written in a COBOL-like language. These
programs describe how the different OS/VS COBOL elements are to be
converted to VS COBOL II. If necessary, you can customize the LCPs to
provide the specific conversions required for your shop. As you can see in
figure 7-2, there are many different LCPs. In fact, there is one for each COBOL
statement to be processed.

After you have the LCPs in the form you want them, you compile them
using the LCP Compiler. The LCP compiler transforms the LCPs into code

that can be interpreted by the driver. In figure 7-2, this code is referred to as a compiled conversion program. There is one compiled conversion program for each LCP.

The driver is the component that reads the specified OS/VS COBOL source program, makes the changes specified by the compiled LCPs, and creates a VS COBOL II source program. As it executes, the driver extracts and converts any COPY members used by the program. It also checks to make sure that data names in the program don't conflict with VS COBOL II reserved words. If a conflict occurs, a suffix, which you can specify, is added to the data name. Finally, the driver creates a diagnostic listing that shows the results of the conversion.

If you use the COBOL Conversion Aids, you should realize that there may be some code that can be only partially converted or can't be converted at all. For example, none of the language elements from the Report Writer or the communication modules have equivalents in VS COBOL II. When that's the case, an appropriate message is printed on the diagnostic listing created by the driver.

If you used Report Writer in your old programs and want to continue using it, a Report Writer precompiler is also available from IBM. It works as illustrated in figure 7-3. As you can see, the precompiler converts a program with Report Writer to a program without Report Writer. Then, the program can be compiled by the VS COBOL II compiler. You can use the precompiler to simplify the conversion of old programs to VS COBOL II, but you can also use it for new program development in conjunction with VS COBOL II if you want to continue using Report Writer in your shop.

Now that you know what the conversion aids are, you can see that the conversion difficulty depends on what you've used in your programs. If your programs don't use Report Writer, the communication module, ISAM or BDAM files, BLL cells under CICS, or language that wasn't approved by the 1974 standards, conversion can be a simple, straightforward process. But even if you have used these elements, the conversion process can be manageable if you use the conversion aids that are available. By the way, there are also some third party products available for converting from OS/VS COBOL to VS COBOL II. And although I won't recommend any specifically, you might want to check into them yourself.

In addition to program conversion, you should realize that you may also have to do some file conversion when you convert a set of programs to VS COBOL II. Since VS COBOL II doesn't support ISAM or BDAM files, you'll have to convert these files to VSAM files before your VS COBOL II programs can process them. For some BDAM files, this conversion process can be difficult.

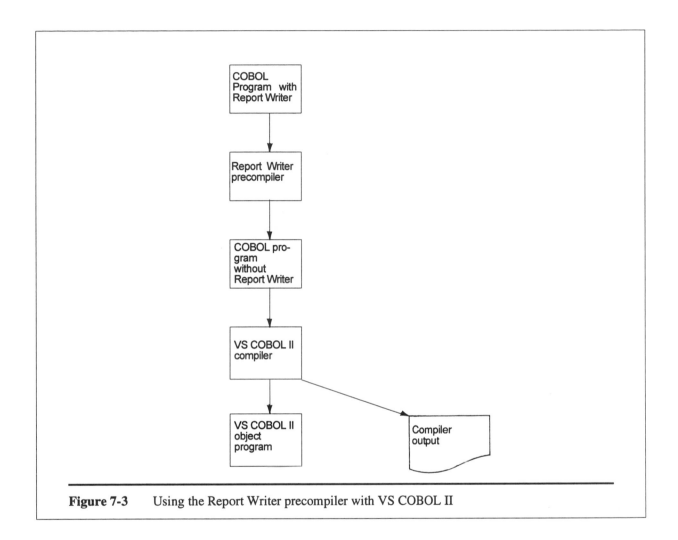

Figure 7-3   Using the Report Writer precompiler with VS COBOL II

Conversion alternatives

Once you decide to install VS COBOL II in your shop, you have to decide when and how you're going to convert your old programs to the new compiler. Because each shop is different, I'm not going to try to give you specific suggestions. But let me outline the three basic approaches you can take.

One extreme is to use the VS COBOL II compiler for new program development and to continue to use OS/VS COBOL for old program maintenance and enhancement. That way you get the benefits of VS COBOL II in your new programs, and you don't have the cost of converting your old programs. However, you do have the cost of maintaining both compilers as well as the cost of training and managing a staff that has to work with both compilers. Also, you're probably going to have to convert your old programs to VS COBOL II eventually, so you're just delaying the process.

The other extreme is to convert all old programs to VS COBOL II as soon as possible after the VS COBOL II compiler is installed. If you're running a small shop with a limited number of old programs, this is likely to be your best alternative. In a large shop with thousands of old programs, though, this alternative will probably be impractical. In a shop like this, the older programs are likely to include many statements that are IBM extensions or statements that are based on the 1968 COBOL standards. Although these statements were supported by the OS/VS COBOL compiler using the LANGLVL(1) compiler option, they aren't supported under VS COBOL II. In addition, the older programs are likely to be written in an unstructured style that will be far more difficult to work with than programs written in a more modern, structured style.

For most shops, the most practical approach to conversion is going to be somewhere between the two extremes. In this case, you develop a plan for converting certain types of old programs over a period of several months or years. One option here is to start by converting the programs that will benefit the most from VS COBOL II. For example, you may begin by converting all of your CICS programs. After they're converted, you can continue with the next set of programs that will benefit the most from being converted. And so on. Eventually, when you're left with a miscellaneous group of programs that haven't been converted, you can make one last plan for completing the conversion job.

In some shops, you may prefer to start by converting the programs that are easiest to convert rather than those that will benefit the most from VS COBOL II. If, for example, you know that 80 percent of your programs don't use any of the elements that will cause problems during conversion, you can convert these first; these conversions should go quickly and easily. Then, you can plan the conversion of the remaining programs in phases that are based on how much the programs will benefit from VS COBOL II or on how difficult they will be to convert.

No matter which approach you take, planning is critical. You need to decide which conversion aids you're going to use and how you're going to use them. You need to decide which programs you're going to convert and when you're going to convert them. And you need to decide which files (if any) you're going to convert and when you're going to convert them.

The costs of converting to VS COBOL II

Before you can decide whether or not you should install VS COBOL II in your shop, you need to know what the costs associated with it are. These costs are

Software costs

    The VS COBOL II compiler
    The IBM COBOL Conversion Aids
    The Report Writer precompiler

Training costs

Conversion costs

    Computer and programmer costs for converting files from ISAM and BDAM to VSAM
    Computer and programmer costs for converting programs from OS/VS COBOL to VS COBOL II

Figure 7-4   The costs of converting to VS COBOL II

summarized in figure 7-4. As you can see, you have to consider the costs of the software that you want as well as the costs related to training and conversion.

As I write this, the purchase price of VS COBOL II, including the compiler and library, ranges from about $15,000 to about $60,000 depending on the system on which it's being installed, plus a monthly charge for software maintenance. Or, you can purchase a license to use the software for an initial charge of about $6500 and a monthly charge of about $1100. If you decide to use the IBM Conversion Aids, you'll pay a one-time charge of $5500 or a monthly charge of $250. And if you decide that you want to use the Report Writer precompiler, you'll pay a one-time charge of $8500. For most MVS shops those charges are relatively trivial.

To train your programmers to use VS COBOL II, you can use a self-instructional book like this one, run informal seminars, or conduct formal classes. Before you can do this, though, you have to decide how you want the features of VS COBOL II to be implemented in your shop. Since it's relatively easy to train experienced programmers to use VS COBOL II once you've made these decisions, your training expense shouldn't be prohibitive.

In most shops, the major cost of VS COBOL II is going to be the cost of converting programs from OS/VS COBOL. At the least, you have to run the Conversion Aids driver on each program you're going to convert and then compile the resulting VS COBOL II source program. If you have a thousand or more programs in your shop, the computer time for the conversion can be a huge expense in itself. To make matters worse, the Conversion Aids won't work for all programs, so some of the conversion work will have to be done by programmers. In addition, if you take the time to test each of the applications you convert to make sure that they still work the way they should, you'll probably discover some minor debugging problems that will have to be resolved by your programmers.

In short, the costs of converting to VS COBOL II can be substantial. Besides that, it can be frustrating to take some of your programmers away from program maintenance or program development while they convert programs from one compiler to another. That's why you have to feel that the costs of VS COBOL II are justified by some obvious benefits before you decide to make the conversion.

The benefits of converting to VS COBOL II

Figure 7-5 summarizes the main benefits you get from VS COBOL II. Obviously, the more programs you convert to VS COBOL II, the more your shop benefits from having this compiler. However, the question for old programs is this: Do the benefits justify the cost of program conversion? If not, you may decide to use VS COBOL II for new program development only.

Although much of the interest in VS COBOL II has been concerned with the new language for structured programming, I don't think that these features will have much effect on the way you code your structured programs. This is particularly true if you code each module of your programs as a single COBOL paragraph as we recommend in *How to Design and Develop COBOL Programs*. On the other hand, if you code each module as a section and you allow more than one paragraph in each section, you'll probably find that some of the structured programming enhancements, such as inline PERFORM statements, will help you improve your programs. In general, though, I think the structured programming enhancements will provide a relatively trivial benefit in a structured shop and no benefit at all in an unstructured shop.

For CICS programs, VS COBOL II provides a significant benefit because it simplifies coding. This means that CICS programs under VS COBOL II can be written so they're easier to read and maintain. In particular, the use of the ADDRESS special register will improve the readability of a CICS program.

In some shops, the VS COBOL II performance improvements justify the costs associated with this compiler. For instance, many shops that needed 31-bit addressing have already installed this compiler. For them, this feature alone justified the related costs.

When it comes to debugging, the improved compiler listings and formatted dumps of VS COBOL II are a definite benefit. But the feature that will have the most dramatic effect on your testing and debugging is VS COBOL II Debug. As I said in chapter 5, VS COBOL II Debug is a much improved and expanded version of the separately licensed IBM product OS COBOL Inter-

---

Structured programming enhancements

Easier CICS coding

Performance improvements

    31-bit addressing
    Reentrant programs
    Improved optimization
    Faster sorting

Improved debugging features

    VS COBOL II Debug
    Improved compiler listings
    Improved dump format

Compiler improvements

    Checking for out-of-range conditions
    Increased compiler limits

Other features

    Controls for reserved words
    Controls for compiler options
    More feedback from VSAM requests
    More flexibility for preloading programs under IMS/VS
    The Extended Graphic Character Set

Standardization

Figure 7-5   The benefits of converting to VS COBOL II

active Debug. Whether you're working in a batch or interactive environment, VS COBOL II Debug simplifies debugging. If you're working in an environment that supports the full-screen mode of the debugger, the development time you'll save using this feature alone will probably justify the cost of VS COBOL II.

The compiler improvements and other features listed in figure 7-5 are nice to have. But the benefits they provide are trivial when compared with the costs of VS COBOL II.

As for standardization, the value of this benefit depends on your shop. In some shops, like government shops, this benefit is an important one because all programs have to conform to the 1974 or 1985 ANS standards. In other shops, standardization is important so programmers can use the same language on both IBM and non-IBM systems. In many shops, though, since the 1985 standards don't provide for the development of interactive programs, the value of this benefit is questionable.

Discussion

As I said at the start of this chapter, I'm not going to try to tell you if, when, or how you should convert to VS COBOL II. What I've tried to do in this chapter is to summarize the information you need for making this decision yourself.

From a practical point of view, though, I don't think you have to ask whether or not you should convert to VS COBOL II. Spokesmen for IBM have already said that no major enhancements will be made to the OS/VS COBOL compiler in the future, and that alone should convince you that you're eventually going to have to convert. In addition, the new compiler provides enough benefits to justify the costs of conversion in most shops. As a result, your primary question at this time should be *when* to convert to VS COBOL II.

Before Release 3 of VS COBOL II was available, I think the consensus was to put off the conversion as long as possible. Now that Release 3 is available, however, I think we'll see more and more shops converting to VS COBOL II. But if it's not essential that you convert to VS COBOL II right away, you might consider putting off the conversion until you're sure that all the bugs are out of the compiler. On the other hand, the longer you delay the conversion, the more programs you'll have to convert later on. So you don't want to put the conversion off too long.

Perhaps the best recommendation is that you make a preliminary plan for conversion as soon as possible, no matter how far off your conversion date is going to be. Then, your programmers can start developing their new programs with the VS COBOL II compiler in mind so they'll be easier to convert later on. They can also start modifying old programs during maintenance activities so they'll be easier to convert. Although this is a simple first step, it's one that can save you thousands of dollars when you eventually do convert to VS COBOL II.

Terminology

COBOL Conversion Aids
Language Conversion Program

LCP
LCP compiler
driver

Objectives

1. Prepare an analysis of the costs and benefits of your shop converting to VS COBOL II.

2. Develop a preliminary conversion plan for your shop.

Appendix
A

VS COBOL II statement format summary

This appendix presents a summary of VS COBOL II statement formats. The summary includes the statements presented in section 2 of this book as well as some that aren't presented anywhere else in this book. If a statement isn't presented in this appendix, you can assume that its format and use are the same as they were under OS/VS COBOL.

Throughout this appendix, I've shaded the elements of each statement that are new in VS COBOL II. If an element is shaded *and* enclosed in a box, that means it's a Release 3 element. In addition, I've included notes that describe functional or operational differences that don't affect the syntax of a statement. These notes are shaded as well. If any elements have been omitted from VS COBOL II, they have simply been left out of the syntax of the statement.

I've divided this appendix into five sections. The first section contains some general information about VS COBOL II. The last four sections correspond to the four program divisions: the Identification Division, the Environment Division, the Data Division, and the Procedure Division.

The rules for the notation used in this appendix are:

1. Words printed entirely in capital letters are COBOL reserved words.

2. Words printed in lowercase letters represent names, literals, or statements that must be supplied by the programmer.

3. Braces {} enclosing a group of items indicate that the programmer must choose one of them.

4. When a single item is enclosed in braces, it means the ellipsis that follow applies to that item only—not to the entire statement or clause (see rule 6 below).

5. Brackets [] indicate that the enclosed item may be used or omitted, depending on the requirements of the program.

6. The ellipsis ... indicates that an element may be repeated as many times as necessary.

7. Underlined reserved words are required unless the element itself is optional. Words that aren't underlined are optional.

8. In general, the clauses and phrases in a statement should be coded in the sequence shown.

GENERAL INFORMATION

Character set

Characters used for words and names

A-Z   Uppercase letters
a-z   Lowercase letters
0-9   Digits
-     Hyphen

Characters used to show relationships

=   Equals
<   Less than
>   Greater than
<=   Less than or equal to
>=   Greater than or equal to

Rules for forming non-numeric literals

1. Maximum of 160 characters or 320 hexadecimal digits.
2. Enclosed in quotation marks.
3. Hexadecimal literal preceded by X.

Subscripting format

```
data-name-1 ( ⎧integer-1                      ⎫
              ⎨data-name-2 [  +   integer-2]  ⎬...)
              ⎩               -               ⎭
```

Condition formats

Relation conditions

$$
\left\{
\begin{array}{l}
\texttt{identifier-1} \\
\texttt{literal-1} \\
\texttt{arithmetic-expression-1} \\
\texttt{index-name-1}
\end{array}
\right\}
\left\{
\begin{array}{l}
\texttt{IS [NOT] GREATER THAN} \\
\texttt{IS [NOT] LESS THAN} \\
\texttt{IS [NOT] EQUAL TO} \\
\texttt{IS GREATER THAN OR EQUAL TO} \\
\texttt{IS LESS THAN OR EQUAL TO}
\end{array}
\right\}
\left\{
\begin{array}{l}
\texttt{identifier-2} \\
\texttt{literal-2} \\
\texttt{arithmetic-expression-2} \\
\texttt{index-name-2}
\end{array}
\right\}
$$

$$
\left\{
\begin{array}{l}
\texttt{identifier-1} \\
\texttt{literal-1} \\
\texttt{arithmetic-expression-1} \\
\texttt{index-name-1}
\end{array}
\right\}
\left\{
\begin{array}{l}
\texttt{IS [NOT] >} \\
\texttt{IS [NOT] <} \\
\texttt{IS [NOT] =} \\
\texttt{IS >=} \\
\texttt{IS <=}
\end{array}
\right\}
\left\{
\begin{array}{l}
\texttt{identifier-2} \\
\texttt{literal-2} \\
\texttt{arithmetic-expression-2} \\
\texttt{index-name-2}
\end{array}
\right\}
$$

Class conditions

$$
\texttt{identifier IS [NOT]}
\left\{
\begin{array}{l}
\texttt{NUMERIC} \\
\texttt{ALPHABETIC} \\
\texttt{ALPHABETIC-LOWER} \\
\texttt{ALPHABETIC-UPPER} \\
\texttt{DBCS} \\
\texttt{KANJI} \\
\texttt{class-name}
\end{array}
\right\}
$$

Reference modification format

```
data-name (leftmost-character-position: [length])
```

Identifier format

$$
\texttt{data-name [(}
\left\{
\begin{array}{l}
\texttt{index} \\
\texttt{subscript}
\end{array}
\right\}
\texttt{...)] [(leftmost-character-position: [length])]}
$$

General program structure

```
IDENTIFICATION DIVISION.
PROGRAM-ID.  program-name...
  .
  .
  .
[ENVIRONMENT DIVISION.
  .
  .]
[DATA DIVISION.
  .
  .]
[PROCEDURE DIVISION.
  .
  .]
[nested-source-program
  .
  .]
[END PROGRAM program-name].
```

IDENTIFICATION DIVISION

```
IDENTIFICATION DIVISION.
  .
PROGRAM-ID.     program-name [IS {COMMON [INITIAL]  } PROGRAM].
                                 {INITIAL [COMMON]  }
```

Note: COMMON can be coded only for nested source programs.

ENVIRONMENT DIVISION

Note: The Environment Division is optional under VS COBOL II Release 3.

Configuration Section

SPECIAL-NAMES   paragraph

```
[SPECIAL-NAMES.

    [function-name-1 IS mnemonic-name] ...

    [function-name-2 [IS mnemonic-name]

        [ { ON STATUS IS condition-name-1 [OFF STATUS IS condition-name-2] }  ]...]
          { OFF STATUS IS condition-name-2 [ON STATUS IS condition-name-1] }

    [alphabet-name IS

        {  STANDARD-1                                                    }
        {  STANDARD-2                                                    }
        {  NATIVE                                                        }
        {  EBCDIC                                                        }
        {          [ { THROUGH }  literal-2              ]              }  ]...
        {  literal-1 [ { THRU    }                        ]              }
        {          [ ALSO literal-3 [ALSO literal-4]...  ]              }
        {                                                                }
        {          [ { THROUGH }  literal-6              ] ]            }
        {  literal-5 [ { THRU    }                        ] ] ...       }
        {          [ ALSO literal-7 [ALSO literal-8]...  ] ]            }

    [CURRENCY SIGN IS literal-9]

    [DECIMAL-POINT IS COMMA].]
```

Note: VS COBOL II accepts S03, S04, S05, SYSLST, SYSIPT, and SYSPCH for
       function-name. Condition-name for a UPSI switch can be used in the
       Procedure Division under VS COBOL II.

Input-Output Section

FILE STATUS clause of the SELECT statement
```
[FILE STATUS IS data-name-1 [data-name-2]]
```

RERUN clause
```
[RERUN ON assignment-name]
```

Note: Under VS COBOL II, a checkpoint isn't taken on the first record.

RESERVE clause
```
[RESERVE integer {AREA  } ]
                 {AREAS }
```

DATA DIVISION

Note: The Data Division is optional under VS COBOL II Release 3.

File description entry format
```
FD file-name [IS EXTERNAL] [IS GLOBAL]

     [LABEL { RECORD IS  } { STANDARD    } ]
            { RECORDS ARE} { OMITTED     }
                           { data-name-1 }

     [BLOCK CONTAINS [integer-1 TO] integer-2 { RECORDS    } ]
                                              { CHARACTERS }

             { CONTAINS integer-3 characters                  }
             { IS VARYING IN SIZE                             }
     [RECORD {    [FROM integer-4] [TO integer-5 CHARACTERS]  } ].
             {    [DEPENDING ON data-name-2]                  }
             { CONTAINS integer-6 TO integer-7 CHARACTERS     }
```

Sort-merge file description format

```
SD file-name
```

```
         ┌ CONTAINS integer-1 characters        ┐
         │ IS VARYING IN SIZE                    │
[RECORD ⟨     [FROM integer-2] [TO integer-3 CHARACTERS] ⟩ ].
         │     [DEPENDING ON data-name]          │
         └ CONTAINS integer-4 TO integer-5 CHARACTERS ┘
```

Data Description entry format

```
level-number  ⎧ data-name-1 ⎫
              ⎨ FILLER      ⎬
              ⎩             ⎭

    [REDEFINES data-name-2]

    ⎡ ⎧ PICTURE ⎫               ⎤
    ⎢ ⎨ PIC     ⎬ IS character-string ⎥
    ⎣ ⎩         ⎭               ⎦
```

```
                    ⎧ DISPLAY          ⎫
                    │ DISPLAY-1        │
                    │ INDEX            │
                    │ POINTER          │
                    │ COMPUTATIONAL    │
                    │ COMP             │
                    │ COMPUTATIONAL-1  │
                    │ COMP-1           │
    [USAGE IS      ⟨ COMPUTATIONAL-2   ⟩ ]
                    │ COMP-2           │
                    │ COMPUTATIONAL-3  │
                    │ COMP-3           │
                    │ COMPUTATIONAL-4  │
                    │ COMP-4           │
                    │ BINARY           │
                    ⎩ PACKED-DECIMAL   ⎭
```

```
      ⎛ OCCURS integer-2 TIMES
      ⎜
      ⎜     ⎡ ⎧ ASCENDING  ⎫              ⎤
      ⎜     ⎢ ⎨           ⎬ KEY IS {data-name-3}... ⎥ ...
      ⎜     ⎣ ⎩ DESCENDING ⎭              ⎦
      ⎜
      ⎜        INDEXED BY {index-name-1} ...
  [   ⎨                                                            ]
      ⎜ OCCURS integer-1 TO integer-2 TIMES DEPENDING ON data-name-4
      ⎜
      ⎜     ⎡ ⎧ ASCENDING  ⎫              ⎤
      ⎜     ⎢ ⎨           ⎬ KEY IS {data-name-3} ... ⎥ ...
      ⎜     ⎣ ⎩ DESCENDING ⎭              ⎦
      ⎜
      ⎝        INDEXED BY {index-name-1}...
```

```
           ⎧ ZERO   ⎫
  [BLANK WHEN ⎨ ZEROS  ⎬ ]
           ⎩ ZEROES ⎭
```

[VALUE IS literal]

```
                        ⎧ VALUE IS  ⎫          ⎧ THROUGH ⎫
  [88 condition-name ⎨           ⎬ literal-1 [ ⎨         ⎬ literal-2]
                        ⎩ VALUES ARE ⎭          ⎩ THRU    ⎭
```

```
                                   ⎧ THROUGH ⎫
                     [literal-3 [ ⎨         ⎬ literal-4]]...]
                                   ⎩ THRU    ⎭
```

[VALUE IS NULL]

[GLOBAL]

[EXTERNAL]

```
    ⎧ JUSTIFIED ⎫
  [ ⎨           ⎬ RIGHT]
    ⎩ JUST      ⎭
```

```
           ⎧ LEADING  ⎫
  [SIGN IS ⎨          ⎬ [SEPARATE CHARACTER]]
           ⎩ TRAILING ⎭
```

```
    ⎧ SYNCHRONIZED ⎫ ⎧ LEFT  ⎫
  [ ⎨              ⎬ ⎨       ⎬ ]
    ⎩ SYNC         ⎭ ⎩ RIGHT ⎭
```

PROCEDURE DIVISION

Note: The Procedure Division is optional under VS COBOL II Release 3.

ACCEPT statement

```
ACCEPT identifier [FROM {mnemonic-name}
                        {function-name}]
```

```
                           (DATE      )
                           |DAY       |
ACCEPT identifier FROM     |DAY-OF-WEEK|
                           (TIME      )
```

Note: Under VS COBOL II, mnemonic-name in FROM phrase can be declared as SYSIPT.

ADD statement

```
ADD {identifier-1} [identifier-2]...
    {literal-1   } [literal-2   ]

    TO  identifier-3 [ROUNDED] [identifier-4 [ROUNDED]]...

    [ON SIZE ERROR imperative-statement-1]

    [NOT ON SIZE ERROR imperative-statement-2]

    [END-ADD]
```

```
ADD {identifier-1} [identifier-2]... [TO] {identifier-3}
    {literal-1   } [literal-2   ]         {literal-3   }

    GIVING identifier-4 [ROUNDED] [identifier-5 [ROUNDED]]...

    [ON SIZE ERROR imperative-statement-1]

    [NOT ON SIZE ERROR imperative-statement-2]

    [END-ADD]
```

ADD $\begin{Bmatrix} \underline{CORRESPONDING} \\ \underline{CORR} \end{Bmatrix}$ identifier-1 <u>TO</u> identifier-2 [<u>ROUNDED</u>]

[ON <u>SIZE</u> <u>ERROR</u> imperative-statement-1]

[<u>NOT</u> ON <u>SIZE</u> <u>ERROR</u> imperative-statement-2]

[<u>END-ADD</u>]

CALL statement

<u>CALL</u> $\begin{Bmatrix} literal-1 \\ identifier-1 \end{Bmatrix}$

[<u>USING</u> $\begin{Bmatrix} [\underline{BY} \ \underline{REFERENCE}] \begin{Bmatrix} identifier-2 \\ record-name-1 \\ \underline{ADDRESS} \ \underline{OF} \ record-name-2 \end{Bmatrix} \dots \\ \underline{BY} \ \underline{CONTENT} \begin{Bmatrix} literal-2 \\ identifier-3 \\ \underline{LENGTH} \ \underline{OF} \ identifier-4 \end{Bmatrix} \dots \end{Bmatrix} \dots]$

[ON <u>OVERFLOW</u> imperative-statement]

[<u>END-CALL</u>]

<u>CALL</u> $\begin{Bmatrix} literal-1 \\ identifier-1 \end{Bmatrix}$

[<u>USING</u> $\begin{Bmatrix} [\underline{BY} \ \underline{REFERENCE}] \begin{Bmatrix} identifier-2 \\ record-name-1 \\ \underline{ADDRESS} \ \underline{OF} \ record-name-2 \end{Bmatrix} \dots \\ \underline{BY} \ \underline{CONTENT} \begin{Bmatrix} literal-2 \\ identifier-3 \\ \underline{LENGTH} \ \underline{OF} \ identifier-4 \end{Bmatrix} \dots \end{Bmatrix} \dots]$

[ON <u>EXCEPTION</u> imperative-statement-1]

[<u>NOT</u> ON <u>EXCEPTION</u> imperative-statement-2]

[<u>END-CALL</u>]

Note: Under VS COBOL II, procedure names aren't allowed in the USING phrase.

COMPUTE statement

```
COMPUTE identifier-1 [ROUNDED] [identifier-2 [ROUNDED]]...

        { =     }
        { EQUAL } arithmetic-expression

    [ON SIZE ERROR imperative-statement-1]

    [NOT ON SIZE ERROR imperative-statement-2]

    [END-COMPUTE]
```

CONTINUE statement

```
CONTINUE
```

DELETE statement

```
DELETE file-name RECORD

    [INVALID KEY imperative-statement-1]

    [NOT INVALID KEY imperative-statement-2]

    [END-DELETE]
```

DISPLAY statement

```
DISPLAY {identifier-1} {identifier-2}...
        {literal-1   } {literal-2   }

    [UPON {mnemonic-name    }]
          {environment-name }

    [WITH NO ADVANCING]
```

Note: Under VS COBOL II, mnemonic-name in UPON phrase can be declared as SYSLST.

DIVIDE statement

DIVIDE {identifier-1 / literal-1} <u>INTO</u> identifier-2 [<u>ROUNDED</u>] [identifier-3 [<u>ROUNDED</u>]]...

    [ON <u>SIZE</u> <u>ERROR</u> imperative-statement-1]

    [<u>NOT</u> ON <u>SIZE</u> <u>ERROR</u> imperative-statement-2]

    [END-DIVIDE]

<u>DIVIDE</u> {identifier-1 / literal-1} {<u>INTO</u> / <u>BY</u>} {identifier-2 / literal-2}

    <u>GIVING</u> identifier-3 [<u>ROUNDED</u>] [identifier-4 [<u>ROUNDED</u>]]...

    [ON <u>SIZE</u> <u>ERROR</u> imperative-statement-1]

    [<u>NOT</u> ON <u>SIZE</u> <u>ERROR</u> imperative-statement-2]

    [END-DIVIDE]

<u>DIVIDE</u> {identifier-1 / literal-1} {<u>INTO</u> / <u>BY</u>} {identifier-2 / literal-2}

    <u>GIVING</u> identifier-3 [<u>ROUNDED</u>]

    [<u>REMAINDER</u> identifier-4]

    [ON <u>SIZE</u> <u>ERROR</u> imperative-statement-1]

    [<u>NOT</u> ON <u>SIZE</u> <u>ERROR</u> imperative-statement-2]

    [END-DIVIDE]

EVALUATE statement

```
          (identifier-1 )      (identifier-2 )
          | literal-1    |      | literal-2    |
EVALUATE  { expression-1 } ALSO { expression-2 } ...
          | TRUE         |      | TRUE         |
          ( FALSE        )      ( FALSE        )

  {{WHEN

    ( ANY
    | condition-1
    | TRUE
    | FALSE
    |        (identifier-3            )  (THROUGH) (identifier-4            )
    ( [NOT]  { literal-3              }  [ THRU  ] { literal-4              } ]
             ( arithmetic-expression-1)            ( arithmetic-expression-2)

  [ALSO

    ( ANY
    | condition-2
    | TRUE
    | FALSE                                                                    }...} ...
    |        (identifier-5            )  (THROUGH) (identifier-6            )
    ( [NOT]  { literal-5              }  { THRU  } { literal-6              }
             ( arithmetic-expression-3)            ( arithmetic-expression-4)

    imperative-statement-1}...
  [WHEN OTHER imperative-statement-2]

[END-EVALUATE]
```

IF   statement

```
IF condition [THEN] { statement-1 [statement-2]... }
                    { NEXT SENTENCE                 }

      [ELSE { statement-3 [statement-4]... } ]
            { NEXT SENTENCE                 }

      [END-IF]
```

INITIALIZE statement

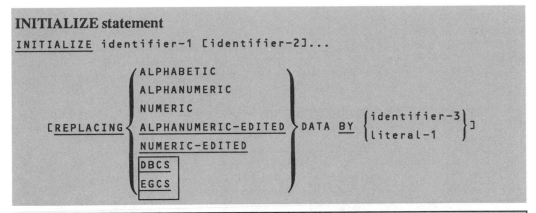

```
INITIALIZE identifier-1 [identifier-2]...

                  (ALPHABETIC
                   ALPHANUMERIC
                   NUMERIC
  [REPLACING    <  ALPHANUMERIC-EDITED  > DATA BY {identifier-3}]
                   NUMERIC-EDITED                 {literal-1    }
                  | DBCS |
                  ( EGCS )
```

INSPECT statement

```
INSPECT identifier-1 CONVERTING {identifier-1}  TO  {identifier-2}
                                {literal-1   }       {literal-2   }

     [{BEFORE}  INITIAL {identifier-3}
      {AFTER }          {literal-3   }
```

MERGE statement

```
MERGE file-name-1

     ON {ASCENDING }  KEY data-name-1 [data-name-2]...
        {DESCENDING}

     [COLLATING SEQUENCE IS alphabet-name-1]

     USING file-name-2 [file-name-3]...

    (OUTPUT PROCEDURE IS procedure-name-1 [{THROUGH} procedure-name-2])
    {                                      {THRU   }                   }
    (GIVING file-name-4 [file-name-5]...                               )
```

MULTIPLY statement

MULTIPLY $\begin{Bmatrix} \text{identifier-1} \\ \text{literal-1} \end{Bmatrix}$ BY identifier-2 [ROUNDED] [identifier-3 [ROUNDED]]...

    [ON SIZE ERROR imperative-statement-1]

    [NOT ON SIZE ERROR imperative-statement-2]

    [END-MULTIPLY]

MULTIPLY $\begin{Bmatrix} \text{identifier-1} \\ \text{literal-1} \end{Bmatrix}$ BY $\begin{Bmatrix} \text{identifier-2} \\ \text{literal-2} \end{Bmatrix}$

    GIVING identifier-3 [ROUNDED] [identifier-4 [ROUNDED]]...

    [ON SIZE ERROR imperative-statement-1]

    [NOT ON SIZE ERROR imperative-statement-2]

    [END-MULTIPLY]

PERFORM statement (basic out-of-line format)

PERFORM procedure-name-1 [$\begin{Bmatrix} \text{THROUGH} \\ \text{THRU} \end{Bmatrix}$ procedure-name-2]

PERFORM statement (basic inline format)

PERFORM [imperative-statement]...

    END-PERFORM

PERFORM statement (inline format with TIMES option)

PERFORM $\begin{Bmatrix} \text{identifier-1} \\ \text{integer-1} \end{Bmatrix}$ TIMES

    [imperative-statement]...

    END-PERFORM

PERFORM statement (out-of-line format with UNTIL option)

```
PERFORM procedure-name-1   [{THROUGH}   procedure-name-2]
                            {THRU    }

    [WITH TEST {BEFORE}]
               {AFTER }

    UNTIL condition
```

PERFORM statement (inline format with UNTIL option)

```
PERFORM

    [WITH TEST {BEFORE}]
               {AFTER }

    UNTIL condition

    [imperative-statement]...

    END-PERFORM
```

PERFORM statement (out-of-line format with VARYING option)

```
PERFORM procedure-name-1   [{THROUGH}   procedure-name-2]
                            {THRU    }

    [WITH TEST {BEFORE}]
               {AFTER }

    VARYING {identifier-1 }  FROM {identifier-2 }
            {index-name-1}        {index-name-2}
                                  {literal-1    }

        BY {identifier-3}  UNTIL condition-1
           {literal-2   }

        [AFTER {identifier-4 }  FROM {identifier-5 }
               {index-name-3}        {index-name-4}
                                     {literal-3    }

        BY {identifier-6}  UNTIL condition-2]...
           {literal-4   }
```

Note: You can code up to seven VARYING identifiers under VS COBOL II Release 3.

PERFORM statement (inline format with VARYING option)

```
PERFORM

    [WITH TEST {BEFORE}]
              {AFTER }

    VARYING {identifier-1} FROM {identifier-2 }
            {index-name-1}      {index-name-2 }
                                {literal-1    }

            BY {identifier-3} UNTIL condition-1
               {literal-2   }

    [imperative-statement]...

    END-PERFORM
```

Note: You can code up to seven VARYING identifiers under VS COBOL II Release 3.

READ statement (sequential access)

```
READ file-name [NEXT] RECORD [INTO identifier]

    [AT END imperative-statement-1]

    [NOT AT END imperative-statement-2]

    [END-READ]
```

READ statement (random access)

```
READ file-name RECORD [INTO identifier]

    [KEY IS data-name]

    [INVALID KEY imperative-statement-1]

    [NOT INVALID KEY imperative-statement-2]

    [END-READ]
```

REPLACE statement

```
REPLACE ==pseudo-text-1== BY ==pseudo-text-2==
        [==pseudo-text-3== BY ==pseudo-text-4==]...


REPLACE OFF
```

RETURN statement

```
RETURN file-name RECORD [INTO identifier]

    AT END imperative-statement-1

    [NOT AT END imperative-statement-2]

    [END-RETURN]
```

REWRITE statement

```
REWRITE record-name [FROM identifier]

    [INVALID KEY imperative-statement-1]

    [NOT INVALID KEY imperative-statement-2]

    [END-REWRITE]
```

SEARCH statement

```
SEARCH identifier-1 [VARYING {identifier-2}]
                             {index-name  }

    [AT END imperative-statement-1]

    WHEN condition-1 {imperative-statement-2}
                     {NEXT SENTENCE         }

    [WHEN condition-2 {imperative-statement-3}]...
                      {NEXT SENTENCE         }

    [END-SEARCH]
```

```
SEARCH ALL identifier-1

    [AT END imperative-statement-1]

    WHEN {data-name-1 {IS EQUAL TO} {identifier-2           }}
         {            {IS =        } {literal-1              }}
         {                           {arithmetic-expression-1}}
         {condition-name-1                                    }

         [AND {data-name-2 {IS EQUAL TO} {identifier-3           }}]...
              {            {IS =        } {literal-2              }}
              {                           {arithmetic-expression-2}}
              {condition-name-2                                    }

    {imperative-statement-2}
    {NEXT SENTENCE         }

    [END-SEARCH]
```

SET statement

$$\underline{SET} \begin{Bmatrix} \text{index-name-1 [index-name-2]...} \\ \text{identifier-1 [identifier-2]...} \end{Bmatrix} \underline{TO} \begin{Bmatrix} \text{index-name-3} \\ \text{identifier-3} \\ \text{integer-1} \end{Bmatrix}$$

$$\underline{SET} \text{ index-name-1 [index-name-2]...}$$

$$\begin{Bmatrix} \underline{UP} \ \underline{BY} \\ \underline{DOWN} \ \underline{BY} \end{Bmatrix} \begin{Bmatrix} \text{identifier-1} \\ \text{integer-1} \end{Bmatrix}$$

$$\underline{SET} \begin{Bmatrix} \text{mnemonic-name-1 [mnemonic-name-2]... } \underline{TO} \begin{Bmatrix} \underline{ON} \\ \underline{OFF} \end{Bmatrix} \end{Bmatrix} ...$$

$$\underline{SET} \text{ condition-name-1 [condition-name-2]... } \underline{TO} \ \underline{TRUE}$$

$$\underline{SET} \begin{Bmatrix} \text{pointer-data-item-1} \\ \underline{ADDRESS} \ \underline{OF} \text{ identifier-1} \end{Bmatrix} \begin{bmatrix} \text{pointer-data-item-2} \\ \underline{ADDRESS} \ \underline{OF} \text{ identifier-2} \end{bmatrix} ...$$

$$\underline{TO} \begin{Bmatrix} \text{identifier-3} \\ \underline{NULL} \\ \underline{NULLS} \\ \underline{ADDRESS} \ \underline{OF} \text{ identifier-4} \end{Bmatrix}$$

SORT statement

$$\underline{SORT} \text{ file-name-1} \begin{Bmatrix} ON \begin{Bmatrix} \underline{ASCENDING} \\ \underline{DESCENDING} \end{Bmatrix} KEY \text{ data-name-1 [data-name-2]...} \end{Bmatrix} ...$$

[WITH DUPLICATES IN ORDER]

[COLLATING SEQUENCE IS alphabet-name-1]

$$\begin{Bmatrix} \underline{USING} \text{ file-name-2 [file-name-3]...} \\ \underline{INPUT} \ \underline{PROCEDURE} \text{ IS procedure-name-1 } [\begin{Bmatrix} \underline{THROUGH} \\ \underline{THRU} \end{Bmatrix} \text{ procedure-name-2}] \end{Bmatrix}$$

$$\begin{Bmatrix} \underline{GIVING} \text{ file-name-4 [file-name-5]...} \\ \underline{OUTPUT} \ \underline{PROCEDURE} \text{ IS procedure-name-3 } [\begin{Bmatrix} \underline{THROUGH} \\ \underline{THRU} \end{Bmatrix} \text{ procedure-name-4}] \end{Bmatrix}$$

START statement

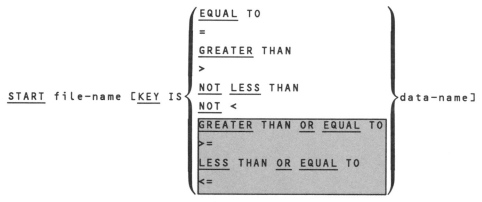

```
                                  ⎛EQUAL TO            ⎞
                                  ⎜                    ⎟
                                  ⎜=                   ⎟
                                  ⎜                    ⎟
                                  ⎜GREATER THAN        ⎟
                                  ⎜                    ⎟
                                  ⎜>                   ⎟
START file-name [KEY IS ⎨NOT LESS THAN       ⎬data-name]
                                  ⎜                    ⎟
                                  ⎜NOT <               ⎟
                                  ⎜                    ⎟
                                  ⎜GREATER THAN OR EQUAL TO⎟
                                  ⎜                    ⎟
                                  ⎜>=                  ⎟
                                  ⎜                    ⎟
                                  ⎜LESS THAN OR EQUAL TO⎟
                                  ⎝<=                  ⎠
```

[INVALID KEY imperative-statement-1]

[NOT INVALID KEY imperative-statement-2]

[END-START]

STRING statement

```
STRING ⎧identifier-1⎫ ⎡identifier-2⎤... DELIMITED BY ⎧identifier-3⎫
       ⎩literal-1   ⎭ ⎣literal-2   ⎦                 ⎨literal-3   ⎬
                                                     ⎩SIZE        ⎭

       ⎡⎧identifier-4⎫ ⎡identifier-5⎤... DELIMITED BY ⎧identifier-6⎫⎤...
       ⎢⎩literal-4   ⎭ ⎣literal-5   ⎦                 ⎨literal-6   ⎬⎥
       ⎣                                              ⎩SIZE        ⎭⎦
```

INTO identifier-7

[WITH POINTER identifier-8]

[ON OVERFLOW imperative-statement-1]

[NOT ON OVERFLOW imperative-statement-2]

[END-STRING]

SUBTRACT statement

SUBTRACT $\left\{ \begin{array}{l} \text{identifier-1} \\ \text{literal-1} \end{array} \right\}$ $\left\{ \begin{array}{l} \text{identifier-2} \\ \text{literal-2} \end{array} \right\}$ ...

    FROM identifier-3 [ROUNDED] [identifier-4 [ROUNDED]]...

    [ON SIZE ERROR imperative-statement-1]

    [NOT ON SIZE ERROR imperative-statement-2]

    [END-SUBTRACT]

SUBTRACT $\left\{ \begin{array}{l} \text{identifier-1} \\ \text{literal-1} \end{array} \right\}$ $\left[\begin{array}{l} \text{identifier-2} \\ \text{literal-2} \end{array} \right]$ ... FROM $\left\{ \begin{array}{l} \text{identifier-3} \\ \text{literal-3} \end{array} \right\}$

    GIVING identifier-4 [ROUNDED] [identifier-5 [ROUNDED]]...

    [ON SIZE ERROR imperative-statement-1]

    [NOT ON SIZE ERROR imperative-statement-2]

    [END-SUBTRACT]

SUBTRACT $\left\{ \begin{array}{l} \text{CORRESPONDING} \\ \text{CORR} \end{array} \right\}$ identifier-1 FROM identifier-2 [ROUNDED]

    [ON SIZE ERROR imperative-statement-1]

    [NOT ON SIZE ERROR imperative-statement-2]

    [END-SUBTRACT]

UNSTRING statement

```
UNSTRING identifier-1

    [DELIMITED BY [ALL] {identifier-2}  [OR [ALL] {identifier-3}]...]
                        {literal-1   }              {literal-2  }

    INTO identifier-4 [DELIMITER IN identifier-5] [COUNT IN identifier-6]

        [identifier-7 [DELIMITER IN identifier-8] [COUNT IN identifier-9]]...

    [WITH POINTER identifier-10]

    [TALLYING IN identifier-11]

    [ON OVERFLOW imperative-statement-1]

    [NOT ON OVERFLOW imperative-statement-2]

    [END-UNSTRING]
```

USE statement

```
                                    {EXCEPTION}               {file-name-1 [file-name-2]...}
USE [GLOBAL] AFTER STANDARD {ERROR    } PROCEDURE ON {INPUT                       }
                                                     {OUTPUT                      }
                                                     {I-O                         }
                                                     {EXTEND                      }


                                    {BEGINNING} {FILE}
USE [GLOBAL] AFTER STANDARD {ENDING   } {REEL}
                                                {UNIT}

                            {file-name-1 [file-name-2]...}
LABEL PROCEDURE ON {INPUT                       }
                            {OUTPUT                      }
                            {I-O                         }
                            {EXTEND                      }
```

WRITE statement (VSAM sequential files)

```
WRITE record-name [FROM identifier]

    [END-WRITE]
```

WRITE statement (QSAM sequential files)

```
WRITE record-name [FROM identifier-1]


  [{BEFORE}  ADVANCING  {(identifier-2)  [LINE ]}
   {AFTER }              {integer       } {LINES}}
                         {mnemonic-name-1         }
                         {PAGE                     }


  [INVALID KEY imperative-statement-1]
```

```
  [NOT INVALID KEY imperative-statement-2]

  [AT  {END-OF-PAGE}  imperative-statement-3]
       {EOP         }

  [NOT AT {END-OF-PAGE}  imperative-statement-4]
          {EOP         }
```

```
  [END-WRITE]
```

Note: Under VS COBOL II, you cannot use a WRITE statement for a QSAM file opened as I-O.

WRITE statement (VSAM indexed files)

```
WRITE record-name [FROM identifier]

  [INVALID KEY imperative-statement-1]

  [NOT INVALID KEY imperative-statement-2]

  [END-WRITE]
```

Appendix
B

VS COBOL II compiler and run-time options

This appendix presents all of the VS COBOL II compiler and run-time options. The underlined options are the IBM defaults. Be aware, though, that your installation may change these defaults when it installs VS COBOL II. Also, note that some of the names of the compiler options have been changed from OS/VS COBOL. And be sure to review the run-time options here, since I didn't present all of them in chapter 4.

VS COBOL II COMPILER OPTIONS

VS COBOL II Option	Equivalent OS/VS COBOL Option	Description
ADV NOADV	ADV NOADV	Causes one byte to be added to the record length of a print file to account for the printer control character. This option is used only with WRITE ADVANCING. The default is ADV.
APOST QUOTE	APOST QUOTE	Specifies whether the apostrophe (') or double quote (") is used as the delimiter character. The default is QUOTE.
BUFSIZE(nnnnn) BUFSIZE(nnnK)	BUF=xxxxxx	Specifies the amount of main storage that's allocated for each compiler work data set. The default is BUFSIZE(4096).
CMPR2 NOCMPR2		Release 3 only. Determines whether compilation results are compatible with Release 2. The default is NOCMPR2.
COMPILE NOCOMPILE NOCOMPILE(W E S)	NOSYNTAX NOCSYNTAX SYNTAX CSYNTAX	COMPILE requests full compilation including diagnostics and object code. NOCOMPILE requests full syntax checking with diagnostics, but no object code is produced. NOCOMPILE(W E S) requests full compilation including diagnostics and object code, but only syntax checking is done after an error at the specified level or higher is detected. The default is NOCOMPILE(S).
DATA(24) DATA(31)		Determines whether storage obtained for data areas during program execution is located below 16M (DATA(24)) or anywhere in storage (DATA(31)). The default is DATA(31).
DECK NODECK	DECK NODECK	Causes object code to be written to the SYSPUNCH data set. The default is NODECK.

DUMP	DUMP	Determines whether a system dump will be produced at compile time. The default is NODUMP.
NODUMP	NODUMP	

DYNAM	DYNAM	Causes subprograms to be loaded dynamically at execution time. The default is NODYNAM.
NODYNAM	NODYNAM	

FASTSRT	Causes DFSORT to perform the processing of input and output files. The default is NO-FASTSRT.
NOFASTSRT	

FDUMP	Causes a formatted dump to be created when an abnormal termination occurs. The default is NOFDUMP.
NOFDUMP	

FLAG(x[,y])	FLAGW	Determines what messages are printed in the diagnostics listing (x) and what messages are imbedded in the source listing (y). See figure 4-12 for the values that are valid for x and y. The default is FLAG(I).
	FLAGE	

FLAGMIG	Release 3 only. Identifies the language elements of Release 2 that may execute differently under Release 3. The default is NOFLAGMIG.
NOFLAGMIG	

FLAGSTD(x[yy][,z])	Release 3 only. Identifies the language elements in a program that do not conform to the specified subset of the 1985 standards. The x identifies the subset, yy identifies optional modules, and z indicates if obsolete elements are flagged. The default is NOFLAGSTD.
NOFLAGSTD	

FLAGSAA	Release 3 only. Identifies the language elements in a program that do not conform to SAA requirements. The default is NOFLAGSAA.
NOFLAGSAA	

LANGUAGE(ENGLISH)	Release 3 only. Determines the language in which compiler output is printed. The default is LANGUAGE(ENGLISH).
LANGUAGE(UENGLISH)	
LANGUAGE(JAPANESE)	

LIB	LIB	Allows the use of COPY statements. The default is NOLIB.
NOLIB	NOLIB	

LINECOUNT(nn)	LINECOUNT=nn	Specifies the number of lines to be printed per page in the compiler source listing. The default is LINECOUNT(60).
LIST NOLIST	PMAP NOPMAP	Causes an assembler-language expansion of your source code to be produced. The default is NOLIST.
MAP NOMAP	DMAP NODMAP	Causes a Data Division listing to be produced. The default is NOMAP.
NAME NONAME		Release 3 only. Determines whether linkage editor NAME control cards are generated during compilation. The default is NONAME.
NUMBER NONUMBER	NUM NONUM	Causes the compiler to use the line numbers in your source program in error messages rather than generating its own. The default is NONUMBER.
NUMPROC(PFD) NUMPROC(NOPFD) NUMPROC(MIG)		Release 3 only. Determines if and how signed decimals are to be converted to the preferred format. The default is NUMPROC(NOPFD).
OBJECT NOOBJECT	LOAD NOLOAD	Causes object code to be written to the SYSLIN data set. The default is OBJECT.
OFFSET NOOFFSET	CLIST NOCLIST	Causes a condensed Procedure Division listing to be produced. The default is NOOFFSET.
OPTIMIZE NOOPTIMIZE	OPTIMIZE NOOPTIMIZE	Causes the optimization features to be applied to your program. The default is NOOPTIMIZE.
OUTDD(ddname)	SYSx	Specifies the name of the data set you want display output written to. The default is OUTDD(SYSOUT).
PFDSGN NOPFDSGN		Releases 1 and 2 only. Indicates that signed fields will use the preferred sign format. The default is NOPFDSGN.
RENT NORENT		Causes your program to be reentrant. The default is NORENT.

RESIDENT NORESIDENT	RESIDENT NORESIDENT	Requests the COBOL Library Management Feature. The default is NORESIDENT.
SEQUENCE NOSEQUENCE	SEQ NOSEQ	Causes the compiler to check that source line numbers are in ascending sequence. The default is SEQUENCE.
SIZE(nnnnn) SIZE(nnnK) SIZE(MAX)		Indicates the amount of storage needed for compilation. The *nnnnn* is number of bytes, *nnn*K is increments of 1K, and MAX is limited only by the space available in your user region. The default is SIZE(MAX).
SOURCE NOSOURCE	SOURCE NOSOURCE	Causes a source listing to be produced. The default is SOURCE.
SPACE (1) SPACE (2) SPACE (3)	SPACE 1 SPACE 2 SPACE 3	Specifies whether you want your source listing single-, double-, or triple-spaced. The default is SPACE(1).
SSRANGE NOSSRANGE		Determines if out-of-range conditions are checked during program execution. The default is NOSSRANGE.
TERMINAL NOTERMINAL	TERM NOTERM	Causes progress and diagnostic messages to be sent to the SYSTERM data set. The default is NOTERMINAL.
TEST NOTEST	TEST NOTEST	Causes the generated object code to be compatible with VS COBOL II Debug. The default is NOTEST.
TRUNC NOTRUNC	TRUNC NOTRUNC	Releases 1 and 2 only. Determines how the sending field in a MOVE statement or the final intermediate result field of an arithmetic expression is truncated when the receiving field is binary. The default is TRUNC.
TRUNC(STD) TRUNC(OPT) TRUNC(BIN)		Release 3 only. Determines how results stored in a binary receiving field are truncated. The default is TRUNC(STD).

VBREF NOVBREF	VBREF plus VBSUM NOVBREF plus NOVBSUM	Causes a verb cross-reference to be produced. The default is NOVBREF.
WORD(xxxx) [*]NOWORD		Specifies a reserved word list other than the system default to be used. The default is *NOWORD. (* means that the option cannot be overridden.)
XREF NOXREF	SXREF NOSXREF	Causes a sorted cross-reference listing to be produced. The default is NOXREF.
ZWB NOZWB	ZWB NOZWB	Causes the sign to be removed from a DISPLAY field when it's compared to an alphanumeric field. The default is ZWB.

VS COBOL II run-time options

VS COBOL II Option	Equivalent OS/VS COBOL Option	Description
AIXBLD NOAIXBLD	AIXBLD NOAIXBLD	Causes Access Method Services to be invoked to complete file and index definition procedures for VSAM key-sequenced and relative-record data sets. The default is NOAIXBLD.
DEBUG NODEBUG	DEBUG NODEBUG	Activates debugging lines (D in column 7) and USE FOR DEBUGGING declaratives in your program. The default is DEBUG.
LIBKEEP NOLIBKEEP		Releases 2 and 3 only. Causes library routines to be retained in memory between calls to COBOL resident main programs. The default is NOLIBKEEP.
MIXRES NOMIXRES		Release 3 only. Allows you to combine RES and NORES and OS/VS COBOL and VS COBOL II programs in a run unit. NOMIXRES is the default.
RTEREUS NORTEREUS		Releases 2 and 3 only. Causes the run-time environment to be initialized for reusability when the first COBOL program is invoked. The default is NORTEREUS.
SIMVRD NOSIMVRD		Release 3 only. Allows you to simulate a variable-length relative organization data set with a VSAM KSDS. The default is NOSIMVRD.
SSRANGE NOSSRANGE		Causes out-of-range conditions to be checked during program execution. The SSRANGE compiler option must be specified for range checking to occur. SSRANGE is the default.
SPOUT NOSPOUT		Causes a message indicating the amount of storage used during the execution of a COBOL program to be issued. The default is NOSPOUT.

STAE   Causes the run-time environment to intercept an
NOSTAE   abend. The default is STAE.

UPSI(nnnnnnnn)   Specifies the setting of the UPSI switches. The
                                        default is UPSI(00000000).

WSCLEAR   Release 3 only. Causes all external records
NOWSCLEAR   acquired by a program and working storage
                                        acquired by a reentrant program for which no
                                        VALUE clauses are specified to be cleared to
                                        binary zeros. NOWSCLEAR is the default.

Appendix
C

VS COBOL II Debug (COBTEST)
command summary

This appendix presents all of the COBTEST commands that are covered in chapter 5 of this book. The first part of this appendix covers the commands that can be used in any of the COBTEST modes: batch, line, or full-screen. The second part covers commands that can only be used in full-screen mode.

The rules for the notation used in this appendix are:

1. Words printed in capital letters are keywords and must be written as shown.

2. Words printed in lowercase letters represent names, literals, or statements that must be supplied by the programmer.

3. Braces { } enclosing a group of items indicate that the programmer must choose one of them.

4. Brackets [] indicate that the enclosed item may be used or omitted, depending on the requirements of the debugging session.

5. The ellipsis ... indicates that an element may be repeated as many times as necessary.

6. In general, the parameters in a statement should be coded in the sequence shown.

GENERAL COBTEST COMMANDS

The AT command

```
{AT}  ENTRY  {[(]program-name-1[,program-name-2,...)]}
{A }         {ALL
```

```
{AT}  statement-list [(command-list)] [COUNT(n[,m][,k])]
{A }
```

```
      [{NOTIFY  }] [DEFER]
      [{NONOTIFY}]
```

The COBTEST command under CMS

```
COBTEST program-name [PARM(?)] [BATCH]
```

Note: The COBTEST command can not be used in interactive full-screen mode.

The COBTEST command under TSO

```
COBTEST {LOAD(load-module-name:ddname)}  [PARM('parameter-string')]
        {load-module-name             }
```

The DROP command

```
{DROP}  [[(]symbol-1[,symbol-2...)]]
{DR  }
```

The EQUATE command

```
{EQUATE}  symbol [program-name.]identifier
{EQ    }
```

The FLOW command

```
{FLOW}  [{ON          }]
{FL  }  [{OFF         }]
        [{PRINT       }]
        [{(n) [PRINT] }]
```

The FREQ command

```
{FREQ}  [{ALL                                    }] [OFF]
{FR  }  [{[(]program-name-1[,program-name-2,...)]}]
```

The GO command

```
{GO}  [statement-number]
{G }
```

The HELP command

```
{HELP}  [[command-name] [⎧ALL          ⎫ ]]
{H   }                  ⎪FUNCTION     ⎪
                        ⎨OPERANDS [(operand-list)]⎬
                        ⎩SYNTAX       ⎭
```

Note: The HELP command can not be used in batch mode.

The IF command

```
{IF}  (expression) ⎧(command-list)⎫
{I }               ⎨ HALT         ⎬
                   ⎩ GO           ⎭
```

The LINK command

```
{LINK}  [USING] [(]data-name-1[,data-name-2,...)]
{LIN }
```

The LIST command

```
{LIST} ⎧identifier-list⎫ [GROUP] [⎧DISPLAY⎫] [PRINT]
{L   } ⎨literal         ⎬         ⎨HEX    ⎬
       ⎩ALL             ⎭         ⎩BOTH   ⎭
```

The LISTBREAKS command

```
{LISTBREAKS}  [PRINT]
{LISTB     }
```

The LISTEQ command

```
{LISTEQ}  [PRINT]
{LISTE }
```

The LISTFREQ command

```
{LISTFREQ}  [⎧ALL                                  ⎫]
{LISTF   }   ⎨[(]program-name-1[,program-name-2,...)]⎬
             ⎩                                      ⎭

          [ZEROFREQ] [PRINT]
```

The NEXT command

```
{NEXT}  [(command-list)]
{N    }
```

The OFF command

```
OFF [statement-list]
```

The OFFWN command

```
{OFFWN}  [(]character-string-1[,character-string-2,...)]
{OFFW }
```

The ONABEND command

```
{ONABEND}  [(command-list)]
{ONAB   }
```

The PRINTDD command

```
{PRINTDD}  ddname
{PRI    }
```

The PROC command

```
{PROC}  [(]program-name-1[,program-name-2,...)] [(command-list)]
{PRO }
```

The RECORD command

```
{RECORD  }
{RE      }
{NORECORD}
{NORE    }
```

The RESTART command

```
{RESTART}
{RESTA  }
```

Note: The RESTART command has no effect in batch mode.

The RUN command

```
{RUN}  [statement-number]
{R  }
```

The SET command

$$\begin{Bmatrix} SET \\ S \end{Bmatrix} \ identifier-1 = \begin{Bmatrix} identifier-2 \\ literal \end{Bmatrix}$$

The STEP command

$$\begin{Bmatrix} STEP \\ ST \end{Bmatrix} \ [number]$$

The TRACE command

$$\begin{Bmatrix} TRACE \\ T \end{Bmatrix} \ [\begin{Bmatrix} ENTRY \\ PARA \\ NAME \\ OFF \end{Bmatrix}] \ [PRINT]$$

The WHEN command

$$\begin{Bmatrix} WHEN \\ WN \end{Bmatrix} \ character-string \begin{Bmatrix} identifier \\ (expression) \end{Bmatrix} \ [(command-list)]$$

The WHERE command

$$\begin{Bmatrix} WHERE \\ WHER \end{Bmatrix} \ [PRINT]$$

FULL-SCREEN COBTEST COMMANDS

The AT command

```
{AT}  [number]
{A }
```

The AUTO command

```
{AUTO}  [{list-command}  ]
{AU  }   {ON          }
         {OFF         }
```

The LIST command

```
{LIST}
{L   }
```

The LISTINGS command

```
{LISTINGS}
{LISTI   }
```

The MOVECURS command

```
{MOVECURS}
{MOVEC   }
{MC      }
```

The OFF command

```
{OFF}  [number]
{O  }
```

The POSITION command

```
{POSITION}  line-number
{POS     }
```

The RESTORE command

```
{RESTORE}
{RESTO  }
```

The SEARCH command

```
{SEARCH}  [delimiter character-string [delimiter]]
{SEA   }
```

The SELECT command

```
S number
```

The SOURCE command

```
{SOURCE}  [{LISTING program-name}
{SO    }   {OFF                  } ]
           {ON                   }
```

The SUFFIX command

```
{SUFFIX}  {ON }
{S     }  {OFF}
```

The VTRACE command

```
{VTRACE}  [number]
{V     }
```

Appendix
D

VS COBOL II file status codes

This appendix presents all the possible file status codes for Release 2 and Release 3 of VS COBOL II. Although the codes for Release 2 are the same as for OS/VS COBOL, some of the codes for Release 3 have been changed. So if you're using Release 3 and you test file status codes in your programs, you'll want to review the material in this appendix.

VS COBOL II Release 2

FILE STATUS code	Meaning
00	The operation was successfully completed.
02	A READ, WRITE, or REWRITE statement was successfully completed, but a duplicate key was detected.
10	A sequential READ statement attempted to read beyond the end of the file, or attempted to read a record in an optional file that wasn't present.
20	An invalid key condition occurred.
21	A sequence error occurred for a sequentially accessed indexed file.
22	A duplicate key condition occurred, and duplicate keys aren't allowed.
23	A READ, DELETE, START, or REWRITE statement was attempted on a randonly accessed file, but the specified record wasn't found.
24	A WRITE statement was attempted on a relative or indexed file, but there was no more space available for the file.
30	A permanent error condition occurred.
34	A WRITE statement was attempted on a sequential file, but there was no more space available for the file.
90	An implementor-defined condition occurred.
91	A password failure occurred on a VSAM file.
92	A logic error occurred.
93	The specified resource wasn't available for a VSAM file.
94	The file position indicator wasn't set for the sequential access of a VSAM file. (Only occurs if the CMPR2 compiler option is specified.)

FILE STATUS code	Meaning
95	Invalid or incomplete information was specified for a VSAM file.
96	No DD statement was specified for a VSAM file.
97	An OPEN statement was successfully executed for a VSAM file and the file integrity was verified.

VS COBOL II Release 3

FILE STATUS code	Meaning
00	The operation was successfully completed.
02	A READ, WRITE, or REWRITE statement was successfully completed, but a duplicate key was detected.
04	A READ statement was successfully completed, but the record length was different than the length specified by the permanent file attributes.
05	An OPEN statement was successfully completed, but the optional file wasn't available. If the file was opened I-O or EXTEND, the file was created.
07	An OPEN or CLOSE statement was successfully completed, but tape file options were specified and the file wasn't stored on tape.
10	A sequential READ statement attempted to read beyond the end of the file, or attempted to read a record in an optional file that wasn't present.
14	A sequential READ statement attempted to read a record in a relative file, but there were more significant digits in the relative record number than were provided by the relative key data item for the file.
21	A sequence error occurred for a sequentially accessed indexed file.

FILE STATUS code	Meaning
22	A duplicate key condition occurred and duplicate keys aren't allowed.
23	A READ, DELETE, START, or REWRITE statement was attempted on a randomly accessed file, but the specified record wasn't found, or a START or READ statement was attempted on a randomly accessed optional file, but the file wasn't available.
24	A WRITE statement was attempted on a relative or indexed file, but there was no more space available for the file, or an sequential WRITE statement was attempted on a relative file, but there were more significant digits in the relative record number than were provided by the relative key data item for the file.
30	A permanent error condition occurred.
34	A WRITE statement was attempted on a sequential file, but there was no more space available for the file.
35	An OPEN statement with the INPUT, I-O, or EXTEND phrase was attempted, but the file wasn't available and wasn't optional.
37	An OPEN statement was attempted, but the file wouldn't support the open mode specified.
38	An OPEN statement was attempted, but the file was previously closed and locked.
39	An OPEN statement was attempted, but the attributes specified for the file in the program conflicted with the permanent file attributes.
41	An OPEN statement was attempted, but the file was already in open mode.
42	A CLOSE statement was attempted, but the file wasn't in open mode.
43	A REWRITE statement was attempted for a mass storage file in sequential access mode, but the last I/O statement executed for the file was not a successful READ statement.

FILE STATUS code	Meaning
44	A REWRITE statement was attempted, but a boundary violation occurred because the record was not the same size as the record being replaced, or a WRITE statement was attempted, but a boundary violation occurred because the record was larger than the largest or smaller than the smallest record allowed for the file.
46	A sequential READ statement was attempted on a file in input or I-O mode, but no valid next record had been established because the preceding READ statement was unsuccessful or caused an at end condition.
47	A READ statement was attempted, but the file wasn't opened in INPUT or I-O mode.
48	A WRITE statement was attempted, but the file wasn't opened in I-O, OUTPUT, or EXTEND mode.
49	A DELETE or WRITE statement was attempted, but the file wasn't opened in I-O mode.
90	An implementor-defined condition occurred.
91	A password failure occurred on a VSAM file.
92	A logic error occurred.
93	The specified resource wasn't available for a VSAM file.
94	The file position indicator wasn't set for the sequential access of a VSAM file. (Only occurs if the CMPR2 compiler option is specified.)
95	Invalid or incomplete information was specified for a VSAM file.
96	No DD statement was specified for a VSAM file.
97	An OPEN statement was successfully executed for a VSAM file and the file integrity was verified.

Index

Comment Form

Your opinions count

If you have any comments, criticisms, or suggestions for us, I'm eager to hear from you. Your opinions today will affect our products of tomorrow. And if you find any errors in this book, typographical or otherwise, please point them out so we can correct them in the next printing.

Thanks for your help.

Mike Murach

Book title: VS COBOL II: A Guide for Programmers and Managers (Second Edition)

Dear Mike:

_____

_____

_____

_____

_____

_____

_____

_____

_____

_____

_____

_____

_____

Name _____

Company (if company address) _____

Address _____

City, State, Zip _____

Fold where indicated and tape closed.

No postage needed if mailed in the U.S.

NO POSTAGE
NECESSARY
IF MAILED
IN THE
UNITED STATES

BUSINESS REPLY MAIL

FIRST-CLASS MAIL   PERMIT NO. 3063   FRESNO, CA

POSTAGE WILL BE PAID BY ADDRESSEE

Mike Murach & Associates, Inc.
2560 W SHAW LN STE 101
FRESNO, CA 93711-9866

Order Form

Our Unlimited Guarantee

To our customers who order directly from us: You must be satisfied. Our books must work for you, or you can send them back for a full refund...no questions asked.

Name & Title _____

Company (if company address) _____

Street Address _____

City, State, Zip _____

Phone number (including area code) _____

Fax number (if you fax your order to us) _____

Qty	Product code and title	*Price
COBOL Language Elements		
___ VC2R	VS COBOL II (Second Edition)	$27.50
___ SC1R	Structured ANS COBOL, Part 1	32.50
___ SC2R	Structured ANS COBOL, Part 2	32.50
CICS		
___ CC1R	CICS for the COBOL Programmer Part 1 (Second Edition)	$36.50
___ CC2R	CICS for the COBOL Programmer Part 2 (Second Edition)	36.50
___ CRFR	The CICS Programmer's Desk Reference (Second Edition)	42.50
MVS Subjects		
___ MJLR	MVS JCL (Second Edition)	$42.50
___ TSO1	MVS TSO, Part 1: Concepts and ISPF	36.50
___ TSO2	MVS TSO, Part 2: Commands and Procedures (CLIST and REXX)	36.50
___ MBAL	MVS Assembler Language	36.50
___ OSUT	OS Utilities	17.50

Qty	Product code and title	*Price
Data Base Processing		
___ DB21	DB2 for the COBOL Programmer Part 1: An Introductory Course	$36.50
___ DB22	DB2 for the COBOL Programmer Part 2: An Advanced Course	36.50
___ IMS1	IMS for the COBOL Programmer Part 1: DL/I Data Base Processing	36.50
___ IMS2	IMS for the COBOL Programmer Part 2: Data Communications and MFS	36.50
VSAM		
___ VSMX	VSAM: Access Method Services and Application Programming	$27.50
___ VSMR	VSAM for the COBOL Programmer (Second Edition)	22.50
DOS/VSE Subjects		
___ VJLR	DOS/VSE JCL (Second Edition)	$34.50
___ ICCF	DOS/VSE ICCF	31.00
___ VBAL	VSE Assembler Language	36.50

❑ Bill me for the books plus UPS shipping and handling (and sales tax within California).

❑ Bill my company. P.O.# _____

❑ I want to **SAVE 10%** by paying in advance. Charge to my ___Visa ___MasterCard ___American Express:

Card number _____

Valid thru (mo/yr) _____

Cardowner's signature _____

❑ I want to **SAVE 10% plus shipping and handling.** Here's my check or money order for the books minus 10% ($_____). California residents, please add sales tax to your total. (Offer valid in U.S.)

*Prices are subject to change. Please call for current prices.

To order more quickly,

Call **toll-free** 1-800-221-5528

(Weekdays, 8 to 5 Pacific Time)

Fax: 1-209-275-9035

Mike Murach & Associates, Inc.

2560 West Shaw Lane, Suite 101
Fresno, California 93711-2765
(209) 275-3335

NO POSTAGE
NECESSARY
IF MAILED
IN THE
UNITED STATES

BUSINESS REPLY MAIL
FIRST-CLASS MAIL   PERMIT NO. 3063   FRESNO, CA

POSTAGE WILL BE PAID BY ADDRESSEE

Mike Murach & Associates, Inc.
2560 W SHAW LN STE 101
FRESNO, CA 93711-9866